# *—1545—*

## *Who Sank The Mary Rose?*

# 1545

## *Who Sank The Mary Rose?*

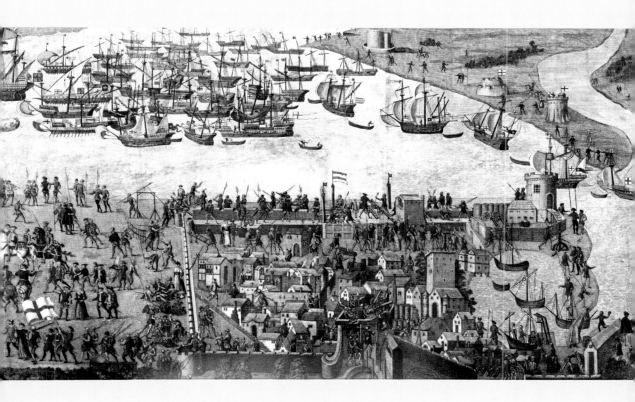

## Peter Marsden

**Seaforth**
PUBLISHING

First published in Great Britain in 2019 by
Seaforth Publishing,
A division of Pen & Sword Books Ltd,
47 Church Street,
Barnsley S70 2AS
www.seaforthpublishing.com

British Library Cataloguing in Publication Data
A catalogue record for this book is available from the British Library

ISBN 978 1 5267 4935 2 (HARDBACK)
ISBN 978 1 5267 4936 9 (EPUB)
ISBN 978 1 5267 4937 6 (KINDLE)

Pen & Sword Books Limited incorporates the imprints of
Atlas, Archaeology, Aviation, Discovery, Family History, Fiction, History, Maritime,
Military, Military Classics, Politics, Select, Transport, True Crime, Air World,
Frontline Publishing, Leo Cooper, Remember When, Seaforth Publishing,
The Praetorian Press, Wharncliffe Local History, Wharncliffe Transport,
Wharncliffe True Crime and White Owl

All uncredited images from the author's collection. Attempts have been made to find all copyright holders, but the publishers
will be pleased to hear of any that may have been omitted.
Typeset and designed by Stephen Dent
Printed and bound in India by Replika Press Pvt Ltd

# CONTENTS

# *Introduction*

Why the English warship *Mary Rose* sank in 1545 with the loss of roughly five hundred lives has been the subject of much debate among historians. We know how it happened, in so far that gunports were left open while she was engaged against the French navy, and that a squall unexpectedly heeled her over and she flooded and sank. But why it occurred has been the problem. At the time the English court blamed the crew; the French believed that gunfire from their galley had caused the disaster; and since the ship was raised other possible reasons, including the pilot possibly being a Frenchman, or that the hired Spanish mercenaries did not understand orders in English, have entered the possibilities. So, the forensic examination of the ship and her contents, when combined with a detailed study of historical records, has complicated the answer. Nevertheless, it has yielded a huge amount of new information and has corrected some long-held but erroneous views as to what actually occurred.

In the year 2000 I was unexpectedly drawn into the matter when Martyn Heighton, Chief Executive of the Mary Rose Trust, invited me to take charge of preparing a book that described the history of the ship. Until then I had observed with awe from afar as Alexander McKee and Margaret Rule, both of whom I knew, had led the discovery, excavation and raising of the ship in 1982, and also the many others who carried out the preservation and exhibition of the ship in a fine new museum at Portsmouth.

I did have some experience relevant to the task as an archaeologist and historian, for in addition to discovering the remains of early London, now at the Guildhall Museum and Museum of London, I had also found Roman, Saxon and medieval ships there, and had obtained a doctorate from Oxford University in maritime archaeology. I had also investigated shipwrecks of the seventeenth, eighteenth and nineteenth centuries elsewhere. My only involvement with the *Mary Rose* up till then had been when my colleagues and I discovered that British law did not recognise the cultural significance of wrecks of historic ships and boats such as the *Mary Rose*, because they were originally designed to move and therefore were considered to be very large chattels, in the same class as domestic pots. Consequently, I became part of a small band of people, including Alexander McKee and Margaret Rule, who successfully campaigned for the British government to recognise and protect historic shipwrecks. And so the Protection of Wrecks Act 1973 was passed, and subsequently the Ancient Monuments Act 1979 included historic shipwrecks. After years of fighting, we were able to ensure that the *Mary Rose* was given a protected status.

After the volume on the history of the ship was published in 2003, I was commissioned to prepare a separate book describing the *Mary Rose* ship herself which was published in 2009. These were part of a series of five volumes, with others on the history of the ship edited by Alexzandra Hildred and Julie Gardiner, that in over two thousand pages described what was then known about the vessel, her history and her contents, and was written by about one hundred specialists in many different fields, from guns to human skeletons.[1]

The books were only ever intended to be interim publications as limited time and funds restricted our research to matters that only related to the ship, with little opportunity to compare her with what was known of other warships in King Henry's navy. Moreover, the ship's story in the Battle of the Solent was restricted to her, with little time to study the wider story of the battle. Consequently, some of our conclusions did not address critical issues, such as where most of the men of the ship were accommodated, and how the ship was managed in battle, so the likely reason for the loss of the ship and the death of hundreds of men remained uncertain. Also, a close scrutiny of some English and French records proved that a few were unreliable, particularly the description of the disaster written by John Hooker about 1575 and some aspects of the memoirs of the French nobleman and diplomat, Martin du Bellay, who died in 1559. Hooker, for example, described the sinking as happening in Portsmouth Harbour, and Bellay that the battle started on 18 July 1545. Both are incorrect.

It is over ten years since the Mary Rose Trust published interim details of the story of the ship. Since then there has been time for specialists to reflect on the results of those publications and to carry out further research which has been much more focused. This has resulted in a more developed reconstruction of the ship, and an under-standing of the wider history of the events in which she was involved, including the publication of the French records. It also examines what should be in the ship but is absent from the archaeological record, including the absence of the lime pots which are listed as being in the ship when she sank. This period of reflection has also highlighted our need to know when the French fleet actually arrived off the east end of the Isle of Wight, and if the French also attacked the then fishing village of Brighton. Answers are to be found in this book.

In the years that followed the Mary Rose Trust publications, it became clear that the human remains found in the *Mary Rose* probably did not represent a balanced selection of everyone on board, for the study of the shoes alone show that that they were mostly slip-ons, and so were probably not suitable for wearing by the 'topmen', sailors, who handled the rigging that was so essential in battle. Also, a programme of DNA studies and a few facial reconstructions was started which opened up new avenues of information.

Then David Potter published his assessment of the Battle of the Solent and opened up many French records that were previously unknown to us. Similarly, the tidal predictions for the day of the battle were calculated and published by the Admiralty, and helped to clarify the circumstances in which the *Mary Rose* sank. Moreover, David Loades and David Knighton published updated transcripts of relevant historical records in 2017, and in 2015 Douglas McElvogue published his reconstruction of the ship based on his intimate knowledge from having recorded the vessel for the Mary Rose Trust.[2]

In spite of all of this new knowledge I was left with the nagging problem of where nearly five hundred men were accommodated in the ship. This forced me to review the contemporary documents as to what the ship looked like. It soon became clear that each of her castles must have had three decks, whereas previously it was thought that there was firstly only one, then two decks. But with three, supported by clear contemporary evidence that had previously been dismissed, the problem was solved, though it left the ship's stability as a matter that needed further attention.

The research also highlighted the need to define the positions of the missing capstans and bitts that held the mooring cables, for although these were missing the holes in the deck beams left by the bolts that once fastened them may still be found. Also needing clarification was the relationship between the partition bulkheads and the rows of stanchions, and even the true positions of the ladders, stairs and access hatches. All of this new information can then be added in a resurvey of the ship so that her interior elevation fits the outboard elevation, which at present they do not. And, most importantly, there needs to be a unified means of research publication to replace the scattered system that now exists, for this can result in vital publications being missed. So, although much progress has been made in research, and in conserving the ship and the objects found in her, much more is needed.

There are still differences of opinion as to what the ship looked like when first built in 1512, in that some people think that she had a squared stern and gunports on her main gun deck from the beginning, and others think that they only occurred after her rebuilding around

1536. In looking at the evidence described in chapter 5, the latter seems to fit best of all as there were great differences in her armament after her rebuild. It may be helpful to treat the ship as a floating castle or country house of that time, and to look at the functions of rooms ashore and see how many can be transferred to parts of the vessel, as this was what was expected by the officers, seamen, gunners and soldiers.

The story of the battle had not been told in full because the *Mary Rose* was at the centre of the research. But now that it has been possible to affirm that the French fleet arrived off the Isle of Wight on the afternoon of Sunday 19 July, we are better able to reconstruct the sea battle. Previously, dates of the arrival have varied from the 17 to 19 July, but this has been based on records written years after the events, particularly by Bellay and Hooker.

As the *Mary Rose* was sunk early in the conflict, the story is not so much about the ship, but rather about the ambitions of two kings, Francis I and Henry VIII, to whom the sea battle was very personal. This followed Henry VIII's seizure of Boulogne in 1544, and King Francis I's response was to assemble a huge invasion fleet to seize the Isle of Wight and possibly Portsmouth as a bargaining counter. This force was far larger than that of the Spanish Armada of 1588, and he delegated his plans to his most senior Admiral, Claud d'Annebault. In England the King, Henry VIII, entrusted the task of opposing the French admiral to his supreme Lord Admiral, Lord Lisle, and as the battle unfolded each admiral tried to outwit the other. The battle is often described as inconclusive with no winner, but in fact Admiral Lisle showed a brilliance that literally saved England, and left Admiral d'Annebault having to reconsider his position. Lisle was particularly fascinated a year later when, for the first time, he privately met d'Annebault on a French field during peace negotiations, and was amazed when the Frenchman claimed that 'There was no battle'. Did that mean that the huge number of men had died for nothing while following their orders? Was it for nothing that both kings had bankrupted their countries? In this conflict the *Mary Rose* was a tool of death and destruction in the ambitions of King Henry, so her loss was of limited consequence. On the French side there were several galleys that were sunk in the Solent together with their unfortunate slave rowers who were chained to the benches. So, by reviewing all this extra information it became necessary to re-examine the place of the *Mary Rose* as a working vessel at the moment that she sank, and as a reflection of what was going on in the other ships.

The circumstances around the sinking of the *Mary Rose* and the drowning of well over four hundred men was clearly not a simple matter, and as I delved ever deeper into her story I became aware of a faint figure lurking in the shadows of history who was responsible for the disaster. This book is about the search for that figure.

To the finders and excavators of the *Mary Rose*, especially Alexander McKee and Margaret Rule, the authors of the previous publications, and to my publisher, I owe a huge debt. Further research and publications will no doubt follow, especially as the internal structures are returned to the *Mary Rose*, but meanwhile this book shows how the permanent Royal Navy was born, how the *Mary Rose* typified what the largest ships were like and how they were used, and who sank the ship.

**Peter Marsden**
Bishopsteignton,
Devon

*Chapter One*

# DISASTER

F our human skeletons lying in the mud that covered the main gun deck of the *Mary Rose* told a horrifying story of the loss of the ship on the evening of Sunday, 19 July 1545. To the archaeologists they gave the lie to the view that 'Dead men tell no tales'. Analysis of the skeletons revealed that they were all young men in their twenties who had drowned beside their great two-tonne bronze gun at the lowest of the ship's gun ports on the starboard side. They were the first of more than four hundred men to have been overwhelmed as the ship heeled to an unexpected gust of wind and cold, dark seawater flooded in through the gunports from the Solent seaway off the south coast of England. And so one of the finest warships of Henry VIII's navy sank in full view of the rest of the fleet commanded by Lord Admiral Lisle, on his flagship *Henry Grace a Dieu*, and of the King standing on the battlements of Southsea Castle a mile away surrounded by his court camped on

A later copy of an original sixteenth-century picture in Cowdray House (later destroyed by fire) shows the sea battle in July 1545 and the sunken *Mary Rose*. It also shows events that happened over several days, with the French moored off the east end of the Isle of Wight, the English navy putting to sea from Portsmouth harbour, and English ships fighting the French galleys. *(Society of Antiquaries)*

Southsea Common. Embarrassingly, it also occurred in sight of the French navy led by Admiral Claud d'Annebault who represented King Francis I (r. 1515–47) and understandably believed that gunfire from one of his galleys had sunk the *Mary Rose*.

Only a few metres away the diving archaeologists found the skeleton of an older man in his thirties, a Boatswain judging from the silver whistle or naval 'call' on a silk ribbon that identified his rank. The sinking occurred so quickly that he drowned while walking along the deck, perhaps checking the readiness of the gun crews for the next attack on the French galley.

King Henry's loss is our gain because the raised and preserved remains of the *Mary Rose* provide us with a unique insight into the beginnings of the English Royal Navy five centuries ago. It also had consequences leading to the better design and use of warships that, only forty-eight years later, enabled the English navy to fight off the mighty Spanish Armada of 1588 when King Philip II (r. 1556–98) tried to invade England. The improved design also enabled English merchants to begin trading globally in ocean-traversing galleons, and so lay the foundation of what was to become Britain's vast trading empire during the eighteenth and nineteenth centuries. Consequently, the discovery of the *Mary Rose* has opened a window to England's maritime past that is out of proportion to her size.

Sir John Dudley, Lord Lisle, as Lord Admiral in charge of the English navy, was responsible for opposing the French invasion of July 1545. *(Wikimedia)*

l'amiral d'annebante

The French
Admiral, Claud
d'Annebault, was
reluctantly in charge
of the French fleet.
*(Bridgeman Art
Library CND 171321)*

As the *Mary Rose* was heading north when she sank, the last thing that those gunners saw were shafts of sunlight shining through her open port side gunports, illuminating the smoky gloom that lingered from gunfire. She had fired some of her guns as she sailed past the French galley, and, with their ears still ringing from the deafening roars, gunners swabbed out their gun barrels to douse any residual burning debris before reloading.

The 'plop' as a sounding lead was dropped into the sea beside them may have been one of the last noises that the four gunners heard. It was heaved on the end of a line by a sailor on the upper gun deck just above them who was checking on the depth of water as the ship approached the shoals of Spitsand only 300 metres away. Judging from the ribbon depth markers of leather, wool and silk he would have shouted the depth of about five fathoms to the ship's sailing Master. Part of the line coiled up in a wooden bowl was found by archaeologists as they cleared mud from the upper gun deck.[1] The Imperial Ambassador of Charles V of Spain (r. 1519–58), Francis Van der Delft, who witnessed the sinking from ashore, heard from a survivor that immediately before the disaster occurred the Captain, or sailing Master, had just ordered the crew to turn the ship to renew the attack on the enemy galley.

The gunport openings, although only about half a metre square and just fifty centimetres above the deck, enabled the gun crews to watch the battle scene as the enemy's galley receded astern, its chained convict crew splashing oars in unison.[2] The hinged watertight gunport lids of the *Mary Rose* should have been slammed shut as the ship heeled over. Instead, they remained open, supported by a rope tied to an iron ring on their outboard faces, the top end of the rope being held by men standing on the upper gun deck above. The gunners must have been aware of the danger of flooding, for the sea was only sixteen inches below, according to Sir Walter Raleigh in an account he apparently wrote many years later.[3]

The ship's Captain, Vice-Admiral Sir George Carew, intended that the *Mary Rose* should sail up to the French galley and drop the great iron grapnel, hanging from a stout iron chain at the end of her bowsprit, onto the enemy's deck to 'capture' it for boarding. Sharp sickle-like iron blades, 'shearhooks', fastened to the ends of her main and foresail yards were intended to cut the enemy's rigging and disable the vessel. Soldiers armed with pikes, spears and daggers were at the ready, waiting at their station under the sterncastle for the order to swarm the ship's side and attack the enemy's crew. But the order never came. Within minutes the

King Francis I of France who sent his navy to England to capture the Isle of Wight and Portsmouth in 1545 as a bargaining counter for the return of Boulogne, which Henry VIII had captured in 1544. *(Bridgman Art Library TWC 62736)*

King Charles V of Spain, the Holy Roman Emperor, whose Ambassador, Francis van der Delft, described the loss of the *Mary Rose* in July 1545. *(Bridgman Art Library XIR 16711)*

soldiers too were drowned, their skeletons and weapons providing the main concentration of human remains discovered by archaeologists when the ship was excavated over four centuries later.

The forensic examination of the ship and the remains of people revealed likely causes of the disaster. Archaeologists have reconstructed those horrifying final moments when frightened men shouted while trying to gain footholds on the steeply inclined deck in the hope of escaping through the gunports. Some of the crew were mortally injured as loose equipment, and heavy iron and stone cannonballs slid down onto them. One of the young men was crushed by a sliding gun carriage only metres away from the four gunners. Even the escape route up the staircase companionway, just forward of the gunners, was blocked as the bodies of two archers fell from the upper gun deck.

In what seemed like seconds, the sea cascaded through the central hatches to the orlop deck below, and then deeper down into the hold where cooks were preparing the next meal. They had no time to escape up the narrow ladder to the decks above, though that would not have saved them as anti-boarding netting covering the uppermost decks would have prevented them from swimming to safety.

Cries of panic and pain were quickly smothered as the ship slid beneath the waves and large bubbles of air burst at the surface, leaving only about forty survivors gripping floating debris. They were mostly the men from the fighting tops high on the four masts, and sailors tending the rigging. Although the ship sank in only ten metres of water, her impact on the clay seabed was so violent that her keel pushed up a ridge of mud, leaving the entire hull lying at sixty degrees, so that her starboard side faced downwards. The *Mary Rose* had suddenly been transformed from a lively home for her crew to a silent coffin as the clothed bodies of hundreds of men sank to their dark muddy grave.

On the battlements of Southsea Castle, Mary, the wife of Sir George Carew, collapsed in horror making 'a sounding' as she realised that she had become a widow.[4] They had been married for just four years and the King tried to console her as he witnessed the event. So sensitive was the disaster that immediately afterwards Lord Admiral Lisle dared not to mention it in a letter to the King while describing the progress of the battle.

Four centuries later the ship was excavated and raised, enabling her remains to become the centrepiece of an award-winning museum at Portsmouth where the only picture of the sea battle is displayed. It was copied from a now-destroyed later-sixteenth-century mural that was in Cowdray House, the home of Sir Anthony Browne, at Midhurst in West Sussex. Browne was a senior courtier and Master of the Horse to Henry VIII and attended the King that day. Rescue boats are shown being rowed around the tops of the masts of the *Mary Rose* which were all that could be seen sticking out of the sea. A lone survivor waves his arms while standing on the crow's-nest 'top' of the main mast; around him float corpses of drowned men being collected by rescuers. When a similar disaster happened nearby to the warship *Royal George* in 1782, the local people also used rowing boats to collect the bloated corpses, tying ropes around their ankles to tow them to the beach where they were stripped of valued possessions before being handed over for burial.[5] Perhaps the same thing happened in 1545.

Why the gunport lids were not closed, and who was responsible for the disaster, has intrigued historians ever since. This is especially puzzling as the ship had survived a long and active service in many conditions of sun and storm, in estuaries and out at sea. Something exceptional must have occurred in 1545. The French were sure that they had fired the fatal shot at the *Mary Rose*,[6] and the family of Sir George Carew was equally sure that her sinking was caused by misbehaving crew.[7] Examination of the gunports revealed an unexpected weakness in the design of the ship, and analysis of the skeletons showed that the crew included hired foreign mercenaries, raising the possibility that they did not understand orders in English to close the gunport lids. Moreover, the Pilot may have been French, judging from where some of his navigation instruments were made, and he may have tried to sabotage the vessel. There seems to be no simple answer, though, as we shall see, important clues have emerged that point to who was responsible.

The discovery and preservation of the *Mary Rose* has focussed attention on how Henry VIII created England's permanent Royal Navy, so it is appropriate that she is now exhibited alongside Nelson's flagship HMS *Victory* in Portsmouth Dockyard just a few hundred metres from where she was built between 1510 and 1512. She also lies within calling distance of the most modern warships in the world that, in contrast to the bows, arrows and massive cannons, now carry missiles that can be targeted precisely at victims hundreds of miles away.

The story of the *Mary Rose* is primarily of a personal vendetta between the kings of England and France, carried out by their most senior Admirals. King Henry VIII had used the ship as a weapon that, from time to time over thirty-three years, had brought terror to ordinary folk living quietly on the coast, mostly in Brittany, and in the year before her loss when Henry seized the French port of Boulogne. Understandably, the angry King Francis had had enough and sent a huge invasion force of French warships and troop carriers to attack England in 1545, with the aim of capturing either the Isle of Wight or Portsmouth as a bargaining counter. The French king placed his ambition on the shoulders of his Admiral Claud d'Annebault, a highly professional French military officer with limited maritime experience. King Henry ordered John Dudley, Viscount Lisle, his Lord Admiral of England, to repel the enemy. He too was a military man, but with more maritime experience. Consequently, for a few days England's future lay in the hands of these two men as they confronted each other in July 1545 in what is known as the Battle of the Solent. The stakes could not have been higher for had the French succeeded, the history of England could have been significantly different.

The story is also of the ordinary people who served on the ships, Englishmen and foreigners, whose names and lives are almost completely unknown. One of the saddest features of the *Mary Rose* is that we cannot know names of the young men on board. We know them intimately by studying their bones, clothing and possessions, and in some cases we even know what they were employed to do. The faces of a few have been reconstructed so that we can look them in the eyes, while they look back at us. Still they remain nameless – simply a number, such as FCS 73, meaning Fairly Complete Skeleton 73. Tudor history is largely about monarchs, nobles, major events, fine houses and palaces, but thanks to the survival of the *Mary Rose* and the efforts of archaeologists and historians, we are able to enter the lives of ordinary people. It is fitting therefore that of the three people whose names

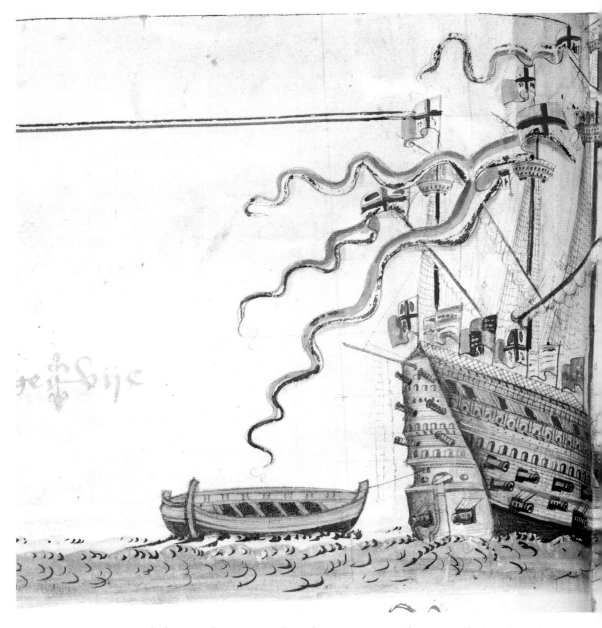

we do know who were on board, one was an ordinary cook, 'Ny Coep', possibly with the name Cooper, who scratched his name and trade on a wooden bowl and on the lid of a wooden tankard.[8] The other two were from noble families, Sir George Carew and Roger Granville, who are, of course, known from contemporary documents.

Historical records only list the approximate total of sailors, gunners and soldiers who died on board. To the nobles, like Sir George Carew, they were replaceable with local farmers, fishermen and foreign mercenaries. But in this story they are important players on the stage

The only contemporary picture of the *Mary Rose* was drawn by Anthony Anthony and was part of a view of ships of Henry VIII's navy. This illustration was given to the King in 1546, and mostly matches what was found of the ship. *(Pepys Library, Magdalene College, Cambridge)*

of history, as men who served and died for their country in the embryonic royal navy of King Henry VIII, leaving the *Mary Rose* as an unrivalled historical record.

In order to find out who was responsible for the sinking of the *Mary Rose* we have to delve into her history to examine why she was so successful for so many years, and then why suddenly everything went so disastrously wrong. To begin, we must return to the year 1510, only months after the young Henry became King of England and signed a warrant for her construction.

*Chapter Two*

# BUILDING THE *MARY ROSE*

As soon as the teenage Henry VIII was crowned on 29 July 1509 he planned to attack France, partly to win extra territory and partly to impress his new Spanish wife, Catharine of Aragon (r. 1509–33), and for that he needed an army and a navy. His main reason, however, was that his realm lay between two threatening powers: France ruled by King Louis XII (r. 1498–1515) to the south, and Scotland, its ally to the north, under King James IV (r. 1488–1513). He had to ensure that England's defences were increased beyond those established by his father, King Henry VII. It was the expanding power and ambition of France that, in 1487, caused Henry's father to build two great warships, the *Regent* and the *Sovereign*, as insurance against attack. This was timely as in December 1491 the then twenty-one-year old French king, Charles VIII (r. 1483–98) married the fourteen-year-old Duchess Anne of Brittany (r. 1491–98, 1499–1514), enabling him to absorb this separate state and so develop the north-western port of Brest as a naval base. To the north, King James of Scotland had already built a huge 1,000-ton warship, the *Michael*, which entered naval service in February 1512. Even though his father, Henry VII, had started building a navy, he felt the need to respond by building an even larger warship, the *Henry Grace a Dieu* which was launched in 1514.

In order to oppose the territorial ambitions of the French King, he joined the Holy League in November 1511, a European alliance between the Emperor Maximilian of the Holy Roman Empire (r. 1508–19), King Ferdinand II of Aragon (r. 1479–1516), the city of Venice and the League's nominal leader Pope Julius II (r. 1503–13).

Henry intended his navy to be led by the largest type of ship in northern Europe known as a 'carrack', but designed as a warship. This had high castles fore and aft and modest size guns to be used for attack before closing on an enemy vessel, allowing soldiers to prepare to board once the sailing Master had manoeuvred the ship alongside.

On 29 January 1510, only seven months after his coronation, Henry

A carrack drawn by 'WA' in the later part of the fifteenth century, not long before the *Mary Rose* was built. She has a rounded stern, a very thick main mast, and a 'steep tub' barrel hanging from the side of her stern. *(Ashmolean Museum, University of Oxford)*

initialled the warrant authorising the building of his first two ships,[1] to be constructed at Portsmouth where his father had built a dry dock and storehouses. By 9 June 1511 they were sufficiently complete to be called the *Mary Rose* of 500–600 tons, named after Saint Mary the Virgin and linked to the Tudor rose of Henry's family, and *Peter Pomegranate* of 450 tons, named after Saint Peter with the pomegranate emblem representing Queen Catherine of Aragon.[2]

They were launched in an incomplete state in the summer of 1511, no doubt with a 'hallowing' ceremony as it was then called – an excuse for everyone to drink a lot of beer! Then in June or July 1511 they appear to have been towed from Portsmouth to the River Thames for fitting out near the Tower of London. This first voyage eastwards along the English Channel and around Kent to the River Thames was undertaken in great style by the sailing Master of the *Mary Rose*, John Clerke, and his small crew of four quartermasters, a Boatswain and twenty-four soldiers, all dressed in coats of the Tudor colours of white and green.[3]

As there are no pictures of either ship at this time, we have to rely on images of large carracks generally, together with a detailed List made in 1514 of fittings in the *Mary Rose* which had four masts.[4] Contemporary pictures of carracks include drawings in a document of the life of Richard Beauchamp, Earl of Warwick between 1485 and 1490.[5] This shows that the guns were normally mounted in the castles and on the upper deck in the waist between. But it is the Schlusselfelder nef, a table decoration made by a silversmith in Nuremberg about 1503, that particularly shows how carracks like the *Mary Rose* set sail and prepared for action.[6] Tiny, silver sailors climb the rigging while 'topmen' sit astride the timber yards, the horizontal spars from which the sails are hung, to untie the ropes that hold the furled sails. Footropes hanging from the yards for the sailors to stand on had not then been invented, so this was a particularly dangerous task. The ship is underway with her anchors tied to the sides of the bow, and the fore-sail is set to give the ship forward momentum as the main sail is unfurled. The main mast is very thick and bound with ropes as if constructed from several timbers, and high on each mast is a crow's-nest 'top'. Soldiers are preparing to be armed with light swivel guns,

The Schlusselfelder nef, a silver-gilt table decoration of a carrack made in Nuremburg about 1503, shows a ship setting sail and is an important clue to what the *Mary Rose* was like when first built in 1510–1512. It includes a massive main mast.

bows and spears, as bags of ammunition are hauled up to them on a rope. Ropes edge the sails, and parrels, an assembly of ropes and wooden balls that encircle the mast, enable the timber yards to be raised, lowered and swivelled around to catch the wind. Soldiers, with their pikes and bows with arrows at the ready, stand on the wooden roof covering the sides of the waist to protect the gunners below, whilst at the top of the forecastle and sterncastle are A-frames supporting anti-boarding netting. Other men are overlooking the stern, two apparently blowing trumpets.

These and other illustrations allow us to compare them with the surviving structure of the *Mary Rose* to show how Henry intended his 'great ships' to look. The tree-ring dating of oak timbers used in her hull show that much of the central part of the ship was retained when she was rebuilt about 1536, leaving her ends to be completely rebuilt. A pump well at her bottom and slots for swivel guns remained from when she was first built, and tree-ring dating has identified six timbers in the central area that definitely belonged to her original construction in 1510 to 1512. Six more were *probably* original build timbers. These seem to show that the ship originally had an orlop, main and upper decks, each about two metres above the other.[7]

The curving bottom and sides of her hull show that she was built to follow the earliest known descriptions of shipbuilding in Europe, written between 1435 and 1620, which were based on a sophisticated shipbuilding geometry to give a vessel the best hydrodynamic shape.

The bottom of the Woolwich ship, found in 1912 when building a power station beside the River Thames in London, is believed to be the carrack warship *Sovereign*. This ship was apparently rebuilt when the *Mary Rose* was built, and had a similar construction, including carvel edge-to-edge planking.

Based on a 'Master-frame' at her widest part, roughly amidship, she had a typical U-shaped hull in cross section, with the upper part of her sides above the waterline sloped inwards, known as 'tumblehome', to make her more stable. She had a strong hull to enable her to carry great numbers of men and equipment, with a wall of oak ribs covered by thick edge-to-edge 'carvel' planking outboard and an inner lining of planking, known as the 'ceiling', inboard. Additional thick longitudinal timbers known as 'wales' and 'stringers', and thick transverse timbers called 'riders', together increased her strength.

Henry VII's old warship, *Sovereign*, was rebuilt at this time showing

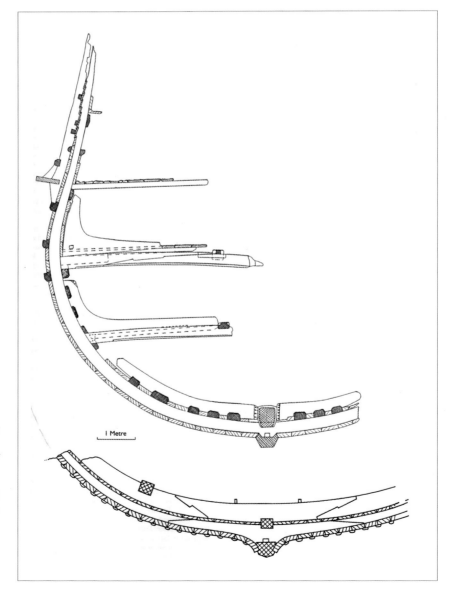

Sections of the *Mary Rose* (top) and the Woolwich ship show that the latter was a larger vessel, and so limits the identity of the ship. There is no reasonable doubt that the Woolwich ship was the *Sovereign*. *(Mary Rose Trust)*

I Metre

how another great ship was built. The bottom three metres of her hull were found preserved in the river bank of the Thames in 1912 when Woolwich Power Station was built near central London. Although larger (800 tons) than the *Mary Rose* (600 tons), the *Sovereign* also had edge-to-edge carvel planking, an inner lining of ceiling planks and similar stringers and riders. One rib in the *Sovereign* was noted as having formerly been notched to take overlapping clinker planks, but which had been largely smoothed off. This helped to confirm the ship's identity since an historical record tells us that she was partly built from timbers of an earlier ship named *Grace Dieu*, which in the fifteenth century would have been clinker built.[8]

On their arrival in the River Thames in London the two new ships became the responsibility of Admiral Sir Edward Howard, with Thomas Sperte taking over as Master of the *Mary Rose* for her fitting out. David Boner, the Purser, managed the purchase of materials under the watchful eye of Robert Brigandyne, Clerk of the King's Ships, while carpenters, riggers and gunsmiths swarmed the vessel, and painters, led by John Browne of London, coloured her full-bodied hull probably with geometric patterns as was then the fashion. Decoration also included coats of arms, the Tudor colours of green and white, and the red cross on a white background of England.[9]

Guns firing stone and iron shot were lifted on board, and provision was made for the soldiers to be based on the upper deck in the waist between the two castles, as well as on the castles. The shot was mostly anti-personnel, to join the arrows fired by the archers. In the waist, the archers were to hide behind a protective row of rectangular wooden shields, some of which could be removed to enable archers and gunners to shoot at the enemy. These were called 'pavesses', some of which were found still in position on the starboard side of the *Mary Rose* when she was excavated. They were made of poplar which did not splinter easily, and measured about eighty-five centimetres high, forty-two centimetres wide, four centimetres thick and were probably as colourfully painted as they were in 1545, judging from the Anthony Roll, with the red cross of St George of England on a white background alternating with the Tudor colours of green and yellow.

An inventory list of fittings in the ship in 1514 only includes those things that were removed and delivered to John Hopton, the clerk controller of equipment storage, possibly at Erith. Most of the guns were given to John Millet and Thomas Elderton of the ordnance office, and the rest were kept on board.[10] Although the list is incomplete, it is also by looking at the fittings removed from the other twelve ships that we can build up a more complete picture of fittings in the *Mary Rose*. We can surmise, for example, that the kitchen galley in her hold had two ovens, as she had in 1545, and that the cooking equipment included a spit, a gridiron, a frying pan, a kettle and hanging hook, a fish kettle, a cresset lamp, shovels, scoops, baskets, a flesh-hook and tongs, and bellows.

Her four masts were probably of spruce as were those on the *Regent* around 1497.[11] The list specifies that the main mast of the *Mary Rose* had three sails hung from horizontal timber 'yards' and that there was a large crow's-nest fighting 'top' to accommodate several soldiers, and that this mast was held upright by thirteen rope 'shrouds' fastened to 'dead mens' eyes' (deadeyes), round wooden fittings, on each side of the vessel. The main mast was probably very thick as was then usual, and in the *Sovereign* was 1.3 metres in diameter, constructed from several timbers bound together. This may be why there was a gap in the bottom ceiling planking of the *Mary Rose* that was filled with timber chocks on either side of the timber keelson to support the later narrow main mast, as if the original mast was about 1.5 metres thick.

The *Mary Rose* then had three sails on her foremast with a crow's-nest fore 'top', her main mizzenmast had two sails and a mizzen 'top', and her bonaventure mizzen probably had only one sail. With them was a range of fittings, most of which in later times are known to have had specific purposes that enable us to reconstruct how they were used: tackes, sheets, bowlines, parrels, trusses, drynges, braces, tyes, halyards, lifts, jeers, stays, 'shyrwyns', shrouds, 'swifting tackle', garlands and 'panlankers'. She also had davits in the forecastle to enable the anchors to be lifted when she set sail. It is amazing how many of the ship fitting terms used in 1514 remained in use until the eighteenth and nineteenth centuries, though the term 'larboard' side, used as early as the fifteenth century, was only changed officially to 'port' side in 1844 to avoid confusion with 'starboard'.

She had a large bower anchor on each side of her bow, next to a pair of sheet anchors in reserve, and elsewhere two 'destrell' anchors, and a small 'caggers' (kedge) anchor. The cables for them all ranging from eight to seventeen inches in circumference. Her kedge anchor was probably stowed in the large ship's boat, also listed, which was towed astern and from where it was dropped, with its cable fastened to the capstan to enable the ship to be moved from one mooring place to another. She also probably had buoys and buoy ropes to mark the place where the anchors lay on the seabed, the buoys being of cork and wood. The navigation of the ship was in the hands of the Master and the Pilot who had three compasses, two sand glasses and two sounding leads. Her large ship's boat had a mast, sail and twenty oars. There was also a small 'cock boat', with a mast, sail and six oars, that was presumably stowed on board in the waist.

The bell of the *Mary Rose* was a feature of the ship when first built, and stayed with her until she sank in 1545. Its inscription says that it was made in 1510.

The *Mary Rose*, as a statement of the young King Henry's power, was decorated with three long streamers at the top of her masts, eighteen gilded flags and twenty-eight small flags.[12] These were supplied by William Botrye, a London dealer in textiles, the flags being of linen and buckram, a coarse cloth stiffened with gum or paste, on which were painted a variety of designs relating to saints, together with the royal coats of arms. Her streamers flew from her fore, main and mizzen masts, and their size may be judged from those used in the much larger warship, *Henry Grace a Dieu*, that were forty and fifty-one yards long on her main mast, thirty-six yards long on her foremast, and twenty-eight yards long on her mizzenmast.[13] But they could only be used on ceremonial occasions when the ship was at anchor, otherwise they would become tangled up in the rigging. A common decoration for the streamers was the red cross of St George on a white background.[14]

Her seventy-eight guns had a variety of names: great curtowes, murderers, falcons and falconettes, demi slings, serpentines, guns firing stone shot, cast pieces and crow's-nest 'top' guns.[15] Eight of the largest were ship-smashing guns, probably mounted on wooden carriages to fire heavy shot through her gunports, and five more fired either anti-ship or anti-personnel shot. The remaining sixty-four fired only anti-personnel shots and were mostly mounted on Y-shaped iron swivel brackets slotted into holes in beams in various parts of the ship, some of the shots having remained in her sterncastle.[16]

Judging from the location of guns in five other ships, it seems that the thirteen heaviest guns, including the great curtowes and the demi slings, were situated on the upper deck, and the remaining sixty-one, all anti-personnel guns, were positioned in the two castles, with three on the crow's-nest 'tops' of the foremast, the main mast and the main mizzen mast.

Henry was so anxious to equip his ships and land-based fortifications with guns of quality that he employed Humphrey Walker, his 'King's gunfounder' to cast so many bronze guns that the price of tin in Europe increased considerably in 1510. Lorenzo Pasqualigo reported to the Venetian Senate that Henry had bought enough to cast one hundred guns. He also purchased twenty-four curtows and twenty-four serpentines from Hans Poppenruyter at Malines in Belgium, and by 1514 Simon Giles, from Malines, was manufacturing guns for the King in Houndsditch, London.[17]

Henry was so determined to build his navy that he acquired fourteen more ships in 1512, at least three of which were new, and seven were bought from as far away as Genoa. The next year he acquired three more ships, two of which he bought, and in 1514 he added another two more great ships. So, by the end of 1514 his navy included five ships that were larger than the *Mary Rose*: the *Henry Grace a Dieu* of 1500 tons, the *Gabriel Royal* of 700–1,000 tons, the *Katherine Fortileza* of 700 tons, the *Great Elizabeth* of 900 tons, and, he still had the *Sovereign* of 800 tons.

In 1512 the *Mary Rose* was complete and ready for war, and at last Henry could plan attacks on France. He appointed the thirty-seven-year old Sir Edward Howard as Lord High Admiral of England to command of his new navy, and in turn Howard chose the *Mary Rose* as his flagship because she evidently had special qualities over the much larger and more prestigious other vessels. He soon arrived on board with his servants and possessions, his quarters in the sterncastle presumably being similar to those of an earlier Lord Howard who went to sea in the 1470s with a feather bed, tapestry, table linen, a small library, and a 'pissing basin of silver'. The *Mary Rose* had her own commanding officers which in 1512 comprised her Captain, Sir Thomas Wyndham, and also her sailing Master, Thomas Sperte, who had gained the confidence of the King and subsequently went on to serve as Master of the much larger *Henry Grace a Dieu*. He was also a Yeoman of the Crown. By Nov 1514 he enjoyed an annuity of £20 a year, and in 1517 led an exploration expedition in another ship.

Whereas the Admiral was in charge of the fleet, the Captain was in charge of the ship, and was normally a person of high social status from a noble family. He did not need maritime experience, but his rank in society enabled him to decide what the ship would do and where she would go. Beneath him in rank was the Master, a man of lower social status, who had considerable seafaring experience and who managed the ship. When the King needed expert naval advice he made sure that he consulted the ships' Masters. The Captain and Master brought their own servants which might have been viewed with wry humour by the 206 sailors, 411 soldiers who served as marines, twenty gunners and two Pilots who joined the *Mary Rose*.[18]

Henry was anxious to test the competence of his new navy, so he ordered Admiral Howard to hold a race off the north and east coasts of Kent. In his great cabin of the *Mary Rose* Howard settled down on 22 March 1513, to write a long letter describing the result. It was an unequal race, not only because, naturally, the flagship won, but also because the fleet comprised a mix of about thirty vessels, warships and armed merchant ships. They had left the Thames estuary and sailed eastwards, driven by a strong wind from astern that forced them to heel over so that 'few ships lacked no water over the lee wales'.[19] These are the thick reinforcing planks on the outside of the ship and can still be seen on the *Mary Rose* today. At North Foreland, off the north-east corner of Kent, they turned right, to starboard, and sailed south to anchor safely off the notorious Goodwin Sands where many ships were wrecked. The crews showed professional seamanship, using bowline ropes attached to the sides of their square sails to keep them taut as they sailed close to the wind, and they added extra strips of canvas, the 'bonnets', laced to the bottom of the sails to maximise speed.

At the end of the race Howard 'called for a pen and ink to make what ships came to me ... to an anchor'. The first to arrive was the old *Sovereign*, and as others followed, Howard noted that the *Mary Rose* was best, 'the noblest ship of sail [of any] great ship, at this hour that I trow be in Christendom'. But there was a large gap between her and the last ships to arrive, from which he singled out the *Christ*, 300 tons, bought by the King in 1512, as 'one of the worst that day ... she is overladen with ordnance, beside her heavy tops which are big enough for a ship of 800–900 tons'. This meant that she had too many guns, and her armed crow's-nest 'tops' high on the masts were far too big and heavy. Maybe her subsequent capture by Barbary pirates from North Africa two years later was not such a serious loss after all.[20] The *Christ* aside, it was clear that by 1512 Henry had built his much desired navy, and was ready to attack the unfortunate people of France.

*Chapter Three*

# INTO ACTION, 1512–1514

King Henry VIII knew that in declaring war on France he was reneging on the peace treaty agreed by his father Henry VII (r. 1485–1509) in 1502, but his plans were in accord with those of his wily father-in-law, King Ferdinand of Aragon, who wanted to possess Navarre, a French territory in the Pyrenees. As a good Catholic monarch, Henry could claim that the ambition of the French King, Louis XII, to capture part of Italy also threatened Pope Julius II. The whole political scene in Europe at that time was a tangle of tensions, greed, rivalry and ambition between these main players. To complicate matters, the Scottish King, James IV, threatened the northern border of England by siding with King Louis and building the enormous warship, the *Michael* of about 1,000 tons. Trouble with Scotland had already flared up in 1511 when the noble brothers, Lords Thomas and Edward Howard, sons of the Earl of Surrey, confronted and killed the Scottish adventurer and 'pirate', Andrew Barton, in a sea battle off the Goodwin Sands, Kent. On the pretext of attacking Portuguese ships as a reprisal for killing his father, Barton had seized and plundered neutral ships, including English vessels. But killing Barton had caused such ill-will between Scotland and England, that when James IV remonstrated, Henry replied 'that punishing pirates was never held a breach of peace amongst princes'.[1]

Henry planned to invade France through the English bridgehead of Calais, a town that was the last remnant of a far more extensive medieval acquisition by England of land in France dating back to the marriage of Eleanor of Aquitaine to the future English King Henry II in 1152. In spring 1512 Henry VIII mobilised his new navy to secure the English Channel and appointed Sir Edward Howard as Admiral on 7 April 1512. The men mustered at Blackheath, now in south-east London. Meanwhile, Henry sent his Ambassador to France to warn King Louis XII that if he did not make peace with the Pope, there would be consequences. Louis was not interested. War was inevitable.

The *Mary Rose* was mainly used to attack the people and towns of Brittany, as on the sixteenth-century map.

Brittany

In April 1512 Howard led the fleet, carrying six thousand men, from the River Thames into the Channel and down to Plymouth, his springboard port to attack Brittany. Within a month he had captured twelve Breton and French ships and landed soldiers who, over four days, burned towns and villages within a thirty-mile radius of Le Conquet close to Brest. His bland report to the King did not convey the terror that the English had unleashed on the unfortunate locals, many of whom did not even consider themselves French following the marriage of the young Duchess Anne, of the former independent state of Brittany, to King Charles VIII of France twenty years earlier.[2]

Howard also attacked neutral merchant ships, and in one captured

Jacques Berenghier, a merchant of Lille, and seized his goods. This unfortunate man was forced to labour as a gunner in the English ship *Mary John*, whose Captain, Griffith Don, persecuted him simply because he spoke French. To get his own back, Berenghier was said to have overloaded guns with two stone shot instead of one which caused the guns to burst open when fired. He also possessed flints for making sparks, and carried gunpowder dangerously loose instead of in the powder horn hung around his neck.

He was court martialled by Admiral Howard on board the *Mary Rose*, and after an initial hearing was sent back to the *Mary John*. There he was tortured on the rack in attempts to uncover the identity of others involved and the torture was so severe that the unfortunate man lost a foot. Afterwards, he was returned to the *Mary Rose* for further judgment and where the Admiral found him guilty. The poor man was then sentenced to have his ears slit, and subsequently, when the fleet returned to Southampton, he was imprisoned and threatened with hanging. Through the cruelty of Tudor 'justice' Berenghier lost his ship, his cargo and possessions, his foot and ears, and he had been traumatised by the threat of death.[3]

In June Howard's fleet sailed from either Portsmouth or Southampton, escorting transport ships carrying an army of ten thousand men under Thomas Grey, Marquis of Dorset, to the coast off Brittany. There they were due to meet Spanish warships for further escort to northern Spain and the army was to join King Ferdinand's forces in an attack on Guienne in south-west France. But the whole expedition was doomed, not only because some of the transports were separated from the fleet in the Bay of Biscay, but also because many of the soldiers were seasick and the sailors robbed victuals. Finally, upon arrival in northern Spain they discovered that Ferdinand's plans had changed so that no preparations had been made for their arrival. The men were simply left in the countryside where they became drunk on wine. On 30 October the disappointed Marquis of Dorset reassembled them back to their transports and sailed home to Falmouth, arriving on 3 November. This fiasco left the Englishmen disillusioned, sick and mutinous.[4]

Howard's next action was to use his flagship *Mary Rose* to lead an attack on other coastal towns and villages in Brittany, and his men even chased Bretons into the castle of Brest before the fleet returned to Southampton to meet the King for further instructions. It is not clear what Henry hoped for him to achieve, but while supplies were being loaded aboard the *Mary Rose*, the King crafted plans with naval officers for his next operation and 'made a great banquet to all the captains, and every one sware to another ever to defend, aid and comfort one another without failing, and this they promised before the King, which committed them to God; and so with great noise of minstrels they took their ships, which were twenty-five in number of great burden, and well-furnished of all things'.[5]

Their main target this time was the port of Brest on the north side of a natural inlet, whose access was through a narrow entrance known as the Goulet, set in a dangerously rocky coastline, and protected by a massive castle on its waterfront. This time the *Mary Rose* carried 365 soldiers, seamen and gunners, as well as thirty-one of the Admiral's servants and sixteen for Sir Thomas Wyndham, the Captain. They sighted the coast on the evening of 9 August 1512, and at 11am the next day a lookout spotted the French fleet of about twenty-two ships under the command of Admiral Rene de Clermont, moored six miles off the port of Brest. The French, taken by surprise as 'the wind was high, with a heavy sea', cut their anchor cables and quickly retreated into the safety of the port leaving behind three ships. The *Mary Rose* attacked the *Louise* and damaged her mast with gunfire, but the French ship managed to escape back to port.[6] This is the earliest record of the *Mary Rose* firing her guns in anger, and reflects her seaworthiness and ability to fight in rough Atlantic seas. It also appears to show that long before battle instructions were written down it was naval policy for rival flagships to attack each other rather than other vessels.

The *Nef de Dieppe*, whose Captain was Rigault de Berquetot, was closely engaged in battle for about seven hours with five English warships before she too escaped. Meanwhile, the *Marie la Cordeliere*, commanded by a very experienced Breton seaman, Herve de Portzmoguer, otherwise known as Primauget, engaged with the *Sovereign* and the *Mary James*, leaving both English ships seriously damaged. *Cordeliere* was then engaged by the *Regent*, the biggest English warship, commanded by Sir Thomas Knyvet. Following an exchange of archery by English bowmen and French crossbows, soldiers from both sides boarded each other's ships and a bloody battle ensued. Nobody knows why the gunpowder magazine of the *Cordeliere* exploded at that moment, but it resulted in both ships quickly sinking. Of 800 men on board the *Regent* only 170 were saved, but the dead included Knivet and Sir John Carew. Of the 1,500 Frenchmen in the *Cordeliere*, only twenty were rescued and were made prisoners. The French dead included Portzmoguer, the Seneschal of Morlaix, and many knights and gentlemen. Sir Edward Howard was devastated by the loss of the *Regent* and vowed 'that he will never see the King in the face till he has revenged the death of the noble and valiant knight Sir Thomas Knyvet'.[7] The French, having retired from battle, left the English fleet free to raise the enemy's anchors that were presumably

The burning of the
English warship
*Regent* and the
French warship
*Cordeliere* off Brest
in 1512.

marked with buoys. Howard spent the next two days landing soldiers
intent on burning places in Brittany and seizing French ships, before
returning home to Dartmouth and Southampton on account of the
stormy weather.[8] Although the ordinary people of Brittany suffered
from these unprovoked attacks, this was a significant occasion in naval
history as the first sea battle by an English fleet in which guns played a
decisive role. The *Mary Rose* was tested and found to be capable,
though the cause was debatable.

There were no further naval actions that year and in October Howard met the King at Eltham Palace near London to discuss where the ships should be moored for the winter. Thomas Spert, Master of the *Mary Rose*, and John Cloge, Master of the *Peter Pomegranate*, offered contributions based on their great experience, and the King decided that some of the biggest ships should sail to the safety of the River Thames. They included the *Mary Rose*, the *Sovereign*, *Peter Pomegranate*, *John Hopton*, *Nicholas Reed* and the *Barbara*, leaving the rest probably at Southampton. The *Mary Rose* was brought to Blackwall, and then laid afloat in a new dock at Erith where minor repairs were undertaken, care of her Master and nine mariners as ship keepers. She was there until at least 11 February 1513 when preparations began for the new season.[9]

Unknown to the English, King Louis XII was preparing to even the score by confronting the English with his own navy, reinforced by a squadron of six galleys and four supply tenders from the Mediterranean, but they had to sail around Spain and Portugal and through dangerous Atlantic seas to reach northern France. They were commanded by the veteran Pregent de Bidoux, and arrived in the autumn of 1512. This was a master stroke by the French King for Pregent, born in Gascony, had a formidable reputation having fought the Turks, defended Naples against the Spaniards, and in 1510 won a brilliant action against the Venetians. The English had already begun to fear the reputation of his galleys whose flat bottoms enabled them to operate in shallow waters where large warships could not sail. Their convict rowers enabled easy manoeuvring so that the heavy ship-smashing gun, a 'basilisk', could be aimed at the high English carracks as they wallowed under sail in light winds.

The galleys arrived safely and on 13 March 1513 Pregent led them from Honfleur, at the mouth of the River Seine. They were to surprise the English by raiding the coast possibly between Plymouth and Falmouth. However, bad weather, a lack of victuals and sickness foiled him and he had to return home, but not for long. About 20 March the main French fleet was mobilised under the new Admiral du Chillon, and sixteen ships left Honfleur in Normandy for Brest where they believed the English would attack. Meanwhile, Henry had ensured that his fleet was also ready for action, having been repaired and enlarged, though it was clear to him that he would have to operate independently as in April 1513 King Ferdinand of Spain had signed a truce with France. There were twenty-three king's ships, five hired vessels and some victuallers, which Cardinal Wolsey was responsible for supplying. From the start Cardinal Wolsey had difficulty in ensuring that Howard's fleet was provided with food and beer, and as soon as

Howard reached Plymouth on 5 April 1513 he wrote a long letter to Wolsey, from his cabin in the *Mary Rose*, asking for supplies and money to pay the suppliers. 'I assure was never [an] army so falsely victualled', he wrote, pointedly. Barrels that were supposed to provide two months' worth of meat lasted only five weeks, 'for the barrels are full of salt … When there should be penny pieces [of meat], they be scant halfpenny pieces'. Where two pieces were to be given to a 'mess' or group of four men, they had to give three. Moreover, he added that 'the *Katherine Fortileza* has troubled me beyond reason. She brought out of the Thames but for fourteen days victuals, and no victualler is come to help her, and so have I victualled her with beer ever since … Sir, for God's sake, send by post all along the coast that they brew beer and make biscuits that we may have some refreshing to keep us together upon this coast, or else we shall be driven to come again to the Downs [off east Kent] and let the Frenchmen take their pleasure' by attacking southern England.[10]

To add to his problems, the 700-ton *Katherine Fortileza*, a carrack that was larger than the *Mary Rose* and which had been purchased from Genoa, became unseaworthy and was prone to sinking. Not only were the crow's-nest 'tops' on her masts too heavy, weakening her stability, but she had been damaged by a crazy carpenter who had left her with 'so many leaks by reason Bedell, the carpenter that worked in her at Woolwich, that we have had much to do to keep her above water. He has bored an 100 auger holes in her and left [them] unstopped, that the water came in as it were a sieve. Sir, this day I have all the caulkers of the army on her. I trust that by tomorrow she will be more staunched'.[11]

It was whilst resolving these problems that Howard heard from the crew of a merchant vessel from Brest that the French were ready to attack the English coast with one hundred warships, in addition to their galleys. He had no option but to order his fleet to sea, and hope that the supply vessels would quickly follow. It set sail from Plymouth on Sunday 10 April 1513, driven south across the western approaches of the English Channel by a northerly wind that 'rose so sore' as he noted in his letter to Henry VIII: 'I need not write unto you what storms we had, for you know it well enough. Sir, I saw never worse, but, thanked be God, all is well, saving the loss of one of our galleys'.[12]

The fleet arrived two days later to find fifteen French ships outside Brest harbour, but these 'fled like cowards' back through the narrow Goulet seaway into the safety of the harbour, joining fifty other ships sheltering under the coastal fortifications. Pregent's galleys were up the coast at St. Malo collecting victuals, and although Howard wanted to attack them, he was prevented by a wind that veered to the east blowing off-shore. He ordered his ships to drop anchor as the weather worsened and on the night of the 12th he heard that a merchant ship of eighty tons and four smaller vessels had run aground. Ever an opportunist, he sent three of his ships to investigate, and they burnt one big ship and seized others which were sent back to England as prizes. With dwindling supplies he waited for the French to come out and fight, but instead, they moored twenty-four hulks as a barrier across the narrow mouth of the Goulet, to be ready as fireships.

By now Howard was beside himself with worry as his crews were on starvation rations. Bypassing Wolsey, he wrote directly to the King on the 12th: 'Sir, [I beseech you] let ships resort with our victuals into the Trade [the English name for the Brest area] … Spare no cost, let pro[vision] be made, for it is a well-spent penny that saves the pound.' Five days later, and still with no sign of victuals from the Thames, he wrote to the King again, this time in utter despair: 'On God's name' let the victuallers come.[13]

Meanwhile, he undertook an attack on Brest harbour which had to be abandoned when the *Nicholas* of Hampton, commanded by Arthur Plantagenet, Edward IV's illegitimate son, struck one of the many rocks on this dangerous coast. Howard gave Plantagenet permission to return home because, as he wrote to the King, 'when he was in the extreme danger and hope gone from him he called upon Our Lady of Walsingham for help and comfort, and made a vow that, and it pleased God and to deliver him out of that peril, he would never eat meat nor fish till he had seen her'.[14]

With supplies exhausted, Howard retreated to Bertheaume Bay, just outside the Goulet entrance to Brest harbour where provisions at last arrived by convoy, commanded by Sir Edward Echyngham. This meant that the men enjoyed a temporary break from the ration of one meal and one drink a day, but it was not to last and they were soon be back on rations.

Howard had no option but to return home, though before doing so he wanted to win at least one naval success to alleviate what was otherwise a failed operation. The opportunity came on Friday 22 April when six French galleys and four other vessels attacked and sank the ship of Master William Compton. They also damaged one of the King's new supply 'barks', commanded by Sir Stephen Bull, and left her leaking. In return, Pregent lost one of his vessels and retired his fleet to the bay of Anse des Blancs-Salons which the English called Whitesand Bay, near Le Conquet.

Howard's final thrust was to tackle the French galleys on his terms, even though they were operating in shallow coastal waters. On Sunday 24 April he sent six thousand men to land on the coast between

Whitesand Bay and Le Conquet, and attacked the galleys from the shore. Meanwhile, he used his shallow-draft oared vessels, the 'rowbarges', which, unlike the French galleys, did not have heavy guns and were not so well suited for battle, to attack from the sea. Dismissing French superiority, Howard personally led the attack next morning on board a rowbarge with eighty men under his command. They were assailed by arrows and gunfire as Howard brought his rowbarge alongside Pregent's galley, threw a grapnel over and tied its cable to a capstan. Howard leapt onto the galley accompanied by a Spaniard named Charrau and sixteen other men. Charrau realised that he had left his hand gun on the rowbarge, and he told his boy servant to fetch it, at which point a French sailor cut the rope to the grapnel, and the two vessels drifted apart.

When the boy returned he found that he could not get aboard the galley, and instead watched with horror as his Admiral was killed. A badly wounded mariner later reported that he saw Admiral Howard being held against the rails of the French galley with morris pikes. Another reported that he saw the Admiral waving his arms, crying out, 'Come aboard again! Come aboard again!' But all was lost and Howard took the Boatswain's 'call' or whistle, his badge of office as Admiral, from his neck and threw it into the sea before he was killed. The fighting had been fierce, with Lord Ferrers' rowbarge having fired two hundred sheaves of arrows, and Sir Henry Sherborne's vessel managing to charge into Pregent's galley and break several oars. Many died on both sides in this senseless battle, before retiring to assess the damage.

With the English fleet leaderless, the three Captains, Sir Henry Cheyne, Sir Richard Cromwell and Sir John Wallop, went ashore under a 'standard of peace' to meet Pregent at Le Conquet, at around noon on 28 April. Pregent told them that Howard's body had been recovered. Subsequently, it was embalmed and sent to Princess Claud, Louis XII's daughter, while Howard's whistle of command, presumably a second one, was sent to Queen Anne.

Dispirited and in mourning from having lost their Admiral, lacking food and drink, and having many wounded and sick from a measles epidemic that had broken out among the crews, the officers ordered the fleet to sail to Plymouth, where it arrived on Saturday 30 April. The sickness was so serious that two seamen fell down dead as they reached the shore. Meanwhile, the officers nervously awaited the King's response as they moved the fleet to the more secure natural inlet at Dartmouth. The whole venture could hardly have been more of a disaster for the English and demonstrated the need for the new navy to have an efficient supplies system when at sea, and clear plans to follow on how to conduct naval actions.

Morale was at its lowest ebb and required immediate and decisive attention. The King was furious on hearing the news and immediately appointed Edward Howard's elder brother, the forty-year-old Thomas, as Admiral on 4 May 1513. Described as 'small and spare of stature', he had only recently returned from a land expedition attack on the French in Picardy when he was ordered by the King to travel to Dartmouth as fast as possible to take control of the fleet and report back what had gone wrong.

He arrived on 6 May at 9am, and four hours later wrote to the King that he was 'as weary a man of riding as ever was any. At which time I assembled in the *Mary Rose* my lords Ferrers and all older noblemen and Captains and most expert Masters of your army.' He found them

The English fleet, including the *Mary Rose*, explored the mouth of the River Dart at Dartmouth in 1522 as a possible haven. From a sixteenth-century map.

an imposing group whose views could not be ignored, for they included Sir Thomas Cheyne, Sir Henry Sherburn, Sir William Sydney, Sir William Fitz-William, Sir Edward Echyngham, Sir Richard Cromwell and two gentlemen Stephen Bull and William Compton. Howard decided to make the *Mary Rose* his flagship and appointed Edward Bray as Captain. He also ordered the dispatch of his brother's servants and it must have saddened him to be surrounded by his brother's possessions.

Thomas Howard listened carefully to what the fleet officers said about why they had returned from France without the King's permission. 'They answered with one whole voice and all in one tale that they did it upon diverse and reasonable grounds.' The officers had evidently rehearsed their statements, and explained that off the coast of France they had only enough victuals for three days, and that the supply ships from London had gone to Plymouth and Dartmouth instead of joining the fleet. Also, they has been worried that if calm weather occurred, the galleys would sink their ships, because the French guns placed inside were 'a thing marvellous'. Howard particularly noted that the English fear of the French galleys was such that the crews 'would rather go to Purgatory as to Brittany'.[15]

The death toll among the English was great, only fifty-six men having survived of the one hundred and seventy-five who attacked the galleys with his brother. Of those with Lord Ferrers, twenty-five were killed and twenty were injured. Howard concluded: 'As far as I can understand by any man's report [it was] the most dangerous enterprise that ever I heard of' and that it had left those involved 'the most angry men in the world'. The ordinary men in the fleet, however, were 'the worst ordered army and farthest out of rule' that he ever saw. As more than half the army was ashore, robbing and causing a lot of damage, he mobilised local magistrates to round up deserters, and ordered that two gallows be erected. By 15 May Howard reported that he expected some men to be 'towtered' the next day as examples what happened to those who absconded.

When Howard told the Captains and Masters that the King demanded they return to Brittany, they answered that the great fortifications and the combined danger of either the galleys if a calm should come or strong winds would all work against any achievement of success. They argued that if the wind blew onshore, from the south-west, the English fleet would be forced into Crozon Bay, where it could be destroyed by the French guns.

Scapegoats for his brother's death were needed, so after the meeting Howard found two men who 'did their part very ill', and should be punished if the case against them was upheld. They were probably men who had escaped just before Sir Edward Howard was cut adrift from Pregent's galley.

Howard moved the fleet to Plymouth where he decided not to return to Brittany until he knew the King's orders, proposing that the hired ships be discharged. He wanted to move the fleet to Southampton Water as he found Plymouth too cramped and the harbour too difficult to leave as the wind was often onshore. After re-victualling he spent frustrated days being delayed in the Cattewater channel due to onshore winds, and even made a false start on 16 May until a south-westerly wind began to blow 'so rudely' that the venture had to be abandoned.[16] On 18 May he reported to the King that he had been ready to depart for six days, but the wind was still onshore and had been so strong that the fleet was forced to lay out the secondary sheet anchors in addition to the primary bower anchors to hold the ships at their moorings, and that many anchors and cables had been broken. The cables were 'of the worst stuff that ever man saw', he added, highlighting the need for quality control in the supply of naval equipment.[17]

Whilst waiting, Howard examined other equipment only to discover that many bows and arrows were of poor quality, with few bows that could 'abide the bending'. Moreover, musters of men showed that many had escaped ashore, and that one hundred of the three hundred and eleven men commanded by Lord Ferres were missing. Hereford gaol, Howard said, was full of his men who had run away, and he wanted the King to command that some of them be executed locally and in Portsmouth. As two were arrested, he decided that if it were proven that they had absconded they would hang.

At least the supplies of beer were good, the brewhouses of Plymouth being the best that Howard had ever seen, and were brewing 100 tuns a day. But, as there was nowhere to store most of the barrels ashore in the hot weather, Howard told William Pawne to dig trenches to bury them and cover them with boards, turf and sedges to keep them cool. In contrast, most of the beer that came from London had to be sent back. Howard wrote 'much of it is as small as penny ale and as sour as a crab. I doubt not your Lordships will see the brewers punished', he added hopefully!

Frustrated by the delay, Howard grew to dislike Plymouth which he described as 'the most dangerous haven in England for so many ships … and when the wind is southwards it is impossible to leave'. He said that the Masters of the ships 'advise assembling at Southampton, where the wind that would bar us in here would carry us to Brittany. Consequently, I will try to bring the fleet to anchor off Portsmouth'.

With adverse winds still blowing on 20 May, Howard received news that the French were apparently strengthening the defences of Brest. On 11 May over sixty ships had sailed from Brittany to Normandy, and two days later eighteen more were seen.[18] Wondering what the French were doing, Howard sent three barks to Brittany to capture a local fisherman for news. On their return, the unfortunate fisherman said that fifteen or sixteen days previously, eighteen ships had sailed to Honfleur, from which Howard concluded that the French fleet was standing down, so that there was no immediate threat. The fisherman also reported that the people of Normandy were in great fear of another English landing and that all 'would gladly yield themselves English so that their country was not robbed … They would gladly be English and be out of his thraldom [the French King's land], saying that, and [if] the war continue one year, Normandy shall be utterly destroyed.'[19]

At last the wind changed and the fleet set sail, and by the time it arrived at Portsmouth, the King had abandoned his plan to send it back to Brittany. Instead, he decided to attack Picardy and on 8 June the *Mary Rose* set sail from Portsmouth to Sandwich to escort the King's 'Army Royal' across to Calais. Payments to the *Mary Rose* refer to John Brerely, Purser, and to Andrew Fysche, a gunner 'to heal him of his hurts'. Other payments that year were to Thomas Spert, Master of the ship, and to 101 mariners and six gunners.[20]

At Calais the troops were joined by others from the Holy Roman Emperor Maximilian. Together they marched south and captured Therouanne on 22 August. Just before their arrival, a French cavalry group, surprised by the huge English force, fled on horseback, thus giving the event the derisory title of the 'Battle of the Spurs' for that was supposedly all the English saw of the retreating enemy. Henry also laid siege to Tournai, nowadays in Belgium but then under French control which surrendered on 23 September.

Louis XII needed relief from the English and urged James IV of Scotland to attack northern England and to send Scottish warships to reinforce the French navy in Brittany. At first James was unwilling, but then he sent his fleet from Leith on 25 July under the command of the Earl of Arran which reached Brest about six weeks later. Meanwhile, the French continued their naval preparations, and, following the arrival of the Scottish fleet, Louis de Rouville was appointed Admiral of this Franco-Scottish naval force, his purpose being to stop Henry returning from Picardy. In the event, the weather intervened and the fleet was scattered by a storm. James IV was reluctant to invade England because of his obligation to a treaty he had made with the English, and on 24 May 1513 he wrote to Henry asking him to desist from attacking France. When Henry refused he felt that he had no option but to attack, so in July he ordered a muster of Scots at Edinburgh, and as many as forty-two thousand men are said to have joined.

Thomas Howard, Earl of Surrey and second Duke of Norfolk, although infirm and seventy-years old, took charge of events in northern England in the absence of Henry who was still in France. On 21 July he began the journey from London to join the muster that he had called as farmers, agricultural workers and traders began the long walk from every direction in the north to the assembly port of Newcastle, chosen because it could be provided with weapons and supplies by sea. The Duke of Surrey also ordered his son, Thomas, the forty-year-old Lord Admiral, to bring his fleet to the port, and to provide about twelve hundred soldiers and ships' gunners to join the land army. In fact the gunners from the *Mary Rose* and the rest of the fleet would make a significant contribution to the forthcoming battle.

On 11 August James IV delivered a final ultimatum demanding that Henry withdraw from the siege of Therouanne, but this was ignored. Eleven days later the Scots crossed the River Tweed into England at Coldstream, and headed south. Surrey reached Newcastle on 30 August and took personal charge of the army of roughly twenty-six thousand men crowding the streets as the English fleet, led by the Admiral's flag-

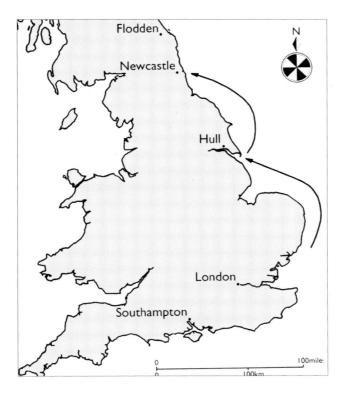

The English fleet, including the *Mary Rose*, sailed to Newcastle in 1513, and reinforced the English army at the successful Battle of Flodden in which the Scottish King, James IV, was killed. (*Mary Rose Trust*)

ship *Mary Rose*, dropped anchor in the wide River Tyne. It was an amazing sight as the port was overwhelmed by men and ships, so much so that Surrey had to order the men to reassemble several miles northwards at Bolton in Glendale. It was there that Admiral Howard arrived at the head of his men who were hauling ships' guns, and it is believed that he wrote with bravado to King James warning him that the Howards were on their way – a reminder that it was they who had killed the popular Scottish privateer, Andrew Barton.[21]

The Scots marched south and by 5 September were camped at Flodden Edge, a hill that dominated the plain below. The English were nowhere in sight. Four days later the Scots discovered that their enemy had quietly circled around to the north, cutting off their escape. On that wet and windy day, the English took up position beside the tiny village of Branxton, and separated into two large divisions. Two hundred mariners led by Maurice Berkeley, Master of the *Mary Rose*, joined a division of about three thousand men with Edmund Howard, Surrey's youngest son, in overall charge. The remaining one thousand soldiers with their ships' Captains and Masters, including Sir William Sydney of the *Great Barque*, Edward Edyngham of the *Spaniard*, and James King of the *Julian of Dartmouth*, joined the other division of about nine thousand men led by Surrey.

The Battle of Flodden began at about 4pm with gunfire on both sides, but the English guns took a terrible toll on the Scots until the tables were reversed and the English were forced back where the exhausted Scots encountered boggy ground. The Scots abandoned their cumbersome long pikes and bills to rely upon their swords, but this was a mistake as the English used their spear-like bills to hack, slash and thrust with devastating effect beyond the short reach of the swords. King James tried to rally his men by charging at the English, but was killed by an arrow and wounds from bills. The battle was over by 7pm and the Scots fled leaving over five thousand dead, whereas the English were said to have lost roughly fifteen hundred men.

Lord Admiral Howard was proud of his ships' companies who had fought bravely under their commanding officers, including Edward Bray, Captain of the *Mary Rose*. Some months later the Admiral claimed his expenses from the exchequer for the 'charges as I and my company were at from the time we landed at Newcastle until the time we took to sea again, by space of 16 days'. Payments were made to men from fifteen ships, including the *Mary Rose*, and included twelve Danish gunners from a hulk and seven men who were injured.[22] When news of the success reached Henry in Tournai on 24 September, he ordered a special victory service to be held in the cathedral next day, before departing on the long journey back to England.

Winter was traditionally the time when naval warfare stopped due to the bad weather, but over 1513–14 things were different, with a heightened tension between England and France. Consequently, the English fleet anchored in readiness at Erith on the Thames, and the French fleet moored at St. Malo, Honfleur and Dieppe. It was a standoff.

Although a truce was agreed in March 1514 it did not stop hostilities. Pregent, commanding the French galleys, sailed from Dieppe in mid-April and attacked Brighthelmstone (Brighton) in Sussex, though the local people counter-attacked and seriously wounded Pregent when an arrow struck his eye. Two months later, and somewhat recovered, he took his galleys back to the Mediterranean, but not before the English noble, Sir John Wallop, had sailed to Normandy and burnt twenty-one towns and villages in reprisal.[23]

Peace with France in 1514 came at a price for Henry VIII, who decided to offer his attractive auburn-headed younger sister, Mary, then only eighteen, in marriage to the aging Louis XII, then fifty-two. This was accepted, and when the wedding took place in Abbeville in October that year, Mary became Queen of France, and the ties between England and France seemed secure. The Holy League against France was dissolved in March and a permanent peace was signed on 7 August. However, Louis died a few months later, worn out, it was said by an Italian commentator, by his excesses in the bedchamber.

*Chapter Four*

# THE SECOND FRENCH WAR, 1522

Henry ordered his fleet to stand down, and in July 1514 the *Mary Rose* and twelve other warships were taken to the Royal Dockyard at Deptford on the Thames for decommissioning. The dockyard had recently been established to build, repair and supply ships. At the same time, the King established the Corporation of Trinity House, initially responsible for safe pilotage on the busy River Thames through the rapidly growing port of London, though in due course its responsibility for pilotage was extended nationally.

The decommissioning was supervised by Sir Henry Wyatt, Master of the Jewell House, and involved making an inventory of everything that was removed from the ships. On 9 August, the *Mary Rose* began to be cleared by a handful of men under a shipkeeper whose list provides a detailed description of parts of the *Mary Rose*.[1] These included her four masts and rigging, some portable inboard equipment, and her flags, banners and streamers whose decoration reflected the King's allegiance to England and Spain, through his marriage. Some had a representation of St Katherine with the arms of England and Castile and the rose and pomegranate, whereas a banner of St. Peter represented his allegiance to the Catholic Church. Curiously there were also five banners with the arms of Boulogne, the French port that Henry was anxious to claim, and, ironically, became the central issue of the sea battle thirty-one years later in which the *Mary Rose* sank.[2]

The anchorage in the River Thames proved unsatisfactory, probably because the ships blocked the tidal passage needed by trading vessels to reach the port of London. As a result, in June 1517 the *Mary Rose*, the *Great Galley*, the *Peter Pomegranate*, the *Great Bark* and the *Lesser Bark* were moved to a huge new 'wet dock' specially excavated for them and which remained their home for several years until events in Europe, outside Henry's control, dictated that the ships' services once again were needed.[3]

Meanwhile, France had a new young King, Francis I, who was entirely different from the aged Louis XII who had died on 1 January 1515. Francis was twenty-years old, close to Henry's age, and was ambitious enough to build a military reputation by conquering parts of Italy. With his armies campaigning in southern Europe he did not want to break the peace with England in the north.

Just as the French people were getting used to their new king, Henry's Spanish father-in-law, King Ferdinand of Aragon, died in 1516, and was succeeded by his sixteen-year-old grandson, Charles of Ghent, who became Charles V of Spain. Soon afterwards the Holy Roman Emperor, Maximilian I, died in January 1519, and Charles succeeded him and inherited much of the Low Countries, Germany and Italy, as well as Spain. This election by the Pope angered Francis I because it left his country almost completely surrounded by potential enemies and he was in need of Henry's support. Peace had suited Henry for a while, though his ambition still remained to seize part of northern France, but he kept this secret when he agreed to hold a friendly meeting with Francis I in the summer of 1520, in Picardy. This occurred between the villages of Guisnes and Ardres on the border of France and the English possession around Calais. Cardinal Wolsey Master-minded the English side of the meeting believing that it would reinforce the Treaty of London in which Tournai was returned to France.

The meeting of the kings was arranged for the 7th to 24th June 1520, but Henry covertly plotted betrayal when he met the Emperor Charles V in England about two weeks earlier. Wolsey had received the Emperor at Dover on 26 May as his fleet docked to a thunderous salute from the guns of the English warships. The *Mary Rose* must have been involved as Charles walked ashore beneath a canopy of gold cloth emblazoned with his badge of a black eagle, and Wolsey escorted him to Dover Castle for the night. When Henry hurriedly arrived the next day he met Charles on the stairs with an informality that was in stark contrast to their subsequent grand progress to Canterbury Cathedral for Whitsun High Mass, where Charles kneeled at the shrine of Thomas a Becket and kissed his holy relics. It was not until 31 May that they parted, Charles sailing home to Spain from Sandwich in eastern Kent, and Henry preparing to sail to Calais from Dover with about six thousand courtiers and servants for his meeting with Francis.

Francis was rightly suspicious of the meeting for it gave Henry and Charles plenty of time to plot against France. Nevertheless, that meeting between Henry and Francis is one of the most absurd events in European history and was like a fantasy from Disney. Only one document mentions the role of the *Mary Rose*, and simply describes the cost of what was necessary to transport the King and his court for his 'interview' with the French king. It specifies that the *Mary Rose*, the *Great Bark*, the *Little Bark* and two small ships were to scour the seas during the King's passage while a huge number of ships transported thousands of people, and massive tonnages of equipment and supplies, from Dover to Calais. Once in France, wagons hauled supplies overland to the fields where the camp was set up.[4] When everything was ready Henry and his queen sailed across the Channel in the *Katherine Pleasaunce*, a voyage that about twenty-five years later was commemorated in a painting commissioned by Henry, probably from a Flemish artist. It shows thirteen of Henry's warships, possibly including the *Mary Rose*, not as they were in 1520 as that was not the artistic style of the day, but as they were about twenty-five years later after their rebuilding.

Cardinal Thomas Wolsey, always a skilled diplomat as well as papal legate to Pope Leo X (r. 1513–21), had his own agenda for bringing peace to Europe. Not only did he aspire to increase Henry's influence in European affairs, but also he helped to bind together the Christian states against the threat to south-east Europe from the Turkish Ottoman Empire, led by Suleman the Magnificent (r. 1520–66).

Each monarch had spent fortunes that he could ill-afford, simply in friendly rivalry to outdo the other. Henry had a huge temporary castle built on a brick base, and set up twenty-eight hundred tents. Red wine flowed from fountains, and a temporary chapel was served by thirty-five priests. So much gold was used by both kings that it gave the place its name that remains to this day, *Camp du Drap d'Or* (Field of the Cloth of Gold). For two weeks in that hot dry dusty summer there were banquets, music, jousting displays and games before the lords, ladies and other courtiers of both kingdoms. The two monarchs wrestled each other, with Francis winning, though later Henry beat him in an archery contest. At the end of festivities, everyone returned home having enjoyed such a unique occasion, the buildings were taken down, and the site returned to its former use as farmland. It is still farmland today, but beneath the surface are the remains of what is one of the most fascinating and closely dated archaeological sites yet to be explored in Europe. The contents of the many rubbish pits alone warrant careful study, and perhaps one day it will be reconstructed to become a major tourist attraction.

Thereafter, Henry turned his attention to deciding when to attack France, and instead of boarding a ship to cross the Channel, he and Queen Catherine rode eastwards to Gravelines, where on 10 July they met Charles V and his aunt, the Regent Margaret of Savoy (r. 1507–30), 'without any pomp'. This pre-arranged meeting seems to have been to plot the invasion of France, after which Henry escorted his imperial visitors to Calais where they concluded a treaty of friend-ship and went their separate ways.

The invasion was not imminent, so the *Mary Rose* and the rest of Henry's fleet were stood down and she returned to her wet dock at Deptford where some minor maintenance repairs were carried out. A payment docket records that she was caulked by two men for several days, and seven men pumped her out over one day and night.[5]

Francis I had spies in the English court, and his suspicions about Henry's ambitions were reinforced when on 14 July he heard that Henry and Charles had agreed a treaty not to make any fresh alliance with France for two years. He did not know that on 25 September 1521 Cardinal Wolsey and Charles V had signed a secret treaty agreeing to declare war on France in 1523.

In spite of having created a navy and being able to muster a substan-tial army on any battlefield that was equal to those of France and Spain, Henry still felt disadvantaged. He considered himself a good Catholic and the Pope's guardian knight, and yet he envied the special religious titles that years earlier a Pope had bestowed on Charles and Francis. He realised that he had to earn a special title, so, in 1521, he published a book in defence of the Pope against the popular but heretical protestant views of the German monk Martin Luther. The Pope, ever mindful of his need for royal friends, duly responded, and on 11 October 1521 rewarded Henry with the grand title *Fidei Defensor* (Defender of the Faith). Each English monarch since then has claimed this title that can still be seen on every British coin, in spite of the fact that seventeen years later Pope Paul III (r. 1534–49) excommunicated Henry from the Catholic Church for seizing supreme power of the Church in England!

Francis did not help his own cause for peace that year by invading Navarre, a small kingdom in north-east Spain that had been fighting for its independence, and by attacking the Low Countries, territories that were ruled by Charles V. These events were part of a much wider European conflict known as the Italian War of 1521–26, in which France and the Republic of Venice jointly opposed Charles V and the Papal States. Charles quickly responded by invading northern France, and urgently claimed Henry's help. This matched Henry's ambition and so, on 29 May 1522, Henry declared war on France and its ally Scotland. The *Mary Rose* was to be in service once again.

The alliance between Charles V and Henry had been sealed three days earlier, on 26 May 1522 during a state visit by Charles to England, ostensibly to mark his betrothal to his six-year-old cousin, the Princess Mary Tudor (r. 1553–58), daughter of Henry VIII and Catherine of Aragon. Charles's fleet had stopped off on its way from the Low

Countries to Spain, and, as before, he was met by Wolsey at Dover. Charles was again conducted to Dover Castle on the high hilltop overlooking the English Channel, where, on a clear day the English coast around Calais could be seen. Later that day he was met by Henry who proudly escorted him around the *Mary Rose* and the *Henry Grace a Dieu* while their guns were fired in salute. Afterwards, both kings and their retinues rode to Canterbury and on to Gravesend, where they embarked on a flotilla of thirty barges for the short voyage to Greenwich for a royal reception in the palace of Placentia where Henry VIII was born. They entered London on 6 June 'in great triumph, not only like brothers of one mind, but in the same attire'.

They signed the Treaty of Windsor on 16 June 1522 agreeing to attack France, with each party committed to supplying at least forty thousand men. Charles also agreed financial terms in return for agreeing to marry Mary, but as events unfolded several years later Charles found that he lacked funds to pay for the war, and in 1525 decided to forgo his marriage to Mary. The unfortunate royal women in those days were treated as pawns in the ambitions of kings, often with arranged marriages to former enemies.

In May 1522 the English fleet was once again at sea, the plan being to bring it from the Thames to Southampton. On 8 June Sir Thomas Howard, Lord High Admiral of England, was appointed by Henry and Charles V as commander-in-chief of the combined fleets of England and the Empire, on the basis that one commander was better than several. With this enormous responsibility, in charge of one of the greatest naval forces in European history up till then, he nevertheless based himself in the *Mary Rose* as his flagship instead of in the more prestigious and much larger and grander *Henry Grace a Dieu*. The *Mary Rose* was clearly a 'special' ship to him, with the experienced John Browne as her Master. As soon as victuals had been stowed, Howard's fleet set sail in fine weather, driven westward past St Helens on the Isle of Wight and on to Dartmouth in south-west England, where he paused to explore the deep-tidal estuary of the River Dart in case it could be used as a wintering place for the navy in the future.[6]

Howard then took the combined fleet to Cherbourg, landing there on 13 June to raid the countryside before returning to England for more supplies. He then re-crossed the Channel and landed near Morlaix on 1 July, where he sacked and burnt the town, massacred the people and burnt seventeen ships – a destruction that is remembered to today. The French view was that the English had dressed several hundred troops as merchants and sent them into the town at night to take them by surprise. The town militia was away at a fair, so with no resistance, the English went on a rampage, breaking open barrels of wine and getting drunk, which enabled the returning French to kill them. In spite of this, Howard returned to Southampton with much booty, leaving Sir William Fitzwilliam to patrol the Channel.

Satisfied by the outcome of this raid, the Emperor Charles boarded his fleet at Southampton on 6 July and sailed for Santander in Spain. Soon afterwards, Howard left the *Mary Rose* when the King put him in charge of fifteen thousand men, the 'Army Royal', to march into France as part of another supposed combined attack with Charles V. Vice-Admiral Sir William Fitz-William took charge of the fleet of twenty-eight ships and used the *Mary Rose* as his flagship, whilst protecting English shipping in the Channel and 'annoying' the French by patrolling the coast of Brittany in mid-August. This was possibly a defensive measure in case of reprisals for sacking Morlaix, and continued until October when the Channel fleet returned to Portsmouth, where the *Mary Rose* was taken out of service for the winter.

With war expected to continue into 1525, it was a surprise when it abruptly ended on 24 February 1525 as Francis was captured by the Emperor Charles' forces at the battle of Pavia, in Italy. Next year, 1526, Charles freed Francis in very advantageous terms to Spain, leaving Francis angry and, privately, even more determined to oppose Charles, to the extent that he even established formal relations with Suleiman the Magnificent, the Ottoman Sultan, as a possible ally.

During 1525 the *Mary Rose* was moved to Deptford where she 'lieth in the pond' and awaited caulking. She was no longer an Admiral's flagship as the top naval posts became purely token, and the infant, six-year-old Henry Fitzroy, Duke of Richmond, King Henry's illegitimate son by his mistress Elizabeth Blount, was appointed Lord High Admiral in succession to Sir Thomas Howard who had succeeded to the dukedom of Norfolk. But when Richmond died in 1536, the office was conferred more appropriately on Sir William Fitz-William.

Even though the wars had caused a great deal of misery for ordinary folk, Henry's creation of a navy with excellent ships like the *Mary Rose* had proved its worth, though the financial administration was in a muddle, inadequate supplies of food and equipment were sent to the fleet at sea, and naval warfare tactics needed careful planning. A report into the state of the King's navy in 1525 specified the maintenance repairs that were necessary. The *Mary Rose*, 600 tons, 'lyeth in a [dock] at Deptford beside the storehouse there, which must [be] ... caulked from the keel upwards, both within and without'. The *Sovereign*, 800 tons, lay in a dock at nearby Woolwich, and must be 'new made' from the keel upwards, 'the form of which ship is so marvellously goodly that great pity it were she should die'. It was evidently decided to abandon her, for her remains were discovered in 1912 when a power station was built on the site.[7] Other ships of Henry's navy needed only slight repair, such as the *Henry Grace a Dieu*, 1,500 tons (another document says 1,000 tons), which was moored not far away at Northfleet and simply needed some caulking between her planks, whereas the *Gabriel Royal*, 650 tons, in contrast, needed rebuilding.[8]

The repairs to the *Mary Rose* were carried out in June and July 1527, the materials purchased showing that they were not extensive. They only included thirty-seven feet of plankboard, five inches thick, to replace some outer hull planking, forty-six feet of square timber perhaps for frames, 120 feet of 'overlop board', two inches thick, for decking, and many iron nails of various sizes to fasten them. They also bought two loads of reeds to burn, soften and remove the old tar caulking, and six hundredweight of oakum, old rope used for caulking, to be used with eight barrels of pitch and two barrels of tar.[9]

For the next ten years the ships would remain largely unused as Henry confronted issues that would change the face of England, and improvements in gun technology meant that he would need to modernise his fleet. It was only a matter of time before the embryonic Royal Navy moved into a new stage of its history, where the lessons of its first two wars with France had to be addressed, but this would expose flaws in his favourite ship *Mary Rose*.

*Chapter Five*

# MODERNISATION

Henry VIII had much more on his mind than going to war against France during the eleven years from 1525 to 1536. He desperately needed a male successor, and by 1527 it was clear that Queen Catherine of Aragon was not going to bear him a son. He decided to divorce her, which, of course, meant upsetting her Spanish nephew Charles V. He also upset the Pope by unsuccessfully trying to obtain his agreement to the divorce. And so his 'Great Matter' dragged on for years, until he married his second wife, Anne Boleyn (r. 1533–36) in 1533. It was not long before that marriage also encountered difficulties which led to his marrying his third wife Jane Seymour (r. 1536–37) in 1536. Serious personal difficulties continued throughout the rest of his reign, made worse by the infection of a leg wound from a severe jousting accident in 1536 which would not heal properly and may have resulted in a change of personality that caused mood swings and obesity in later life.

Separating the Church in England from the papacy's control was another matter that occupied Henry over several years. It was unacceptable to him that monasteries were hugely profitable and provided a rival source of power in his kingdom, so he closed them down, seized their property, sold their lands and buildings to his nobles and took personal control over the Church. This act isolated him from Spain, France, Scotland and the rest of the Holy Roman Empire and he was formerly excommunicated by Pope Paul III (r. 1534–49) in 1538. Henry did not care about the political and religious upset that he generated. He even boldly claimed his status as head of the Church in England on some of the fine new bronze guns carried by the *Mary Rose*. On one was inscribed 'Henry the eighth, by the Grace of God, King of England and France, Defender of the Faith, Lord of Ireland', and on another he added that he was 'Defender of the Faith, of the Church of England and also of Ireland, in Earth the Supreme Head'. Modesty was not one of his attributes!

Henry knew that it was only a matter of time before France or Spain would decide to invade England to restore papal control, and was alarmed when in 1538 he heard that Pope Paul III had managed to negotiate the Treaty of Nice between those two kingdoms. Of paramount importance was his need to keep control of the English Channel as a defensive moat separating England from Europe, and for this he built a chain of coastal forts and modernised his navy.

Known as the 'Device of the King', his coastal defence system made

An inscription on a bronze gun from the *Mary Rose* claims that the English King was 'Henry the Eighth, by the Grace of God, King of England, France and Ireland, Defender of the Faith, and of the Church of England and also of Ireland the Supreme Head'.

of thirty new fortifications armed with heavy guns, was constructed from 1539 onwards and included Camber Castle in Sussex, Southsea Castle at Portsmouth and Pendennis and St. Mawes Castles guarding the entrance to Falmouth in Cornwall. Others were built beside the River Thames at Tilbury and Gravesend, further north at Harwich and Hull, and another in south-west Wales on the Pembroke coast. There were also minor coastal defences, including a town wall across the seaward end of the narrow valley in which nestled the fishing Cinque port of Hastings in Sussex, and at Teignmouth, Devon, where a gun battery was constructed on the beach to protect the entrance to the River Teign.

The King had been adding ships to his fleet for some years: the *Trinity Henry* of 250 tons in 1530, the *Mary Willoughby* of 160 tons in 1532, and the *Sweepstake* of 300 tons in 1535. Importantly, he also modernised his older ships, the *Henry Grace a Dieu*, the *Mary Rose*, the *Peter Pomegranate*, the *Lyon*, the *Katherine Galley*, the *Less Bark*, *Primrose* and the *Minion*.[1] It is not precisely clear when the naval modernisation began, for in 1536 the Imperial Ambassador, Eustace Chapuys, reported to the Emperor Charles V that all of Henry's 'great ships' were in such a poor state of repair that it would take eighteen months to get them to sea. And yet in that same year Thomas Cromwell, Henry's Principal Secretary, wrote that the *Mary Rose* was one of six warships that he had caused to be 'new made'.[2] What they looked like after modernisation is shown in the pictures on the Anthony Roll of 1546, as well as in a painting of about 1540 that supposedly represented the departure of the King at Dover in 1520 to meet Francis I at the Field of the Cloth of Gold. In addition, armament lists trace the increased firepower of guns in the navy, and although we do not know how a ship's tonnage was then calculated, it is clear from the tonnage measurements of the *Mary Rose* that she was enlarged from 500–600 tons to 700–800 tons.

This modernisation is reflected by the date of cutting down of some of the trees used in the ship. Martin Bridge, a dendrochronologist, or tree-ring dating expert, drilled cores of wood in a selection of timbers from various parts of the ship to reveal tree rings that could be precisely measured. The dating is based on the fact that oak trees grow one ring each year, and that the width of each ring largely depends upon the weather, a wet year giving a wide ring, and a dry year giving a thin ring. Other factors, such as the density of the forest, also enters the equation, but basically oak trees in the same region should have the same pattern of thick and thin rings. This has allowed the pattern of tree ring growth in northern Europe to be traced back over thousands of years, enabling experts to ascribe exact dates to each ring. In the

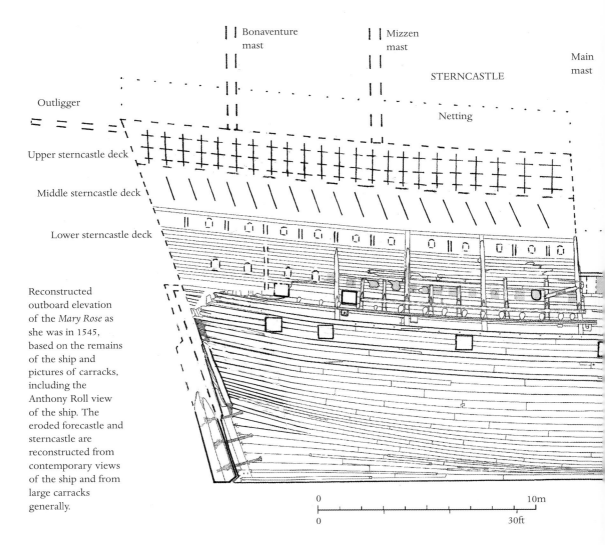

Reconstructed outboard elevation of the *Mary Rose* as she was in 1545, based on the remains of the ship and pictures of carracks, including the Anthony Roll view of the ship. The eroded forecastle and sterncastle are reconstructed from contemporary views of the ship and from large carracks generally.

*Mary Rose* 108 samples were taken from planks, frames, knees and deck beams, forty-one of which were successfully dated because they had a sequence of at least fifty rings that matched with the master dated pattern for the region. But, as the latest soft sapwood growth had mostly been cut away by the shipwrights, leaving only the older harder heartwood, it was not possible to show exactly when each tree was cut down. Samples, however, did give dates after which felling occurred and this was sufficient to show that most trees belonged to the rebuilding around 1536. This is particularly shown by the tree-ring dating of the horizontal knees of the squared stern which are dated well after 1525, for they are dated after 1521 (sapwood missing), 1524 (sapwood missing) and 1525 (twenty sapwood rings).[3]

The conclusion is that *Mary Rose's* bow and stern ends were completely rebuilt, and that her keel was lengthened to enable her to

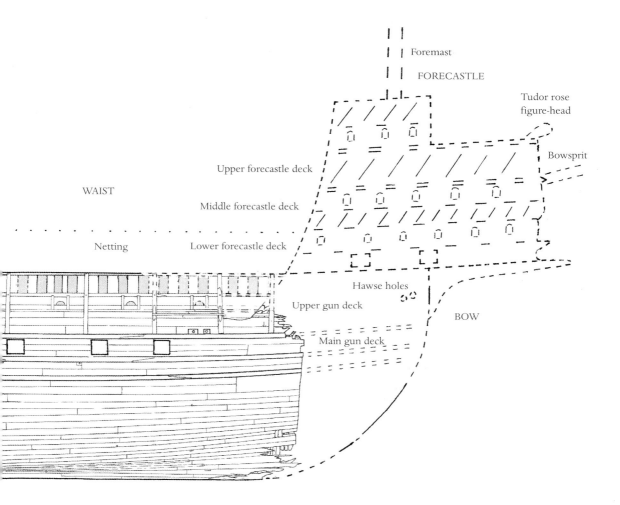

Foremast

FORECASTLE

Tudor rose figure-head

Bowsprit

Upper forecastle deck

WAIST

Middle forecastle deck

Netting

Lower forecastle deck

Hawse holes

Upper gun deck

BOW

Main gun deck

be enlarged from 500–600 tons in 1512–5, to 700–800 tons in 1545–6. For this to happen, she must have been hauled ashore or fitted out in a dry dock where the shipwrights had access to her bottom. This probably occurred at Erith or Deptford, downstream of London, for in 1539 she is recorded as being there with the *Peter Pomegranate* and the *Minion* having been 'new made, standing in their docks' though their masts were still in storage.[4] It was then estimated that it would take at least three months to make them ready for sailing and would require five hundred hundred shipwrights, caulkers and mariners.

James Baker was probably the Master Shipwright involved, his reputation having outlived all others of his generation. He was appointed to the special status of King's Shipwright in 1538, and given an annuity of four pence a day which was increased to eight pence a day in 1544 when he was described as 'skilful in ships'.[5] This increase suggests that

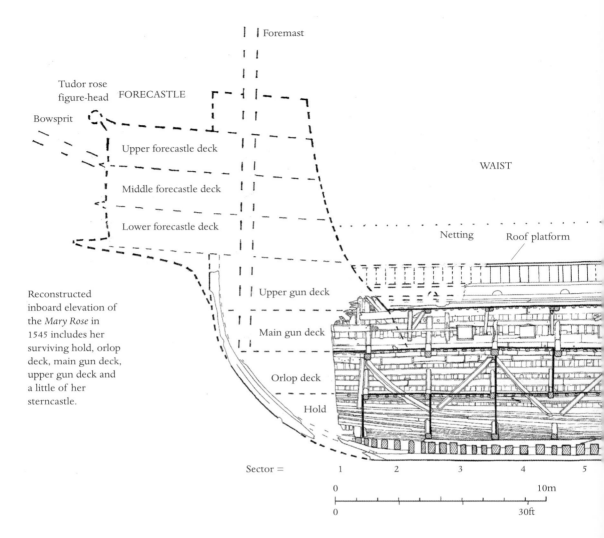

Foremast

Tudor rose
figure-head   FORECASTLE

Bowsprit

WAIST

Upper forecastle deck

Middle forecastle deck

Lower forecastle deck

Netting          Roof platform

Reconstructed
inboard elevation of
the *Mary Rose* in
1545 includes her
surviving hold, orlop
deck, main gun deck,
upper gun deck and
a little of her
sterncastle.

Upper gun deck

Main gun deck

Orlop deck

Hold

Sector =          1          2          3          4          5

0                              10m

0                              30ft

he had either a longer service or was in a more senior position than others who received half of his pension. He was still remembered in the reign of King James I (r. 1603–25) in the seventeenth century, as the first to adapt English ships to carry heavy guns. It seems likely therefore that Baker was the naval architect responsible for cutting the gunports in the sides of the *Mary Rose* to create the main gun deck. It also explains why it was to him the King referred in 1545 when asking for extra guns to be put in the ship. His professional abilities saved him in 1546 when he got into trouble for possessing forbidden religious books and Henry ordered him to be examined. The conclusion was that 'His Majesty thinketh you shall find him a very simple man, and therefore would that, without putting him in any great fear, you should search of him as much as you may.'[6] James was said to be the father of Matthew Baker, the royal Master Shipwright to Queen Elizabeth I

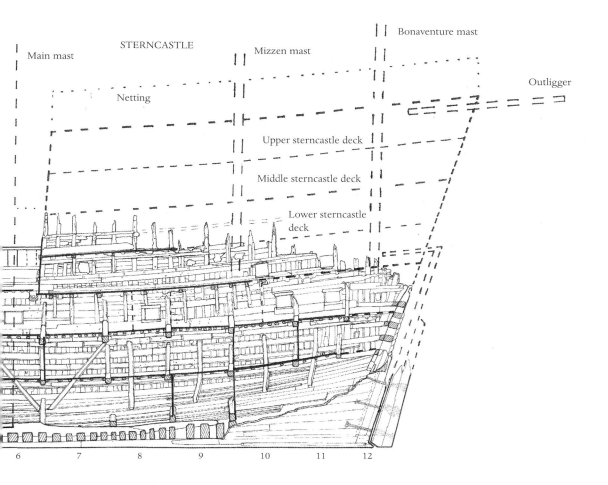

(r. 1558–1603), who was the first in England to publish how ships should be built and their tonnage calculated. He no doubt learned much of his trade from his father to whom he would have been apprenticed.[7] The other Master Shipwrights responsible for modernising the navy probably included John Smyth, Robert Holborn and Richard Bull who in 1548 were granted pensions from the Exchequer of four pence a day 'in consideration of their long and good service, and that they should instruct others in their feats'.[8]

The rebuilding required the removal of all of her masts and rigging, after which her bow and stern were dismantled, including the ends of her keel, leaving only the central portion of her hull partly intact. Deck planks were also stripped out leaving only some deck beams to hold the hull's sides together.[9] The ends of the original oak keel were extended with elm, carefully scarfed onto the old central section of

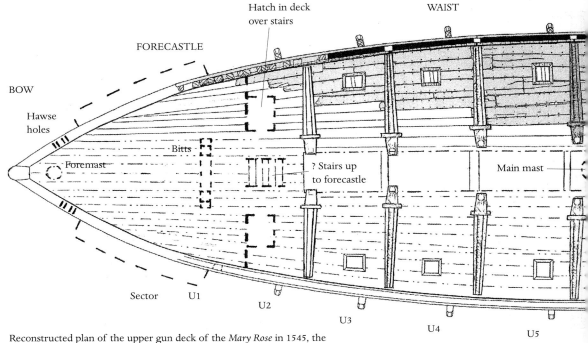

Reconstructed plan of the upper gun deck of the *Mary Rose* in 1545, the
toned area being what was found. The waist between the forecastle and
sterncastle was partly covered by a raised platform (not shown) that
protected the gunners and archers, and by an anti-boarding net. This net
held sailors and soldiers underwater when the ship sank, drowning them.

oak. Tree-ring dating shows that the rebuild included the great horizontal angled knee timbers of oak that gave her stern a wide squared
shape that enabled her to carry stern-chaser guns as shown on the
Anthony Roll. Her hull bottom was also strengthened with massive
transverse timber 'riders' and longitudinal 'stringers', as well as upright
and diagonal timber braces fastened inboard to her sides to support the
extra weight of heavy guns. Major parts of her decks had to be
removed to achieve all of this which would explain why her lowest
deck, the orlop, was re-planked mostly with elm instead of oak as on
the other decks.

The decks inside the hull lay about two metres above each other
giving enough room for most men to stand upright. The major deck
beams across the ship were spaced three metres apart, with the areas
between filled by 'half beams' and fore-and-aft timber 'carlings'. The
whole structure was then covered by planks leaving gaps for hatches
mostly along the centreline. The hatches in the orlop deck were about
2.5 metres long fore and aft and 1.70 metres wide, each having three
covers, with a pair of holes in opposite corners for rope lifting handles.
There is nothing to show that the ship ever had gratings in any decks
to allow light and ventilation below as in later large ships. As such,

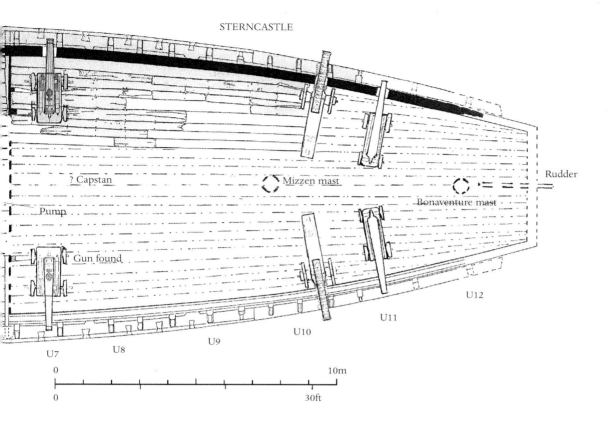

STERNCASTLE

? Capstan

Pump

Gun found

Mizzen mast

Bonaventure mast

Rudder

U7  U8  U9  U10  U11  U12

0              10m

0              30ft

there was always the risk of someone falling down an open hatch and breaking a limb. The conversion of the main deck from its former use as living quarters and storage areas into a gun deck with square gunports cut through her hull, was a major reason for the rebuild. One deck beam on the main gun deck still had its latest bark growth which enabled the cutting down of the tree to be dated to 1535, fitting the rebuild date of 1536.

That the *Mary Rose* was a much more effective fighting ship after her renovation is reflected by the increase in the number of her guns.[10] In 1514 she had only five anti-ship guns, plus seven guns that could fire either anti-ship or anti-personnel shot, and sixty-six anti-personnel guns, whereas in 1545 she had twenty-six anti-ship guns, twelve anti-ship or anti-personnel guns, and fifty-three anti-personnel guns. Moreover, some of these ship-smashing bronze guns bear dates (1535 on three guns, 1537 on one gun, 1542 on three guns, and 1543 on another gun), showing that the modernisation continued on an annual basis after 1536.

As the anti-personnel guns were reduced in number, so some of their old swivel positions in the central part of the ship were covered by the overlapping planks that clad the lower part of the sterncastle. Even

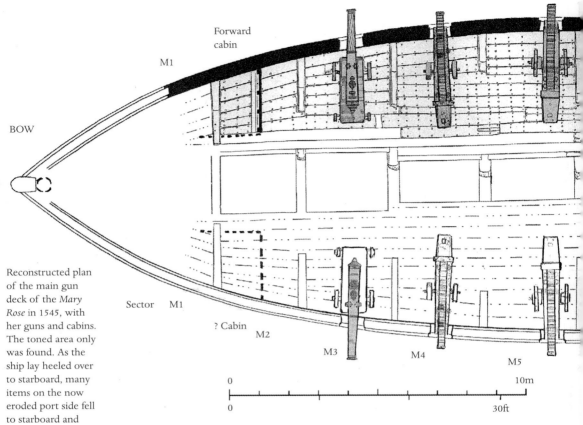

Forward
cabin

M1

BOW

Sector    M1

? Cabin

M2

M3          M4          M5

0                                      10m

0                                      30ft

Reconstructed plan
of the main gun
deck of the *Mary
Rose* in 1545, with
her guns and cabins.
The toned area only
was found. As the
ship lay heeled over
to starboard, many
items on the now
eroded port side fell
to starboard and
therefore survived.

some of the 'pavasse' shields in the sides of her waist, protecting the
archers on the upper gun deck, had been put back carelessly as if
archery were not so important once the large guns were located there.
Another major change was in the diameter of her main mast which
appears to have been reduced from about 1.5 metres to about seventy
centimetres. This was done to fit a new socket and narrower
supporting keelson timber, as if the importance of the anti-personnel
fighting from the tops of the original mast had been downgraded, and
to reduce her top-heavy weight.

Whether or not there were gunports on the main gun deck in 1512
or only after 1536 has been a major question on which scholars have
been divided. However, as it is only after the 1530s that lists show that
the vessel had extra ship-smashing guns it seems reasonable to
conclude that they were added around 1536. This would explain why
pictures of carracks around 1512 when the *Mary Rose* was built do not
show such gunports with lids on the main gun deck, and that in the
*Mary Rose* the extra gunports seem to have been slotted between
existing cabins as if the cabins pre-existed. This would also explain why
the gunports were constructed roughly between the pre-existing cabins

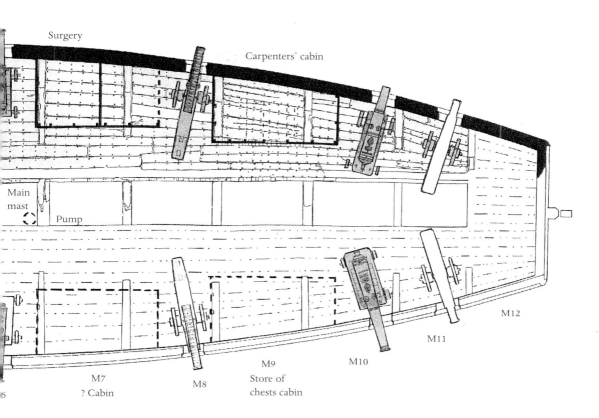

Surgery

Carpenters' cabin

Main mast

Pump

M7

? Cabin

M8

M9

Store of chests cabin

M10

M11

M12

to the extent that the wheel of a guncarriage had to be made smaller to fit in, and why the main gun deck was reinforced with standing knees beside the new gunports some years after 1530.[11] With her conversion complete, her principle purpose remained to disable enemy ships so that they could be boarded after her great iron grappling hook was dropped onto an unwilling enemy deck, and the sharp scythe-like iron 'sheerhooks' on the yardarms cut through enemy rigging.

We lose track of the *Mary Rose* for some years as if she was moth-balled, or, in naval terms, 'in ordinary', until suddenly in 1539 she burst onto the stage of history under an incredibly rare spotlight that exposed her maintenance crew to serious trouble. That summer she was moored off Deptford and on the night of Monday 9 June 1539 her shipkeepers did something very silly for which they subsequently had to account in an Admiralty Court.[12]

After supper on board, around 8pm, Richard Baker, a mariner from St Nicholas Lane in the City of London, Robert Gryggan from Suffolk, William Oram and Marmaduke Colman, from Ipswich, with a few others from nearby ships, went ashore to 'make merry' in a beer house in Deptford. They stayed till 10pm, by which time 'some of

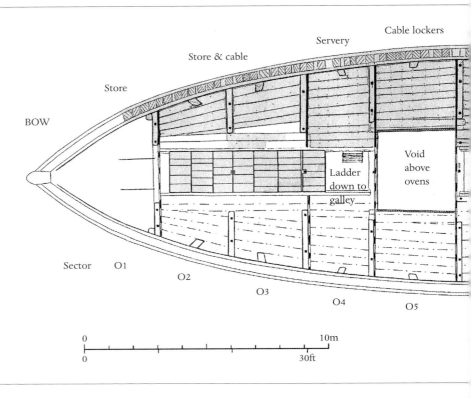

Reconstructed plan of the orlop deck of the *Mary Rose* in 1545, with its anchor cable lockers, food 'servery', and stores which included archery equipment. Access hatches to the stores in the hold below existed along the centre of the deck. A ladder gave access to the galley cooking ovens below the 'servery'.

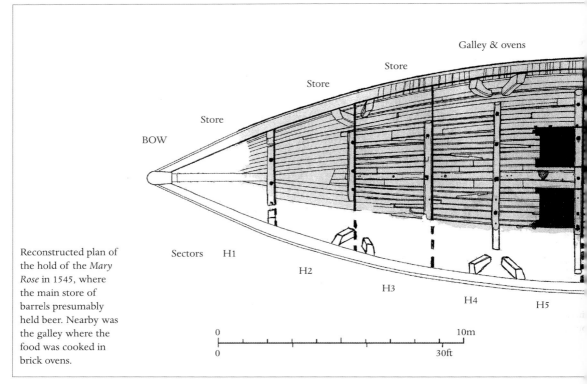

Reconstructed plan of the hold of the *Mary Rose* in 1545, where the main store of barrels presumably held beer. Nearby was the galley where the food was cooked in brick ovens.

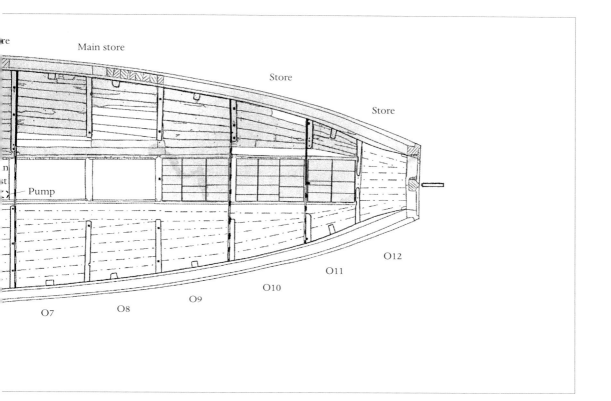

re

Main store

Store

Store

Pump

O7    O8    O9    O10    O11    O12

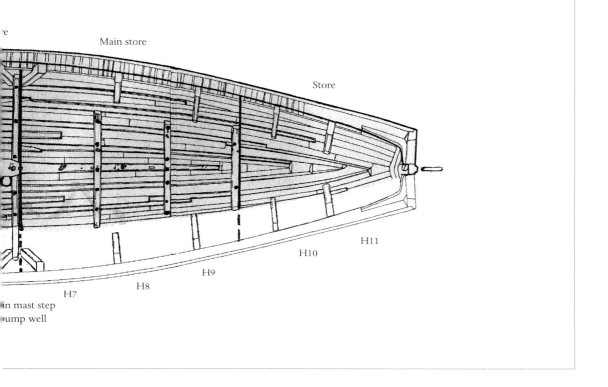

re

Main store

Store

in mast step
ump well

H7    H8    H9    H10    H11

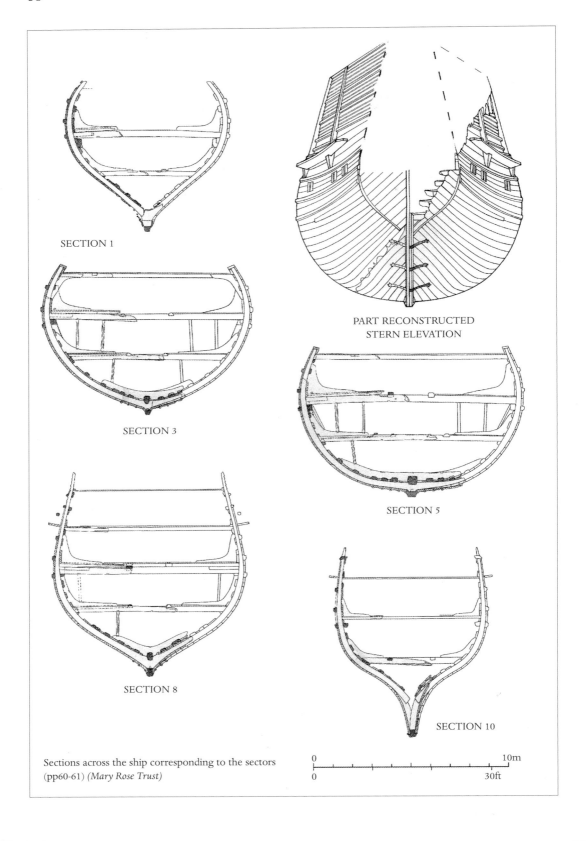

SECTION 1

SECTION 3

PART RECONSTRUCTED
STERN ELEVATION

SECTION 5

SECTION 8

SECTION 10

Sections across the ship corresponding to the sectors
(pp60-61) *(Mary Rose Trust)*

0                                          10m

0                                          30ft

them were overseen with ale'. They returned to the waterfront and called across to the *Mary Rose* for someone to pick them up in the ship's boat, but nobody heard them. In their drunken state, they got hold of a wherry, a rowing boat used to carry passengers on the river, to reach their ship, and although its owner had removed the oars for security they found two boards to use as paddles. They launched the wherry but found the ebbing tide too strong, and as it carried them past the *Mary Rose* one of the men managed to grab an oar from the ship's boat moored to the stern.

A little downstream they struck the anchor cable of a Portuguese merchant ship, the *Sante John de Cangas,* moored off Deptford Creek and Greenwich. The men later claimed that the Portuguese crew threw stones, injuring Oram's head, which made them angry, so they climbed on board 'to give them a blow or two'. According to Robert Grygges, who was 'well drunk', one of his companions called out 'Vengeance on him, here lies a Portingale' (Portuguese). Oram and Baker climbed on board the ship leaving Grygges in the wherry, but when he heard the Portuguese cry out, he joined them in case his companions were injured. Baker said that on entering, Oram drew his sword and struck at three Portuguese with the flat of the blade, drove them below and closed the hatches. Nobody else had a weapon except Grygges who had a knife about eighteen inches long.

The Portuguese had a different story which was that they were taken by surprise by the *Mary Rose* men who arrived past midnight. At that time, Gonsalianus Cassado of Villa Viano, Pilot of the ship, Petro Falcon of Cangas, merchant, and the Master, Roderigo de Pyncta, were asleep in their cabins below deck, as were two sleeping mariners, John de Vale and Edwarde Roderigus. Supposedly guarding the hatches were the two ship's boys, also asleep. As Oram guarded the hatch to keep everyone below, the others searched the ship for about an hour, breaking into three chests and unlocking a fourth. The Portuguese claimed that they took money, a shirt and a sugar-loaf belonging to Petro Falcon, rolls of coloured cloth, some belonging to the merchant Anthony Roderyckej of Cangas, and two shirts belonging to Roderigo de Pyncta. Richard Baker claimed that they took nothing and did not hurt the Portuguese crew, though Grygges admitted that they took two shirts and two hose cloths which they threw into the wherry as they left. They also cast the Portuguese ship's boat adrift so that they would not be caught. The Portuguese crew managed to break out from below and saw the *Mary Rose* men drifting away, and 'cried out and made such a noise' that people ashore in Greenwich shouted to them. Next morning they found the stolen cloth left in the mud where the *Mary Rose* men had landed at Backwall on the opposite north shore of the river.

Baker stayed the night in his house in Nicholas Lane, just north of London Bridge, and next morning returned to the *Mary Rose*. He would have walked across old London Bridge, with its many stone arches supporting crowded houses, into Southwark, and then east-wards until he reached the shore at Deptford, a journey of about four miles. Meanwhile, Grygges and Oram slept the night in a hay barn at St Katherine's, just east of the Tower of London, and it was there that Grygges finally awoke from his drunken stupor at 10am, to find himself 'so foul arranged with oose'. In other words, smelling of the Thames mud that even today has a strong acrid smell. He noticed that Oram's 'head was broken' but did not know how. From there they walked across old London Bridge into Southwark, and found their way back to their ship.

The angry Portuguese moved their ship on a rising tide two miles upstream, away from the *Mary Rose*, to a safer mooring off St. Katharine's pool. On that Thursday the Master and his colleagues went to the home of a Portuguese merchant in the City of London, and, in the presence of a notary public, made a statement about what had happened, putting the matter before an Admiralty Court. Depositions from Richard Baker and Robert Grygges were taken, and it is these that have survived. Sadly, the result of the case is not known, but it is not hard to imagine that the drunken behaviour and inconsis-tency in the stories of the men from the *Mary Rose* resulted in them being found guilty. But how justice was delivered can only be guessed at, particularly as they probably did not have the money to repay the Portuguese.

From then on, the spotlight of historical documents switches off, and apart from a list of her guns in 1540, there are no more references to the *Mary Rose* for several years. As peace continued from 1539 to 1544 we can only assume that she, and the rest of Henry's navy, remained 'in ordinary', moored in rivers and docks, fully modernised and awaiting orders to go into action when needed.

*Chapter Six*

# THE FRENCH KING'S VENGEANCE

It was the birth of a Scottish baby called Mary in 1542 that started the chain of events that sank the *Mary Rose* in 1545. On 14 December 1542 when the young King James V (r. 1513–42) of Scotland died, his six-day-old baby daughter became Queen of the Scots (r. 1542–67). This unfortunate infant almost immediately began to be traded by her guardians as an international asset. Henry VIII of England wanted her eventually to marry his son Edward to reduce the threat of invasion by Scotland, whereas Francis I of France wanted her to marry his son, Francis, the Dauphin (r. 1559–60), and so strengthen the 'auld alliance' between France and Scotland. In spite of his bullish behaviour and having been at war with James, Henry was surprisingly successful in getting his way, and on 1 July 1543 James Hamilton, Earl of Arran, the Scottish Regent, agreed to the future marriage at a ceremony known as the Treaty of Greenwich.

Cardinal David Beaton, Archbishop of St Andrews, a strong supporter of Francis, opposed the match and tried to block the treaty. He gladly received French diplomats who arrived in a fleet of armed ships in September 1543 whose aim was not only to quash the treaty, but also to offer incentives of military aid to fight the English, and to pay cash 'pensions' to key Scottish lords. King Francis was successful, and on 11 December the Scottish Parliament rejected both the Treaty of Greenwich and the English marriage proposal. Years later Mary, Queen of Scots married the Dauphin.

Henry was beside himself with anger at this reversal, and in the spring of 1544 ordered Edward Seymour, Earl of Hertford, to unleash an attack on Scotland with such terrifying force that the Scots would not want to upset Henry again. This started seven more years of war between England and Scotland as Henry continued to force the marriage, jokingly known by historians as the 'War of Rough Wooing'. The war, however, was no joke. Instruction from the King's Privy

Council on 10 April 1544 to the Earl of Hertford reflect Henry's fury
that is still chilling over four centuries later. He was to:

> Put all to fire and sword, burn Edinburgh town, so razed and defaced
> when you have sacked and gotten what you can of it, as there may
> remain for ever a perpetual memory of the vengeance of God light-
> ened upon [them] for their falsehood and disloyalty … and as many
> towns and villages about Edinburgh as you may conveniently, do
> your best and to beat the castle, sack Holyrood House and sack Leith
> and burn and subvert it and all the rest, putting man, woman and
> child to fire and sword, without exception where any resistance shall
> be made against you and this done pass over to the Fifeland and
> extend like extremities to all towns and villages whereunto ye may
> reach conveniently, not forgetting among all the rest so to spoil and
> turn upside down the Cardinal's [Beaton] town of St Andrews, as the
> upper stone be the nether, and not one stick stand by another,
> sparing no creature alive within the same.[1]

The English troops unleashed terror, murder, pillage and destruction
on Leith on 3 May 1544, and then moved on to Edinburgh where they
did likewise. Fortunately, the impregnable Edinburgh Castle held out,
and, as the troops were unable to reach St Andrews in the time available, Cardinal Beaton's city was spared.

Sir John Dudley, Viscount Lisle, had been put in charge of the naval
force that escorted the troop transports carrying twelve thousand
soldiers to Scotland. This provided him with valuable experience to
draw on the following year when he opposed the French in the Battle
of the Solent. He had already gained some experience on a relatively
small scale in February 1537 when he set out with the then Lord
Admiral, Sir Thomas Seymour, to tackle pirates menacing merchant
vessels off southern England. He so impressed the King that he was
appointed Vice-Admiral in March 1537 and led a modest task force 'to
keep the seas' in the English Channel and in the estuary of the River
Severn. In 1539, following the formal excommunication of Henry from
the Catholic Church by Pope Paul III, Lisle became involved in the
general mobilisation of forces to man England's coastal defences, and
on 27 January 1543 he was appointed Lord Admiral of England.

Although the voyage from Newcastle to Leith in 1544 was fairly
short, it required careful planning, and Hertford's instructions on how
the fleet was to operate must have been compiled in collaboration with
Admiral Lisle. The two hundred ships were to sail in three divisions,
each led by a senior officer in a warship.[2] The plan was modelled on
how troop movements took place in battle on land, and followed naval

battle instructions set out by the Spaniard, Alonso de Chaves, around 1530, a copy of which had been previously presented to Henry VIII. The King subsequently ordered Thomas Audley to compile a version as English naval fighting strategy.[3] The *Mary Rose* was not involved in this expedition as she was presumably involved with preparations for Henry's invasion of France.

The Vanward division with seven ships was to be followed by the Battle division of five ships, and then by the Rearward, all escorting troop transport vessels. Leading the Vanward was Lord Lisle's flagship the *Pauncey* (Pansy), a carrack of 450 tons that had been built in 1543. She had four masts with sails and high castles fore and aft, and was attended by the small *Bark of Calais* for Lisle's personal use to maintain contact with other ships. Next was the *Minion*, a carrack of 300 tons carrying Lord Hertford and the King's money for the expedition. She was followed by the *Swallow*, a small warship of 240 tons that had been built in 1544, and then by the highly decorated *Galley Subtle*, a new rowing galley of 200 tons with a single mast and sail. The remaining two ships of this division were the *Gabian* of Ipswich and the *John Evangelist* which presumably carried supplies. The Battle division was led by the *Sweepstake*, a small carrack of 300 tons that had been built in 1535. And, finally, the Rearward division of five ships was led by the *Great Galley*, apparently a carrack of about 900 tons, with the Earl of Shrewsbury in command.

A measure of the care with which the fleet was organised is reflected by the method used to identify the leading ships. Lord Admiral Lisle's flagship had a flag of St George on her fore topmast, and at night two lights high in her rigging. Lord Hertford's ship carried a similar flag on her main topmast, and at night two lights high in her shrouds. And the Earl of Shrewsbury's ship carried a similar flag on her mizzen topmast, with at night a cresset lamp on her poop deck at the stern.

Hertford was anxious to maintain communication with the other commanding officers, so he flew a flag above his forecastle when he wanted Lord Admiral Lisle to join him on board. When he wanted the Captain of the Rearward division, the Earl of Shrewsbury, he flew a flag from his poop at the stern. And when he wanted all of the Captains of the Battle division on board he would set out 'a banner of council' on the middle of his main mast. To avoid any confusion 'his lordship straightly chargeth and commandeth that no ship shall spread any flag in any place above the hatches, nor any lights in the night above the decks.'

In June 1544 Henry invaded France with forty-two thousand troops supported by four thousand auxiliaries sent by Charles V. At the English enclave of Calais they were divided into two groups, one led by Charles Brandon, Duke of Suffolk, which marched south to the port of Boulogne, and the other, led by Thomas Howard, Duke of Norfolk, that advanced further south to the city of Montreuil. Both cities were put under siege. Boulogne lasted from 19 July to 18 September when the city finally surrendered and Henry VIII entered as the glorious victor. But at Montreuil, when Howard heard that a large French force of thirty thousand troops was advancing, he retreated north to Boulogne where he found that King Francis had laid siege to the city. It was about then that Henry was shocked to learn that Francis and Charles V had privately signed a peace treaty on 18 September, leaving him alone to face the might of France.

Henry's seizure of Boulogne was the last straw for the French king who now had an extra reason for putting a stop once and for all to Henry's harassment and invasions that had occurred throughout his reign. The English had killed the ordinary folk of Brittany and Normandy, burned towns, seized property and sunk ships without any apparent purpose other than gratuitous destruction and killing.[4] Henry's crimes had extended from discarding several of his six wives in favour of those who might bear him a son, to claiming to be head of the Church in England instead of the Pope. He thereby encouraged the Protestant movement that spread across Europe and threatened to break up the Catholic Church.

It is on 22 May 1544, after Henry had ordered the attack on Leith and Edinburgh and before Boulogne was seized, that we first hear of Francis's intention of visiting his own vengeance on Henry in an anonymous letter acquired by the Emperor Charles V. The writer reported that a French Captain had heard that:

> The King of France has visited all the ports of Normandy and in all of them has had prepared and laden all the ships for war. Among them was a carrack of 500 tons [presumably the *Philippe*]. These ships are being prepared for an invasion of England. The Captain-general is the Vicomte of Dieppe. The ships are to land at a port I understand is called Southampton and from there they shall go further to a place called Rye.[5]

In December 1544 Francis sent Antonine Escalin des Aimars, known as 'Captain Polin' and also as Baron de la Garde, to Marseilles to assemble a fleet of twenty-six galleys. He was to move them to northern France, even though they were not designed to sail in the rough tidal Atlantic Ocean or in the Channel. The Ferrarese Ambassador noted on 28 December 1544, that for them to sail from the Mediterranean north-wards was 'a long journey and some say very dangerous because the

English seas are so uncertain'. Added to which the convict rowers were in a poor physical condition. The former Imperial Spanish Ambassador, Eustace Chapuys noted in May 1545, that a French galley had even been found abandoned at La Crotoy, on the French coast south of Boulogne, with all of its rowing slaves dead from plague.[6]

Francis I was then aged fifty, his thin trimmed moustache, thick beard and sly eyes shown in his portrait do not reflect his sensitive nature as a patron of the arts and a man of letters who had built a royal library and very fine chateaux, including the beautiful royal palace of Fontainebleau. Militarily and politically he was not very successful, for he had failed to be elected by the Pope as Holy Roman Emperor, and when he pursued wars in Italy in 1525 he was captured by Charles V in the Battle of Pavia near Milan. He was only released after making various promises that he did not intend to keep. Initially, he had tolerated the Protestant movement led by Martin Luther who denounced the corruption and self-indulgence of the Roman Catholic Church, but later he persecuted its followers by censoring printing and forcing John Calvin into exile. His views hardened with age, and finally he ordered the massacre of his own countrymen, a Protestant group known as Waldensians, in April 1545 in over twenty villages around Merindol, near Aix-en-Province and Marseille in southern France. Some of the men were captured by la Garde who, as one of the two leaders of the massacre, probably used them as convict slaves chained to the rowing benches in the French galleys that were to fight the English in the Battle of the Solent. Merindol has not forgotten this outrage, and today there is a monument commemorating those who suffered.

Henry VIII and Francis I were kings of similar age, and following the fall of Boulogne to the English in 1544, each delegated the task of leading his navy in the forthcoming battle in the Solent to his most senior naval officer: Admiral Claud d'Annebault in France and Admiral Sir John Dudley, Viscount Lisle, in England. The gauntlet was thrown down between them, as reflected in a letter of 7 May 1545 from the Imperial Ambassador to France, Jean du Saint Mauris, to Francisco de los Cobos, Secretary to the Holy Roman Emperor Charles V in Spain:

the French insist upon recovering Boulogne, and the English insist upon keeping it. The Admiral of France recently sent his Secretary to discuss the matter with the Admiral of England, and to offer an increased pension [i.e. a payment] part of it to be paid in ready money, if they would surrender Boulogne. The English Admiral replied that they had better reduce the pension and let the English keep Boulogne.[7]

Admiral Lisle heard that de la Garde's galleys were sailing from the Mediterranean, so in June 1545 his English fleet sailed to meet them as they entered the Channel. This came to nothing as his fleet was driven back by south-west winds, though subsequently, when the galleys sailed past the island of Alderney on 6 July, he engaged them in an inconclusive gun battle for five or six hours. This, however, did not stop the French continuing on their way eastwards to Le Havre.[8]

Admiral d'Annebault soon faced serious trouble in that La Garde's position in charge of the galleys was challenged by the Italian brothers Piero and Leone Strozzi, noble exiles from Florence, for La Garde had elected Claud de Manvile to command the merchant ships that were to carry troops and supplies on the invasion of England. The elder brother, Piero Strozzi, was both a naval commander and marshal of France, and Leone Strozzi was prior of Capua, a knight of Malta and a galley commander. Their animosity towards La Garde was to fester and affect the outcome of the Battle of the Solent. But La Garde continued as he wished, and chose as his flagship the magnificent *La Reale*, a quinquereme galley, with rows of oars on several levels, and garnished with clothes of gold and crimson satin hangings – ornamented with the salamander of Francis I, crowned 'F's' and *fleur de lys*.[9]

In his determination to recover Boulogne Francis increased pressure on Henry by ordering the construction of two coastal forts outside the entrance to the harbour so that English supply vessels could be attacked as they arrived. This was quite successful as they soon sank an English supply ship and forced the rest of the fleet to return to England. The fleet's departure meant that life for the besieged English inside Boulogne became increasingly unbearable as food stores were depleted and perished in the heat, and the people suffered from the 'cruel ravages' of plague. This situation was only temporarily relieved when Lord Admiral Lisle attacked Normandy in October 1544 and diverted French attention from Boulogne, enabling the newly appointed Vice-Admiral, Thomas Seymour, to convey supplies to the port. Lisle also tried to attack French warships at Étaples but was repelled.

Edward Hall, the contemporary English historian, explained the build-up to the impending great sea battle, for King Henry 'had knowledge by his spies that the French army intended to land in the Isle of Wight'.[10] In fact Francis I had made no secret of his intentions, for he deliberately ensured that news of his plans was freely available in the royal courts of Europe. On 18 December 1544 Giulio Alvarotti, the Ambassador to France from the province of Ferrara in north-east Italy, reported to Ercole II, the Duke of Ferrara, that there was talk in France of a plan 'to make war against the island of England' and that 'His Majesty is so committed to this enterprise that he will do everything to pursue it' and that the French Admiral, Claud d'Annebault, would lead it in person. Ten days later the Imperial Spanish Ambassador to France, Jean de Saint Mauris, reported to Charles V that at the French court 'all maps of England and Scotland have been consulted to understand the routes necessary. The Admiral [Lisle] intends to command the navy.'[11]

Francis needed all the support he could muster, and on 3 January 1545 he instructed Christophe Richer, his Ambassador in Denmark, to ask King Christian III (r. 1534–59) for a contribution to his navy so as to compel Henry to return Boulogne and 'make amends for all his wrongs'. Furthermore, he issued letters of permission to his subjects in Normandy to arm their ships and make war against his enemies. He also forbade commerce with the Channel Islands.

As early as the beginning of 1544, Francis intended that Admiral d'Annebault would take charge of the expedition, supported by Vice-Admirals La Meilleraye in Normandy and de la Garde in Provence. The assembly of the French fleet and its supplies at ports on the north coast of France became the responsibility of Joachim de Matignon, Governor of Normandy. King Francis gave Matignon 'oversight of all matters concerning the coast of our land of Normandy … and power to assemble provisions', and he was to continue transporting supplies to the fleet after it sailed. The food for the soldiers included chicken, bacon, beef, lamb and wine and cider. The magnitude of the task became so huge that on 10 January 1545 King Francis ordered Matignon to prepare supplies for an army of eight to ten thousand men along the River Somme. This invasion force would be one of the largest ever assembled in north European history.

By 7 May 1545 the plans had become more detailed as Jean du Saint Mauris, wrote from Paris to Francisco de los Cobos, Secretary to Charles V:

With regard to the preparations here against England, it is certain that they have decided upon war both by land and sea. The plans are for the French to send to sea 300 ships and 25 galleys, with five galleasses and 10,000 men, in order to make incursions on the island of England where they intend to make a fort on the coast, avoiding proceeding inland. When this is done, they will land men near Boulogne, where the King of France expects to be able to force the harbour with wooden booms, and to construct a fort on the beach like that which was demolished by the English. The object of this will be to prevent the English from revictualling the place. They [the French] intend to have a large number of pioneers to fill the moat [around the town] and enter over the walls [of Boulogne]. This is the exact plan of the French up to the present time. The fleet [of galleys] from Marseilles was to leave port on the 1st of this month.[12]

The port in which the French fleet was assembled was Le Havre ('The Haven'), also known as Havre-de-Grace, whose creation by King Francis in 1517 was a direct response to King Henry's earlier war with France in 1512–14. It was strategically placed at the mouth of the River Seine and opposite the main English naval port of Portsmouth. It provided a base in times of trouble that protected the river route to Paris. Assembling the infantry troops there was a vastly complex operation which at times resulted in confusion. One group of four companies of men, for example, was initially directed from Normandy and Brittany to Honfleur on the opposite side of the River Seine to Le Havre, but then was redirected inland to Abbeville. And in May ten thousand foot soldiers brought from Guyenne overwhelmed Le Havre, and the cost of feeding twenty-five thousand men in June while awaiting embarkation was astronomical. At the end of June the Prince of Melfi was commissioned to oversee the musters and the embarkation of the men, but because there was a food shortage in France he found himself confronted by numerous extra soldiers who had flocked to Normandy in the hope of being employed. Francis brutally ordered them to be cut to pieces!

Acquiring enough transport ships to carry the troops and supplies to England posed further problems for Francis, for although he had hired many vessels, he also embarked on a programme of building about one hundred and fifty vessels and twenty more galleys. Six of these were to be constructed under the supervision of Pierre de Caux, 'capitaine general des galeres', to a design by Baptiste Auxilia, in the Normandy ports of Dieppe, Rouen and Pont de l'Arche.[13]

Initially, all of the ships of his armada assembled at ports from Bordeaux to Dieppe, with the greatest number, forty-six, being at Dieppe, before being forwarded to Le Havre. The records of Rouen are full of detail on how the fleet was fitted out. For example, in March 1545 Pierre de Saint-Martin, Captain of three galleys, contracted to supply three months of cider, wheat, beans, peas, barrels of beer, bacon and meat both salt and live. Artillery was brought from various stores, including from Compiegne which also contributed cannons and gunpowder.

The three hundred ships were in a great variety of types termed 'navire', 'nef', 'galion', 'barques', 'chaloupes', 'carvelles', as well as 'carracks'. Many were large and owned by courtiers who hired them to Francis to supplement those that he owned. A planning document for

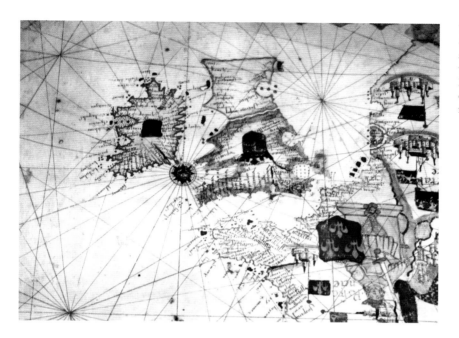

The coastal defences of southern England were built by King Henry VIII as part of his protection from French attack.

early 1547 lists the ships used by the King at Rouen, many of which would have taken part in the invasion of England. They included the *Gallaire royalle*, the *Dauphine*, the *Duchesse*, the *Gallion du roy*, the Prior of Capua's *nef*, the *nef* of Nix Johannin, the galleon *de la Renterie*, the galleon *Sermanie*, the galleon *Vento*, the *nef de Vento*, the *nef Bilhoty*, Hubert Rostaing's *nef* and Cabogne's *nef*. To these was added the *Philippe*, usually described as a carrack, and the *Grande Maistresse*, probably a galley or galleass, an oared sailing ship. Most could carry two to four hundred soldiers and had crews of fifty to ninety.[14]

The royal ships were highly decorated with banners and flags coloured in the gold, silver and azure of the King, the dauphin and the Duke of Orleans. Some standards were in red, yellow and blue cloth and had the monarch's arms of a blue shield with three gold *fleurs de lys* surrounded by a gold collar on a white background. The quadrireme galley *La Couronne*, built at les Damps near Pont de l'Arche, had particularly fine interior panelling in its cabins.

Admiral Lisle monitored the build-up of the invasion fleet through spies, and in June 1545 decided to mount a pre-emptive attack on it as it was moored at the mouth of the River Seine. He told King Henry that he aimed 'either to make a present of some of the best of them to Your Highness, or at least to set fire on them'.[15] When Lisle's fleet of forty or fifty ships, including the *Mary Rose*, arrived it started firing from a distance of half a league (1.5 miles). He had issued an order of battle in which he separated the fleet into the usual divisions of Battle and the Wing. The Battle division included the largest carrack warships with a few large transport vessels led by the *Henry Grace a Dieu* (1,000 tons), *Mary Rose* (800 tons) and *Peter Pomegranate* (600 tons), the list of Captains including Sir George Carew who was presumably in command of the *Mary Rose*.[16] In the Wing division were the manoeuvrable oared vessels and more transports that included the *Great Galley* (500 tons), *Strewse* (450 tons), and the *Mary of Hamburg* (400 tons).

Thanks to light winds the French were able to venture some of their galleys out towards the English, and twice attacked, but then, 'suddenly the wind rose so great that the galleys could not endure the rage of the seas, and the Englishmen were compelled to enter the main seas for fear of flats [shoals]', wrote Edward Hall.[17] The threat of an English landing terrified the French king who was staying only nine miles away at the time, and but for one of his Captains he would have fled at midnight with all of his baggage.[18] With the weather against him. Admiral Lisle realised that he could not tackle the galleys, and so he ordered his fleet to return to Portsmouth.

In spite of his preoccupation with the invasion, Francis did not forget his ally Scotland which he hoped would threaten England and divert some of Henry's forces. He sent a small fleet there, but Captain L'Orges informed Francis that although he was warmly welcomed, and the Scots were prepared to attack northern England with thirty to forty thousand men, this could not be done without money. Nothing happened.

Francis originally intended that his armada would sail on 8 July, but it was delayed by a week due to the late arrival of some vessels. With the fleet assembled at last he undertook a grand royal review of his force of three hundred ships from the nearby cliffs at Chef-de-Caux on 12 July. He saw that well over half of the vessels were large transport merchant craft carrying twenty-five to thirty thousand men with supplies of arms, equipment and food, and the rest were warships.

Claud d'Annebault was fifty years old and an accomplished military officer who had been elected Admiral of France in 1543, and, as he had been Governor of Piedmont and Normandy, he knew the northern coastline very well. His dark bushy beard, determined veiled eyes, firm nose and a look that suggested he smiled easily, seemed to mask an uncertainty – perhaps because he was a family man, married to Francois Tournemine, at home with their son, Jean. Any doubts that he had about this enterprise may have been heightened as disaster struck on 15 July while the fleet was about to sail. An accident in the cooking galley of his flagship, the great carrack *Philippe* of 800 tons, caused the ship to catch fire, and although the crew managed to bring her into port, more than two hundred people were drowned having thrown themselves into the sea. The artillery and the gold and silver were saved, but the ship was completely burnt.[19] On hearing the news Thomas Wriothesley, King Henry's Secretary, gleefully commented, with gross exaggeration, that the ship that he called 'Rumpye La Conte … by misfortune of fire was burnt, many lords, ladies and gentlemen being in her, with great ordnance and subsistence and a million of gold in her, which was to have paid his men of war their wages, was burnt and lost and no creature saved'.[20] Once again the sailing had to be delayed as Admiral d'Annebault transferred his flag to the *Grande Maitresse*, probably a large galley.

The armada eventually set sail on 17 July to the accompaniment of gunfire from the ships and from the cliffs where King Francis watched and hoped that within months Boulogne would be his again.[21] It sailed in the usual three divisions of warships followed by the mass of transport vessels, with the Admiral leading the main Battle division, followed by the Van, commanded by the senior military officer Jean de Taix, after which the Rearguard division was commanded by Guig Guiffrey Boutieres.

The main French source of information about the Battle of the Solent is the memoirs of the nobleman, Martin du Bellay, a senior French official who had access to records. However, these were written sometime after the events that they describe and were published in 1569 after his death in 1558.[22] According to him, the French fleet arrived off the Isle of Wight and the sea battle commenced on 18 July. This is incorrect for on that Saturday the Imperial Ambassador of Charles V, Francis van der Delft, was being 'very handsomely entertained' on board the English flagship, the *Henry Grace a Dieu*, in Portsmouth harbour, before having an audience with King Henry VIII. In fact Van der Delft's letter to the Emperor, written as the events occurred, makes it clear that the French fleet arrived off St Helen's Point at the east end of the Isle of Wight on the afternoon of Sunday 19 July.[23] There seems to be no doubt that the events that du Bellay described actually occurred, but the dates need to be adjusted to fit a time framework based on contemporary letters and documents that include the reports and letters of the English Privy Council.

When he arrived off the east end of the Isle of Wight, Admiral d'Annebault was surprised to find that the English navy was not at sea to meet him. Instead, it lay at anchor safely inside Portsmouth Harbour as if Admiral Lisle was too scared to challenge him. In truth, Lisle was caught off-guard and unaware that the French had sailed. It was only when his men saw the masts of the enemy appearing over the horizon that afternoon that he ordered his fleet into action. This was a surprising lapse by the usually well organised Lord Admiral who must have realised that he should have stationed a vessel off Le Havre to give him advanced warning of their sailing. One can only think that this oversight was due to the pressure of organising the royal review of the fleet at Portsmouth and the arrival of King Henry. Whatever the case, there is no hint that he was chastised by the King.

Admiral d'Annebault took immediate advantage of this situation and sent five of his long sleek galleys in through the entrance of Portsmouth harbour right under the shore batteries to attack the English ships at their moorings, and they had orders to report back on the size and readiness of the English for battle.[24] This highly dangerous opening gambit must have horrified the local people in Portsmouth, for it looked as if the invasion had begun, and many probably collected their valuable possessions and escaped into the countryside. As the galley slaves pulled on their oars in unison, they were assisted by the rising tide that carried them into the harbour where 'our galleys were able to manoeuvre at their pleasure,' wrote Bellay, 'to the disadvantage of the enemy who, not being able to move for want of wind, remained exposed to the fire of our artillery, which had greater power on the ships than they had on it, the ships being higher out of water and more bulky; added to which our galleys, by using their oars, could retire out of danger and gain the advantage'. The Battle of the Solent had begun, and the fate of England hung in the balance as tens of thousands of French soldiers prepared to land.

*Chapter Seven*

# TRAPPED IN PORTSMOUTH HARBOUR

Francis Van der Delft, the Emperor's Ambassador, reminded members of the English Privy Council when he met them at Portsmouth: 'When I spoke to the King', on 18 July, 'there was no knowledge of the coming of the enemy'.[1] Also, Cornelius Scepperus and Van der Delft jointly wrote to the Queen-dowager mentioning that 'the King [Henry] being on the flagship, and as he himself told us, [was] not expecting the coming of the French'.[2] This explains why Admiral Lisle's fleet was not in the Solent to meet the French. However, King Henry knew that the French force was due to arrive at some time to seize the Isle of Wight or Portsmouth which is why he decided to hold a royal review of the English navy at Portsmouth. He intended to show French spies that they would be repelled with force, and that the French King and his Admiral, d'Annebault, would do well to think again.

Henry's situation in July 1545 was very serious for he had bankrupt the country so could hardly afford the war, and the English fleet was smaller than the French. He was also concerned that the Scots, allied to the French, might invade from the north. Moreover, the French siege of the port of Boulogne was reinforced by two forts being built by the French outside the harbour entrance to stop the arrival of English supply ships. Henry's reserves of manpower for the army and navy were exhausted and he was having to employ foreign mercenaries, particularly from Spain and Germany. Indeed, some of his naval Pilots were French, including possibly on the *Mary Rose* judging from the European manufacture of some of the navigation instruments.[3] Although the Emperor, Charles V, had refused to sanction Henry's employment of Spanish soldiers, many had nevertheless entered into English service,[4] as is indicated by the analysis of the oxygen isotope in the teeth of a random small sample of eighteen men from the *Mary Rose*. It shows that many of them had grown up in the warmer

Mediterranean region, and were probably Spanish which could explain the presence of Catholic rosaries among the personal possessions of the men on board.

Henry's financial crisis existed because he had spent much of the income from the sale of monasteries in rebuilding his navy and strengthening the defences of England, so he was having to borrow money from European financiers. In the previous two years before 1545 he had reduced the silver and gold content of coins from 75 per cent down to 50 per cent, and was about to reduce it to a third. This caused social unrest as the value of money fell and inflation rose, adding distress to the ordinary folk. All of the silver coins found in the *Mary Rose* were of debased types, so we can imagine that there was discontent among her crew.[5] Financial administrators ashore knew that peace was the only way out, but Henry did not listen. He did not allow himself to worry that people suffered from the loss of work following the closing of monasteries, or from the enclosure of common land by new noble landowners.

The King's plans for the royal review at Portsmouth that weekend just before the French arrived were described by the Imperial Ambassador, Francis Van der Delft, who on the Saturday had admired the English ships when 'The Queen's Chancellor [showed] ... me the fleet which is in this harbour ... The fleet did not exceed 80 sail, but 40 of the ships were large and beautiful.'[6] His presence in Portsmouth is crucial to our understanding of what happened for in his letter to the Emperor, Charles V, he described the events as they unfolded over those few days, including giving us the most detailed description of the loss of the *Mary Rose*.[7]

King Henry had given Van der Delft permission to join the royal court at the naval review, and he hoped to speak to various nobles who might encourage Henry to seek peace with the French. He had set out on horseback around 12 July, following the sixty-three miles road to Portsmouth from his home in the pretty village of Mortlake, just upstream from London. His house was substantial, with accommodation for himself and his wife, secretaries, messengers and servants, and he had stables and rooms for high ranking guests such as Cornelius Scepperus, a senior envoy sent by the Emperor to stay with him temporarily. The house was 'very appropriately situated on the Thames', wrote Cornelius Scepperus to President Loys Scors on 21 August 1545, for Van der Delft had access by water to Hampton Court Palace, Westminster and the City of London. The earliest known map of Mortlake, dating from 1768, shows that the only row of houses lay between the High Street and the river, so one of them was presumably his house. Leyden House is all that survives from Van der Delft's time, but it has since been extensively modified and looks nothing like it did in 1545. Mortlake is, of course, famous nowadays for marking the end of the annual Oxford and Cambridge Boat Races.

Van der Delft's journey to Portsmouth became highly significant as he followed the ancient highway that is now largely the A30 trunk road. It took him four days to complete, and he was accompanied by his servant, 'my man' to whom he referred, and had sent another man ahead to book lodgings on the way so that messengers knew where to find him. The journey had started uneventfully as he rode his horse along the well-worn highway with its patched and mended wheel ruts, through forests and open fields until that evening he arrived at an inn, possibly in the village of Cobham with its long straggling high street. However uncomfortable the international politics were, he knew that his status as Imperial Ambassador ensured that he would be well looked after.

The second day took him through the North Downs, stopping for lunch probably at the fortified market town of Guildford overlooked by its Norman motte and bailey castle and surrounded by hills. It was dominated by St Mary's Church, and there are still a few buildings that were probably standing there when Van der Delft passed by.

By the evening of 14 July he had reached the rolling countryside of the Weald and stopped at a village, probably near Godalming, a Saxon town that still has a few medieval houses. No doubt uncomfortable from riding, he welcomed his reservation at a village inn. Using the last of the evening light he took up his quill pen, ink and paper and started making notes for the long letter to the Emperor that would become a cornerstone historical record on the loss of the *Mary Rose*. He described his delight at having spotted, at another inn in the same village, an English noble who was close to the King whose ear he might bend to find peace. He then retired to bed, having quietly instructed his servant or the innkeeper to wake him at daybreak.

He arose as the pink dawn spread across the eastern sky around four o'clock which heralded another warm summer day. Sadly, no picture of Van der Delft is known to exist, but we can imagine that he followed the fashion of the day and had a carefully trimmed beard. Having hurriedly completed his ablutions, followed by breakfast, he dressed in his finest travelling clothes, probably black like the Emperor's. He had recently bought them 'at considerable expense' to be as handsome as possible 'out of respect for my office', he told the Emperor, 'because it behoves me to shine brilliantly in these gloomy times'. Speed was of the essence if his ruse was to succeed. Still tired from the short night, he knew that he would be even more exhausted when he reached Portsmouth and became caught up in official events.

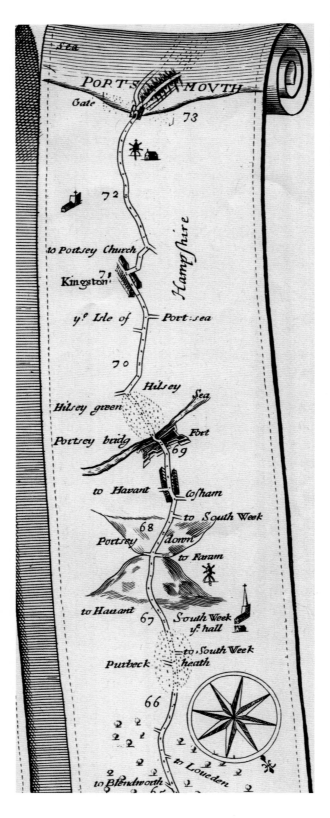

The journey from Mortlake to Portsmouth took Francis van der Delft, the Spanish Ambassador, several days. It can be followed on later maps such as this from John Ogilby's *Britannia*, published in 1675.

Quickly, he and his servant mounted their horses and set off south-wards through the fields towards the coast. As there was nobody ahead he knew that the first part of his scheme had succeeded. All he needed to do, he wrote, was to ride slowly and await events. The retinue behind him belonged to no less than Sir Thomas Wriothesley, the thirty-nine-year-old Lord Chancellor of England. Maybe, thought Van der Delft, a long relaxed chat with the Chancellor might clarify what was in King Henry's mind regarding how peace in Europe might be achieved.

'I rode on gently', he explained, 'in order that he [Wriothesley] might overtake me, which he soon did, and after some civilities, we rode together all day and had much interesting discourse. When we arrived in the evening at the village where we were to sleep, he asked me to sup with him, he himself coming to my lodging to invite me. After supper he resumed the conversation that we had had on the road about the peace.'[8]

During this time the two men got to know and like each other, though Van der Delft would have realised that Wriothesley was well known as a 'scheming' nobleman in the court of Henry VIII.

The Chancellor explained that he too wanted peace, but that there were two major problems. Firstly, although a treaty of mutual support existed between England and the Emperor, Henry was mystified as to why the Emperor had not rallied in his support against the French King. Van der Delft knew the answer, but could not tell the Chancellor that there was a secret clause in a recent treaty which committed the Emperor to support France militarily against an enemy. Consequently, the Emperor was in a quandary since both of his treaty partners were at war with each other! This was all rather embarrassing, and Van der

Sir Thomas Wriothesley, the Lord Chancellor of England. (*Wikimedia*)

Delft's only option was to veer discussions away from battles towards how peace might be achieved.

The second problem was that in December 1544, Henry had authorised English seafarers to attack enemy trading ships which the English had widely interpreted as including those belonging to Spanish, Flemish and German merchants, subjects of the Emperor, on the pretext that they were carrying supplies to France. In retaliation, the Emperor's officials had arrested English trading ships in Spanish ports and at Antwerp. Van der Delft and the Chancellor agreed that the whole tense situation was in danger of spiralling out of control, though they realised that it was Henry's seizure of Boulogne in 1544 that was now the main issue, giving an immediate aggressive purpose to the French. The questions surrounding the future marriage of the infant Scottish Queen Mary had faded away, though it had left strong anti-English feelings in Scotland.

When the two men arrived at the next village where they were to sleep, somewhere near Petersfield, they supped together until a courtier arrived with letters for Wriothesley, before the two men went to their lodgings. Another messenger awaited Van der Delft at his lodging with a letter from the Emperor. This instructed him to stress somewhat bluntly to Henry the Emperor's 'extreme displeasure at the continuance of the war', and his wish to aid in a reconciliation.

The 16th of July was another warm day during which the two men continued their discussion on horseback, Van der Delft elaborating on the Emperor's views, and the Chancellor responding by 'asking me to use my best influence in the interests of peace'. Both men knew how volatile, angry and rude the disease-ridden Henry could be, so Wriothesley added that: 'If the King perchance let slip any angry words, he prayed me [Delft] not to notice them.' Eventually they parted at a road junction three miles from Portsmouth, Van der Delft riding south towards Portsmouth and the Chancellor 'to visit some other places and villages of his'. In fact Wriothesley was visiting his home, the former Titchfield Abbey that lay about eight miles by road to the west. This delayed his attending the Privy Council meetings at Portsmouth until 19 July, as there seemed to be no reason for him to rush since the French were apparently unready to sail. He would not have made this diversion had he known that the French armada was already underway, carried forward by a light breeze towards the Isle of Wight and Portsmouth. The time for peace discussions was over.

Van der Delft had already tried to discuss peace with the King in London only a month earlier, but had found Henry's notorious temper unpredictable. He was new to the job as Ambassador, having taken over from the elderly Eustace Chapuys who had so impressed the

Emperor. At first the King had received Van der Delft at court 'very politely' and 'caused a stool to be brought, and, notwithstanding my excuses, insisted upon my being seated exactly opposite and quite close to him'. Using 'the sweetest words' Van der Delft modestly asked that redress be given to the Emperor's maritime subjects whose property had been impounded by the English. Henry 'displayed great astonishment' declaring that he could not understand the complaints against him, and pointed out that his own subjects had been seized in Antwerp and Spain without any hearings, and the export of goods to England had been blocked. Van der Delft respectfully replied that the Emperor had done all he was obliged to do, to which Henry angrily responded: 'What do you mean by obliged? There is a treaty between us; and that should either be binding or declared nul.' The fact that the Emperor had also signed a peace treaty with France had caused Henry to feel 'bitterly that he was deserted, and left alone at war'. Van der Delft explained that Henry had given consent to the treaty with France, to which Henry 'immediately exclaimed that no consent was given!' And so what began as a pleasant meeting ended in bitterness and anger. Had Henry known about the secret clause in the treaty whereby the Emperor had agreed to support the French king militarily then his reaction would have been incandescent.

Van der Delft stayed in a country lodging outside Portsmouth overnight so as to arrive fresh in the town next morning, Friday 17 July. His initial view of the heavily fortified port was of its defensive wall of timber and earth interrupted by stone towers. It was surrounded by a defensive ditch with a bridge giving access to a gateway known as the Town Bulwark that was almost hidden on its north side.[9] This entrance

*Portsmouth in 1545, overlooking the narrow mouth of Portsmouth harbour, is shown on the Cowdray picture. (Society of Antiquaries)*

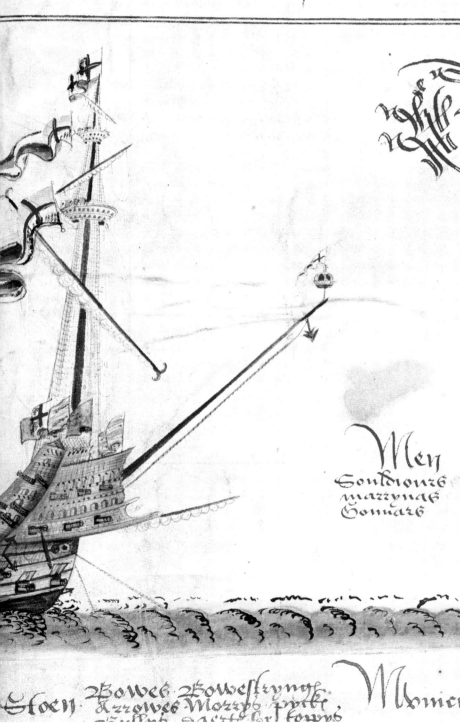

iery of the sayd Shippes agaynst theyr enem

Men
Souldiours
marrynars
Gonners

Stoen
Bowes Bowestrynge.
Arrowes Morres pyke,

Women

The *Henry Grace a Dieu*, the largest carrack warship in the English navy and flagship of Lord Admiral Lisle, was illustrated on the Anthony Roll of 1545–6. *(Pepys Library, Magdalene College, Cambridge)*

must have been incredibly busy as Portsmouth was overflowing with men preparing for the royal review, and with sailors collecting supplies for their ships. Around twelve thousand troops were mustered on nearby Southsea Common, apart from the large number of court officials and their families also encamped there in colourful tents.[10] It is not clear where the King and his immediate staff stayed, but as the Privy Council met in a building in the town it seems likely to have been in Portsmouth. The scale of work to maintain food, latrines and rubbish disposal for everyone is mind-stretching, for it has been estimated that if only half a loaf of bread was provided daily for each soldier it would require six thousand loaves to be baked, using three tons of flour.[11] In addition, the ships were apparently supplied with fresh bread judging from the analysis of silt samples from the *Mary Rose* which revealed no trace of bran residue from biscuits.[12]

As soon as Van der Delft arrived at his lodgings among the narrow streets on Friday 17 July, he sent a message by his servant to Sir William Paget, the King's Secretary, asking for an audience with the King himself on a very important matter. Henry, probably hoping that the Emperor had decided to declare war against France, answered that Van der Delft 'could come at any time', though courteously preferred next Sunday the 19th. That date would be etched in English history as the day when the King and Van der Delft would witness the sinking of the *Mary Rose*.

Meanwhile, the King instructed Sir Thomas Arundel to entertain the Ambassador that Friday afternoon. He was the chief adminis-

Henry VIII is shown on the Cowdray picture riding on horseback to Southsea Castle to watch the sea battle between the English and French fleets. *(Society of Antiquaries)*

trator and financial officer to Queen Catherine Parr (r. 1543–48), Henry's sixth wife who, although aged thirty-three and twenty-one years younger than the King, comforted him through the final years of his life.

The forty-three-year-old Sir Thomas Arundel escorted Van der Delft through the streets to the waterfront to view Henry's navy at anchor in the wide expanse of its natural harbour, with the naval dockyard just to the north of the town. The Ambassador could see why the King had chosen this for his naval base, with the fortress-like town on the east side of a narrow waterway entrance to an enormous natural tidal basin and gave protection to the dockyard. The entrance and the seaward coast were heavily defended by towers, including Southsea Castle that the King had built in 1544 as a protection against French attacks. The Solent seaway outside the harbour entrance separated the mainland of England from the diamond-shaped Isle of Wight whose grey hills were clearly visible only four miles away, so the island not only shielded Portsmouth from the worst of storms, but also gave exceptional access to shipping on its double high tides that surged around the island, first from its west and then from its east ends.

The Ambassador was impressed by the English fleet with its forest of masts, furled sails, colourful flags and long streamers, though they hung limp in the light breeze. Sir Thomas Arundel told him that about sixty more ships were expected soon to join them from south-west England. We know the names of the King's warships from Admiral Lord Lisle's fleet lists of June and August 1545 and also the names of most of the forty-two hired ships that supported the fleet.[13] Henry's warships are also pictured on three rolls of velum documents completed in 1546 by Anthony Anthony, the King's clerk of the ordnance office. He was responsible for the issue and return of military supplies from stores, and the rolls list the armament and complement of mariners, gunners and soldiers of each ship, though the officers and their servants are not included.[14]

Arundel and Van der Delft then embarked on a boat and were rowed out to the largest warship, the *Henry Grace a Dieu* where 'the Admiral received me very civilly, and asked me to dinner for the following day'. The flagship was a four masted 'carrack' of 1,000 tons, whose painted sides and flags were decorated with the red cross of St George on a white background, a traditional design that was widely adopted as the flag of England, and also the Tudor livery colours of green and white.[15] At the top of her main mast was a flag with the royal arms boldly stating that she was the King's premier ship and the flagship of Lord High Admiral of England, John Dudley, Lord Lisle. She housed a formidable array of guns together with a fighting force of 301 mariners, fifty gunners and 349 soldiers in addition to the nobles and gentlemen who served as 'officers' and their servants.

Lord Admiral Lisle was about forty-one years old, and, judging from his portrait, had piercing dark eyes and a neat pointed dark beard. He was a formidable man who expected to be obeyed, and could handle the King's temper and bad moods, even though he might have hidden some resentment as his father, Edmund Dudley, had been executed by the young Henry VIII for high treason in 1510. Lisle had taken part in Cardinal Wolsey's diplomatic voyages of 1521 and 1527, and was knighted for his involvement in the invasion of France, after which he became Knight of the Body of the King, and from 1534 was responsible for the King's body armour as Master of the Tower Armoury. He was a skilled horseman, and excelled in wrestling, archery and royal court tournaments. He was also a royal intimate who played cards with the ailing monarch. In January 1537 he was made Vice-Admiral which gave him sufficient seafaring experience to assure his promotion to Lord Admiral in 1543 as well as a Knight of the Garter and Privy Councillor.[16] In 1544 he commanded the fleet that successfully carried the force of Edward Seymour, Earl of Hertford, to attack Leith and Edinburgh, and later that year was appointed Governor of Boulogne with responsibility for rebuilding the fortifications to King Henry's design.

As Lord Admiral of England he put naval administration on a firmer basis than before, and created the Council for Marine Causes that coordinated, for the first time, the many tasks needed to maintain the navy. Moreover, he updated naval fighting instructions so that they were at the forefront of tactical thinking, describing how squadrons of ships should manoeuvre in formation and use coordinated gunfire.

Eighteen large warship carracks in Portsmouth harbour formed the core of Henry's navy, each having four tall masts, a bowsprit and characteristically high fore and aft castles that were bristling with guns. After the *Henry Grace a Dieu*, the next largest warship was the carrack *Mary Rose*, of 700 tons, which the Anthony roll shows as having rows of square gunports in her sides for ship-smashing guns, and high castles with many openings for smaller anti-personnel guns. Her castles were painted with diagonal stripes of red and white, and just above her waterline could be seen the top of her underwater coating of protective 'white stuff' that limited damage by marine growth. The upper sides of the ship's waist and sterncastle were lined with rows of rectangular shields, 'pavesses', some of which could be removed to enable archers to fire arrows at the enemy. They were decorated with the red cross of St George on a white background alternating with yellow designs.

Sir George Carew.
*(Bridgman Art Library WES 32299)*

A flag on a standard flew from each corner of her forecastle, some with the red cross of St George on a white background and others had the King's livery colours of green and white. More flags on poles were at the sides of her waist, the low part of the ship between the high castles, some having the royal liveries of green and white, and others the *fleur de lys* on a blue background that were the colours of France to which Henry laid claim. The sterncastle, then known as the 'summer-castle', had yet more flags of St George, together with the royal arms and royal livery. Long streamers decorated with the arms of St George and the King's livery colours, hung from the tops of her masts. Four centuries later this Anthony Roll picture provided vital clues that enabled archaeologists to define how much of the ship had survived. The eroded remains of the only carved decoration, a large Tudor symbol of a red rose projecting from the forecastle at the bow like a figurehead, seems to have been found.[17]

The Anthony Roll shows the fixed ropes of her 'standing rigging' mostly rising from the ship's sides to support the high masts, and the 'running rigging' that the crew pulled to manipulate the long horizontal spars, the 'yards', from which the sails were hung so that they could catch the wind. At the ends of the longest main and fore yards were evil-looking sharp curved iron knives known as 'sheerhooks', whose purpose was to cut the rigging of an enemy vessel as it came alongside. Hanging from an iron chain at the far end of her bowsprit was a huge wrought iron grappling hook ready to be dropped onto the deck of an enemy ship to 'capture' it for boarding. She normally had thirty gunners to operate her heavy brass and iron guns, 185 soldiers who were in effect marines armed with bows and arrows and long spear-like pikes and bills for close combat once the enemy vessel was boarded, and two hundred sailors to manage the ship on the orders of the ship's sailing Master. Her Captain, the most senior officer on board who determined what the ship was to do, was Sir George Carew whose name occurs on a list of ships and their Captains that was probably compiled on 20 June 1545.[18]

There was one other 700-ton carrack, the *Jesus of Lubeck* which had been hired by the King in 1544, and was purchased by him about a year later probably as a replacement for the *Mary Rose*. There were two 600-ton vessels, the *Matthew Gonson* and the *Peter Pomegranate*, the former captained by Sir Gawain Carew, uncle of Sir George Carew, which had 138 soldiers, 138 mariners, and twenty-four gunners. The latter was the almost identical but slightly smaller sister ship to the *Mary Rose* which had been built alongside her at Portsmouth and also entered naval service in 1512. She carried well over four hundred men plus officers, gentlemen and their servants, though we do not know the name of her Captain. Thereafter the carracks reduced in size down to the *James* of sixty tons, with just forty men.

Eleven galleasses comprised the next group of warships ranging in size from the *Grand Mistress* of 450 tons down to the *Dragon* of 140 tons.[19] These mostly had four masts with their sails, and could also be rowed from oar ports in their sides, the rowers normally being convicts who were classed as mariners.[20] Only the largest of these carried soldiers for boarding enemy vessels, and in the bow of each was a heavy forward firing gun and a substantial wooden ram to disable the enemy. For good measure they also carried a variety of brass and iron guns in their sides. Two of the galleasses, the *Salamander* and *Unicorn*, had been captured from the Scots at Leith in 1544, each of which had on the top of its ram a carved figure, a salamander on one and a unicorn on the other.

There was only one true galley, the *Galley Subtle*, of 200 tons, which had one mast and square sail. She too was built to ram enemy vessels, and was propelled by many oars at her sides leaving no doubt about her power. Her stern had a rounded canopy, topped by a dragon's head to give shelter to the officers in charge of the convict crew. A man standing on a platform holding a whip drove the rowers. She had two smaller guns at her bow, together with a variety of guns of brass and iron in her sides. Unusually, she had a fixed entry staircase on the side of her hull, just forward of the canopy. She was classed as having 242 mariners and eight gunners.

The smallest warships were four pinnaces, small lightly armed scouting vessels of eighty and forty tons, with three masts with sails and a bowsprit, and just a few guns. They too were rowed, and had oar ports just below the gun deck. They were crewed by mariners and gunners, but the absence of soldiers shows that they were not intended to be used for boarding. Many of the hired vessels were simply transports for men and supplies, ranging in size from the *Venetian* of 800 tons down to four boats from Rye. The King, desperate to enlarge his navy, had already ordered some 'row barges' to be built, but they were not ready in time for the Battle of the Solent.[21] The King was aware that his great sailing carracks were slow and ponderous in a light wind on that Friday afternoon, and were vulnerable to the manoeuvres of the French rowing and sailing galleys with their large forward firing guns. English sailors feared the French galleys as they could be positioned to fire at the poorly defended 'quarters' of the carracks.

The scene of the fleet from the deck of the Admiral's flagship must have been colourful and noisy with busy crews carrying out their daily routines as watch bells rang out each half hour, and crews practiced setting and hauling in sails, firing guns, and adjusting their mooring position with their kedge anchors.

Francis van der Delft was thrilled when on Saturday 18 July, another calm day, he was again taken by boat out to the moored flagship, the *Henry Grace a Dieu*, and either climbed up the ladder hung on the ship's side or was lifted on board on a Boatswain's chair. He again met Lord

An entry ladder on the side of a carrack warship, in the Embarkation picture of *c*. 1540. This presumably shows the normal method of boarding that was probably used in the *Mary Rose. (Royal Collection Trust, Her Majesty Queen Elizabeth II)*

Admiral Lisle and had dinner, 'with three or four knights of the Garter', who, judging from those attending the meetings of the Privy Council at Portsmouth, were probably Sir Anthony Browne, Sir John Gage, Sir Thomas Wriothesley and Sir William Paget, the King's Secretary. After dinner, at which he was 'very handsomely entertained … the Admiral told me that he had the King's orders to take me to His Majesty as he would rather see me that afternoon, in consequence of the whole of his time being occupied the next day visiting his ships and dining on the flagship.'

The meeting with the King took place in the upstairs room of a building in Portsmouth rather than in one of the palatial tents that were set up for the courtiers on Southsea Common.[22] Henry was disappointed to hear that the Ambassador could not confirm that the Emperor would support England against France with military force, so he reiterated his need for help. Although the thorny matter of Henry's capture of Boulogne was broached by Van der Delft, there was no change in attitude from the King over the English seizure of Spanish ships. His intransigence puzzled the Ambassador, until Sir William Paget later said in confidence 'that the King was quite determined to give battle to the French, and if the worst came to the worst, and the English were defeated, he intended to make use of these [seized] ships'. Van der Delft later hopefully suggested to the Emperor could it be 'that he [King Henry] might by some means be induced to yield Boulogne if he could safeguard his prestige?'[23] As it was, any hope of a last-minute peace on that Saturday was about to be dashed as the French Armada neared the Isle of Wight.

The fateful day of Sunday, 19 July dawned bright and warm with a gentle breeze.[24] King Henry prepared for dinner on board the *Henry Grace a Dieu*, with Lord Admiral Lisle and the Captains of his warships. They arrived in their jolly boats, tied them up at the rigging chains on the ship's side, and climbed the portable wooden entry ladder that was hung against the inward sloping 'tumblehome' side of the ship. The ladder presumably looked like that in the 'Embarkation' painting,[25] and in the stone carvings of ships at that time found at St Peter's Church, Tiverton, Devon, as well as on the view of the *Galley Subtle* on the Anthony Roll. They were no doubt greeted by a welcoming call from the ship's trumpeter as they stepped onto the waist.[26] An officer, or 'principal', then led them to the quarters of the Lord Admiral in the sterncastle to meet the King. Henry was a sick man and unable to climb the ladder, so was probably hoisted on board in a Boatswain's chair hung from the yard of the main sail. This wooden seat was operated by a system of pulleys, and in later times continued to be the normal method of bringing a Royal Navy

The sixteenth-century Carew monument in Exeter Cathedral refers to Sir George Carew (Vice Admiral and Captain of the *Mary Rose*), Sir Peter Carew (Captain of the *Great Venetian*), and Sir Gawen Carew (Captain of the *Matthew Gonson*), all of whom took part in the Battle of the Solent in 1545.

warship's Captain on board, to save him from the possible indignity of falling from the entry ladder.[27]

The Lord Admiral's state room in the sterncastle was prepared for the lunch, presumably on a long collapsible table with trestle legs, and was probably timed for the then fashionable lunch hour of around 11am. Sir George Carew, Captain of the *Mary Rose*,[28] was among those attending, his servants having brought some of his personal pewter plates each stamped with his initials 'GC' to supplement the Lord Admiral's tableware.

The presence of the King was, naturally, the highlight of this occasion. In spite of his difficulty walking, he would have enjoyed a tour of his flagship escorted by his Lord Admiral, before returning for dinner with his noble officers. The formalities of dinner in aristocratic houses would have been observed with a gentleman usher overseeing proceedings. Cooks had prepared dinner in the galley far below, and the meal was no doubt served by gentlemen waiters. The meal may have included venison prepared by the official 'carver', and it has been suggested that the deer bones found in the *Mary Rose* may represent the remains of uneaten venison that was sent back from the flagship with George Carew's pewter tableware later that day.[29]

The readiness of the navy to respond to the impending French invasion would be the main subject of discussion, with Admiral Lisle explaining how each ship, equipped with guns, ammunition and gunners, mariners and soldiers, was well able to tackle the French. Sightings off La Havre had shown that the French had a larger fleet than the English so it was important that the back-up ships sent from south-west England by Sir John Russell in Bodmin, should arrive as soon as possible. But Lisle may also have referred to the problem of sickness and the fact that there were insufficient numbers of men to crew all of the ships adequately. The King's reply would have been that he had taken steps to employ German, Spanish and Italian mercenaries some of whom Sir George Carew knew were serving in his ship.

The arrival of the French fleet was described by Van der Delft 'Whilst the King was at dinner in the flagship, news came that the French were only five short leagues away.'[30] That was about fifteen miles, at which distance the tops of the masts and sails appeared over the horizon. According to John Hooker, the Elizabethan biographer of the Carew family writing about thirty years later, Sir George's brother Peter, of the *Great Venezian*, and their uncle Gawain Carew of the *Matthew Gonson*, were also present at the dinner as ships' Captains. Hooker explained that the King expected the French to arrive that day and wanted someone to climb to the masthead to see if they were in sight. It is Peter Carew who was recorded as 'forthwith climbing up to the top of the ship, and there sitting, the King asked him, what news?' Peter Carew replied that he could see three or four ships which he thought were merchant vessels. Soon after he saw a great number of ships, and 'he cried out to the King, that there was, as he thought, a fleet of men of war'. The King, realising that it was the French fleet, then ordered every man to return to his ship, whilst he himself prepared to go ashore in a long boat.[31]

John Hooker is a notoriously unreliable historical source and has to be treated with caution for elsewhere he made important mistakes in his biography of the Carews. For example, he said that the *Mary Rose* sank inside Portsmouth harbour, whereas she sank far outside in the Solent. He also said that she carried seven hundred men, whereas contemporary documents state that they varied from four hundred and fifty to six hundred men. Furthermore, Van der Delft made it clear that the arrival of the French was completely unexpected, so the King would not have sent someone up the mast to look out for the enemy. It is far more credible that during lunch a member of the crew unexpectedly saw the enemy masts on the horizon and reported it to Lord Admiral Lisle, and that the King then asked Sir Peter Carew to climb the rigging to the masthead to see for himself.

With this news the King abandoned his planned tour of the fleet, and instead ordered the naval battle plan to swing into immediate action. Lord Admiral Lisle was ready for this, based on his experience only a month earlier off Le Havre when he confronted the French warships. The plan was based on one that the King himself had approved around 1530 when he instructed Thomas Audley to write down the naval battle instructions.[32] The fleet would sail in three squadrons, the Van, Battle and Wing, with the smaller and more manoeuvrable galleasses on the Wing to protect any vessels that were damaged. The Lord Admiral would lead the central Battle squadron, but he needed a Vice-Admiral to lead the Van squadron. Only a nobleman could hold such an important office, however temporary, which is why Sir George Carew was promoted for the occasion, just as Sir Thomas Seymour had been appointed when he took command of the supply ships to the newly captured Boulogne in 1544. In spite of the errors in Hooker's account we can be sure that Sir George Carew was promoted because Francis Van der Delft refers to him by this rank too.[33]

John Hooker explained that just before the King left the flagship he had 'secret talks with the Lord Admiral' who presumably asked for authority to appoint Sir George Carew to lead the Vanward squadron. Hooker continued,

and then hath the like with Sir George Carew, and at his departure from him, took his chain from his neck, with a great whistle of gold pendant to the same, and did put it about the neck of the said Sir George Carew, giving him also therewith many good and comfortable words ... It was the King's pleasure to appoint Sir George Carew to be Vice-Admiral of that journey, and had appointed unto him a ship named the *Mary Rose*, which was as fine a ship, as strong, and as well appointed as none better in the Realm.

Pewter tableware found in the *Mary Rose* bears the owner's initials 'GC', presumably Sir George Carew.

Several pewter plates found in the *Mary Rose* have the coat of arms of Lord Lisle, and were incorrectly collected by servants of Sir George Carew in the rush to return to his ship after lunch with the King on board the *Henry Grace a Dieu*.

Musical instruments from the *Mary Rose* show how some of the crew passed their time in recreation, though, as the men had designated stations whilst in battle, the drum could have been last used to 'beat to quarters', ready to attack the enemy.

A game of backgammon was found in the carpenters' cabin on the main gun deck of the *Mary Rose*.
(*All photographs by the author*)

Sir George was now both Captain of his ship and Vice-Admiral of his squadron.

The time of arrival of the French fleet is made clear by two letters sent by the Privy Council meeting in Portsmouth that afternoon. The first was sent at 2pm to the previous Lord Admiral, Sir John Russell, who was arranging the dispatch of reinforcement vessels from the south-west. It made no reference to the arrival of the French, so it is clear that the invasion fleet had not yet been seen. The second was written urgently at 5pm and said that the French fleet 'are arrived a great number of galleys and ships, among which the Lord Admiral intends shortly to be' and were two miles to the west of St Helens Point at the eastern end of the Isle of Wight.[34] As the letter from Van der Delft to the Emperor states that it took two hours from when the French fleet was first seen about fifteen miles to the south-east, to when it was moored off Portsmouth,[35] we can surmise that time the arrival of the French fleet was at about 3pm.

This fits what is known of the tides that day, from the 'Easy Tides' program of the modern Hydrographic Department. This uses astro-. nomical data to calculate the tides then, though an eleven-day adjust-ment in date is needed to switch from the Julian Calendar in use in 1545 to the Gregorian calendar of nowadays. Consequently, the date of Sunday 19 July in 1545 corresponds to Sunday the 29 July on our modern calendar. Sunrise occurred at 04.24, high tide followed at 05.38 and at 07.48, the double high tide being caused by the Isle of Wight. Low tide was at 11.48, the next high tides were at 18.17 and 20.17, and sunset was at 19.54. Therefore, the tide was rising all afternoon from low water at 11.48am, with the current in the Solent flowing from east to west carrying the French towards Portsmouth. There was also a southerly breeze mentioned in Van der Delft's letter to the Emperor in which he said that after the arrival of the armada 'the wind has always been in favour of the French'.[36] As the tidal flow into Portsmouth harbour lasted until about 6pm this gave the English fleet the afternoon to prepare for departure at high tide, but even then it needed wind. Van der Delft referred to this when he wrote, 'the English could not get out [of the harbour] for want of wind'.[37]

The speed of the English reaction to the arrival of the French is reflected by a seemingly insignificant event that four centuries later helped archaeologists to identify conclusively that the wreck was the *Mary Rose*. As the King prepared to leave the *Henry Grace a Dieu* the servants hurriedly cleared away the dinner, and, without checking, a servant of Sir George Carew inadvertently collected up three of Lord Admiral Lisle's own pewter plates bearing his coat of arms and these were taken back to the *Mary Rose*.[38]

As the King's Privy Council, his chief advising ministers, urgently met ashore to issue orders for the strengthening of coastal defences,[39] the size of the French fleet continuing to grow as more and more ships appeared over the horizon. It was soon clear that the transport vessels were carrying thousands of troops. Van der Delft eventually counted about three hundred sailing ships, plus twenty-seven galleys.[40]

Admiral d'Annebault was no doubt delighted to have taken the English by surprise, and took immediate advantage of the situation by sending seventeen galleys forward under the command of Baron de la Garde to report back on the size of the English fleet. Five of the galleys had orders to brave English gunfire from the battlements at the harbour entrance and dared to enter the harbour on the still rising tide. Van der Delft described what happened next: 'The English fleet at once set sail to encounter the French, and on approaching them kept up a cannonade against the galleys, of which five had entered the harbour, whilst the English could not get out for want of wind.'[41] One galley was sunk before they returned to St Helen's Point where la Garde reported to Admiral d'Annebault that, 'The enemy's fleet consisted of 60 picked ships, well manned and equipped.'[42] The fact that the English fleet was smaller than the French must have heartened d'Annebault and confirmed that he had the upper hand.

Although the audacity of Admiral d'Annebault sending five galleys into Portsmouth harbour on the incoming tide frightened the English, it gave him no hope of engaging the English there, because, as du Bellay reported:

The entrance was by a channel where only four ships could go abreast and could be easily defended by the enemy bringing forward a like number to oppose them. Besides, one could only enter on a favourable wind and tide, and when the said four ships should be obstructed the current would carry those following upon them and shatter them. Added to this, the enemy would be fighting on their own ground, whence they would be aided by their artillery, to our detriment. Again, it had not been considered that if the ships fouled and damaged one another, the force of the current would assuredly drive them ashore on top of one another.[43]

As the English had to wait for the tide to turn at about 6pm before they could emerge into the Solent where the battle would take place, this gave the rival Admirals time to plan how to outwit each other. Each knew that the rules of engagement required that their flagships would begin by attacking each other.[44] This would have worried d'Annebault as Lisle's 1,000 ton carrack towered over his Venetian galley, *Contarina*, enabling the English gunners and archers to fire down onto its deck and rowers. The one positive aspect, however, was that his galley could use its slave rowers to manoeuvre into a position where he could fire at the weakly defended quarters of the English flagship.[45] Both knew that a critical English audience was standing ashore on Southsea Common watching every move, and that King Henry VIII and his court of nobles and gentlemen might notice mistakes that would later demand Lisle's explanation.

*Chapter Eight*

# THE ENGLISH SET SAIL

Admiral Lisle was expected to follow the naval battle instructions which decreed that the battle plan was 'forseen beforehand, and every Captain and Master made privy to it beforehand'.[1] Judging from the number of warships at anchor in the harbour there were at least forty Captains who would have assembled in the great cabin of Lisle's flagship to agree tactics. The Captains then dispersed back to their ships in their small 'jollyboats'.

On his return to the *Mary Rose* the new Vice-Admiral Carew found it a short climb of only 3.5 metres (about 10ft) up the ship's entry ladder to reach a gap in the colourful wooden pavesses shields that topped the side of the waist. He might have recalled hearing the old sailors grumbling about the square gunports being dangerously close to the water-line – only sixteen inches (40cm) according to Sir Walter Raleigh decades later.[2] Or was his confidence bolstered by the knowledge that behind the gunports were the latest ship-smashing weapons that could deal fatal blows to the French?

The busy upper gun deck in the waist seemed narrow as he clam-

King Henry VIII in the waist of a large carrack warship. This embarkation picture supposedly represents the King sailing to Dover to meet the French King Francis I in 1520, but as it was painted about 1540 it shows warships after their rebuilding in about 1536 with flat sterns. *(Royal Collection Trust, Her Majesty Queen Elizabeth II)*

bered between the guns and their gunners beneath the protective roof-like platform that covered each side of the waist. Its collapsed remains in the wreck suggest that it was three metres wide.[3] Similar platforms are shown in pictures of other carracks, such as on Henry VIII's 'Embarkation' painting of *c.* 1540, the drawing of a 'kareck' of *c.* 1490 by 'WA', as well as in an engraving by Peter Breughel the Elder of a Flemish carrack. In the 'Embarkation' painting King Henry is seen standing on the platform, his legs characteristically astride and with his hands on his hips, and in Breughel's picture a man is also standing on the roof. In the *Mary Rose* there was a gap about three metres wide along the centre of the waist between the platforms which allowed access to the main hatch, but now that the ship was at 'battle stations' the gap was covered by anti-boarding netting, apparently on an arched framework judging from the Anthony Roll picture. Fragments of the netting were found by the archaeologists, still carefully knotted together.[4]

Five heavy guns on wooden carriages lay on each side of the upper gun deck in the waist, and were aimed through small semi-circular gunports just beneath the pavasse shields. At the after end of the waist, immediately in front of the towering sterncastle, was the main mast. Next to it on the port side was the top of the main pump shaft that the crew used to empty bilge water periodically into a wooden trough known as a 'dale', that carried the water into the sea. A jeers capstan may have existed somewhere along the middle of the deck, but its position is not known.

On reaching his quarters high in the sterncastle Carew would have called together the Master and other senior officers to explain the battle plan, and instructed them to prepare to sail. He also probably ordered that the crew and gunners had supper, the five partly burned logs found in her galley ovens indicating that food was still simmering when the *Mary Rose* sank. The skeletons of several men beside the galley ovens were evidently cooks preparing the next meal.

The orders of command came from the 'Principals', as the senior officers were then called. They were nobles and gentlemen whose status gave them the right to command. The Captain, Sir George Carew, was the most senior in the *Mary Rose*, and would have told the 'Master to what port he will go … In a fight he is to give direction for the managing thereof'.[5] Carew had some naval experience under Admiral Lisle eight years earlier when in the English Channel he attacked pirates who were menacing merchant shipping. He also had military experience ashore whilst in command of the English frontier fort of Rysbank near Calais. In 1543 he joined the army of Sir John Wallop and was in charge of horses, and, with his brother Peter, was almost killed in action by the French near the towns of Therouanne and Landrecies. On one occasion he was even captured by the French but quickly freed at the request of Henry VIII. Thereafter he re-joined the navy under Lord Admiral Lisle and appears to have had command of the *Mary Rose* in June 1545.

It is not surprising therefore that Lord Admiral Lisle chose him for immediate promotion to Vice-Admiral in temporary command of the Van division. Carew was then about forty-one-years old, his dark hair, piercing eyes and neat bushy beard suggesting someone with determination. Success was important to him, not just to impress the King but also his wife Mary, whom he had married only four years earlier and who was standing with the King on the battlements of Southsea Castle a mile away watching events.[6] She knew the other members of the Carew family who were probably also present, though her husband's thirty-five-year-old brother, Peter Carew, was unmarried then whilst Captain of the *Great Venezian*, unlike his forty-two-year-old uncle, Gawen Carew, Captain of the *Matthew Gonson*, who was married to Mary.

Roger Granville, the son of a noble family in south-west England, was on board the *Mary Rose*. He was about sixty-eight-years old and married to Thomasine Cole who was also probably present ashore on that royal occasion. One of their children became the famous Sir Richard Granville, Vice-Admiral of England, who was killed while fighting the Spanish in the *Revenge* in 1591.[7] His lack of seafaring experience means that there is absolutely no reason to believe that he was the ship's Master as has been suggested.[8] He would die that evening.

It is possible that the remains of one of these men were found, for parts of a skeleton lay in the collapsed sterncastle on the upper gun deck of the *Mary Rose* with four pear-shaped buttons covered in red silk and threads of a garment also probably of red silk that he seems to have been wearing.[9] The Acts of Apparel of Henry VIII passed in 1510, 1514 and 1515 determined that 'None shall wear ... velvet in gowns, cloaks, coats, or upper garments, or embroidery with silk, or hose of silk ... except ... knights, all above that rank, and their heirs apparent.'[10] It is notable that the only known painting of Sir George Carew shows him wearing a red upper garment, presumably of silk to display his status.[11] Also found in the same area was a brass purse hanger of quality indicating that it was worn by someone of high status.[12] Maybe one day this man may be identified by comparing the DNA of his bones with those of living descendants of both families, rather as happened to identify the remains of King Richard III.

The presence of other men of at least modest status on board is suggested by pewter tableware bearing their owners' initials, though their names have not been identified. One of them had a pewter mug-like wine measure with a hinged-lid bearing the initials 'R' or 'BWE'[13] and there was a pewter saucer with the initials 'HB'. The initials 'GI' on a pewter bowl are particularly interesting as they also occur on a boxwood seal inside a personal wooden chest that was stored in the chests cabin on the main gun deck, and therefore may have belonged to the same man.[14] Although the chest had smashed open as it fell against a gun carriage wheel in the sinking, its contents were assembled and show that the owner was a practical man with a skill in carpentry. His possessions included several woodworking tools. His clothing had disintegrated leaving only brass lace ends and some leather shoes, but other personal items reflect a man of some substance with several silver coins, a dagger, a pouch, a comb, rings for the finger and thumb, a signet and the seal. He may also have had an interest in catching fresh fish as he owned two possible fishing weights.[15]

It was normal for the nobles and gentlemen to have their own servants or stewards to look after them whilst on board. Van der Delft mentioned that they were among the survivors: 'about five and twenty or thirty servants, sailors and the like'.[16] The remains of two possible servants were found, one, a young adult [FCS 53] aged in his twenties and about 1.68 metres tall, whose skeleton was in the collapsed stern-castle. His bones were 'gracile', showing that he had not suffered from

A reconstruction of the fragments of the anti-boarding netting that covered the waist of the *Mary Rose*. The netting stopped many of the crew from being saved in 1545.

Red dress fastenings from the collapsed sterncastle of the *Mary Rose* may be from the jacket of a nobleman, such as Sir George Carew or Roger Granville. Only people from noble families were allowed by law to wear such expensive material.

a hard working life unlike almost all other men found in the ship. They were 'very eroded' from exposure to the currents and had evidently fallen from a deck high in the sterncastle where the men of status had their accommodation. The other young man, in his mid-twenties [FCS 78], was found near the forward end of the main gun deck, and his remains were described as 'gracile, with delicate, poorly muscled bones'. Perhaps he was carrying a message when the ship sank.

The Master was the most senior sailor on board after the Captain, and was often of yeoman class and certainly had great experience in sailing large ships: 'The Master and his Mates are to direct the course, command all the sailors, for steering, trimming, and sailing the ship.'[17] His quarters were therefore in the sterncastle adjacent to the Captain's and to the steering helm that lay aft of the bonaventure mizzen mast. Steering was then probably by 'whipstaff', a stout vertical timber lever,

Part of a spare sail from the *Mary Rose*, found stored on the orlop deck.

in this case at least four metres long, that passed down through slots in the sterncastle decks, through a pivot point, to the horizontal tiller of the rudder.

The Master communicated his orders to the crew through the Boatswain and the Boatswain's mates who often relayed them by a silver 'call' or whistle:

> The Boatswain is to have the charge of all the cordage, tackling, sails, fids and marlin-spikes, needles, twine, sail-cloth, and rigging the ship. His Mate the command of the long-boat for the setting forth of anchors, weighing or fetching home the anchor, warping, towing or mooring, and to give an account of his stores.[18]

Judging from his rate of pay the Boatswain was roughly equivalent to the Master Gunner. The discovery of Boatswain's calls with skeletons in the *Mary Rose* suggests where he and his mates were at the moment of sinking. One man [FCS 84] was on the main gun deck nearly amidship, and his call was found by his lower abdomen as if it had hung around his neck. He was in his thirties, and a bit older than most of the crew, and was quite short (about 1.63m tall, 5ft 4in) and had well developed hands reflecting heavy manual work. His back had suffered from the stress of hauling heavy equipment, but his strongly muscled ankles and feet showed that he was used to working in the unstable environment of ships. His health was not good, for he was in constant pain from abscesses in both his upper and lower jaws and caries in his teeth. His head, reconstructed from his skull by Richard Neave a leading forensic artist, gives us a glimpse of one of the leading members of the crew who was overwhelmed while going about his duties.

Another man was in the forward Boatswain's store of the orlop deck where spare pulley blocks and other rigging equipment was kept, including a spare folded sail. He was evidently leading a small group of men collecting spare equipment, but which of the two men [FCS 72, 73] owned the silver call with a silk ribbon is not clear. They were in their twenties, and had seriously stressed backs due to hard labour, and at least one of them may have been wearing round-toed slip-on leather shoes.[19] With them was a young lad aged thirteen–eighteen [FCS 71]. A Boatswain's possessions were found stored in a personal chest in the chests compartment on the main gun deck, and included two more silver calls, or whistles, books with leather covers showing that he was literate, a silver pendant cross, and silver finger rings showing that he was fairly affluent.

The two hundred sailors in the *Mary Rose* were trained to work in teams to carry out highly demanding seafaring tasks in all weather conditions of day and night. They followed orders to get the ship under sail from being at anchor, set and take in sails, hoist the timber 'yards' on which sails were hung, tack the ship by sailing in a zig-zag route so as to move her forward against the wind direction, 'wear' the ship (now commonly called 'gybing') so that the stern is turned through the wind to get onto a new course. They also had to increase or decrease sail areas by fastening or removing extra canvas or 'bonnets' laced onto the bottom of existing sails (in later times sails were shortened by being reefed), and bring the ship to a halt known as 'heaving to'.[20] The sailors and soldiers must have been accommodated on the upper gun deck beneath the sterncastle where a timber drain might have been a 'piss dale' or urinal, its outflow found projecting from the ship's starboard side. They were also accommodated on the lower sterncastle deck above, since these were the only areas available.

Each man probably had a personal bag of possessions, including spare shoes and clothing, but in general they carried their valuables with them in pouches, which explains why there was a wide scatter of ordinary possessions in the ship, including combs and multi-purpose daggers that were used to spear food for eating because forks were then not used.

The skeletons of at least twenty men that could have been sailors were in the hold and on the orlop deck, areas of the vessel that were frequented by sailors rather than by the soldiers who, at the moment of sinking, were at their battle stations high in the ship.[21] Fifteen were in their twenties and only three were in their thirties, their heights varying from 1.65 metres (5ft 5in) to 1.78 metres (5ft 10in). Almost all had stressed spines, arms and legs from heaving heavy loads, and most had painful caries in their teeth. Some even had abscesses in their jaws. Violence was part of their life and had left its mark. One [FCS 9 (sector H2)], had fractured his left hip at some time because his leg bone had been forced out of his pelvis socket, as if he had fallen from the rigging. Yet another man had a healed spiral fracture in his right leg as if he had fallen while his leg was caught in the rigging [FCS 25 (H8)]. One man [FCS 30 (O7)] had an old healed wound just above his left ear caused by a blow from behind, and FCS 31 (O7) had spondylolysis, a stress defect, resulting from an old healed compression fracture to the base of his spine, perhaps also from a fall from the rigging. Spondylolysis was also found in the spine of FCS 22 (H7). FCS 80 (O6) had an old healed wound on his forehead, and his spine and upper arms were very stressed. FCS 81 (O9), aged thirty-forty, had caries and an abscess in his jaw that must have been very painful, and an old wound on his right eyebrow. The oxygen isotope analysis of his teeth showed that he was probably from southern Europe, presumably Spain, and was one of the foreigners hired by the King.

Most of the many leather shoes found in the ship were of slip-on types, with fewer of the more secure ones that had a fastening strap and buckle over the instep or were ankle boots. They show that most of the men in the lower part of the ship were the less able 'deck men' of the crew, which would explain their poor physical health. A pair of leather shoes with abnormal wear indicating that the owner walked badly due to injuries, was found with skeleton FCS 73 who did have serious damage to both legs, which had healed, so they could have been his.[22] Elsewhere, a shoe had a slash across its top to relieve pressure on a bunion, and a foot bone was found with a partly healed fracture, showing that the man had suffered a serious accident only about two weeks before the ship sank.[23] How much of these injuries were work related or were due to the men fighting among themselves cannot be known, but it is clear that they were a rough bunch.

There was no naval uniform in those days, so they wore a ragbag of clothing, often old and mended. Leather clothing in the *Mary Rose* had survived very well unlike textiles that tended to leave only metal fittings, such as brass lace ends, buttons and metal buckles. However, five woollen jerkins managed to survive on the orlop deck and two of these may have been worn by the men FCS 18 (O4) and 72 (O3). FCS 33 (O8) was found with a leather jerkin.

At least eight teenage boys were working in the hold and on the orlop deck when the ship sank.[24] Judging from how ships' boys served in the navy in later times, they may have been apprenticed seamen, or possible servants. They may have been servants to the ship's Master, Purser, Surgeon, Boatswain and cooks, with tasks that probably included collecting food and carrying gunpowder from the magazine store to the gunners. Most of them had noticeably strained spines, arms and legs, and the heights of three of them, 1.63 metres (5ft 4in) [FCS 2 (H4/O4)], 1.68 metres (5ft 6in) [FCS 21 (H7)], and 1.80 metres (5ft 9in) [FCS 36 (O8)], show that their ages were nearer eighteen than thirteen.[25] A few had suffered serious accidents and malnutrition, and came from poor families. FCS 21 had severe unhealed compression of the spine caused by a recent fall, and FCS 28 had healing spondylolysis caused by severe mid-back stress. The legs of FCS 29 were bowed from childhood rickets, and FCS 2 had a fractured left ankle, as well as osteoarthritis and partly severe Schmorl's nodes on his spine, a form of spinal disk herniation, caused by stressed activity.

One boy, however, stands alone from the rest for he had no abnormal growth or damage on his, admittedly few bones that were found [FCS 71]. He was in a storage compartment at the forward end of the orlop

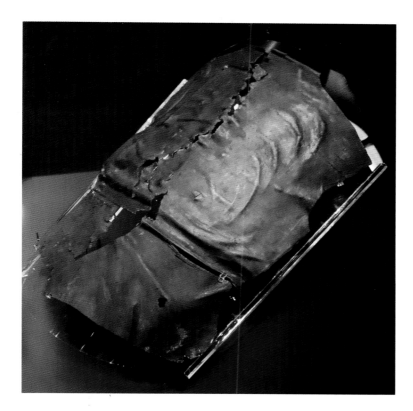

A leather jerkin from someone on board, with an impression of his ribs.

deck in sector O3, and no doubt wore the small beautifully made boy's leather jerkin with a pocket that was also found there.[26] He seems to have come from a caring family and his parents had proudly prepared him for service in the King's navy. Perhaps he was a servant to a gentlemen or officer.

The cooks feeding the crew during those three hours before high tide worked beside the two brick ovens and their large copper cauldrons, one of 600 litres and the other of 360 litres, down in the hold. The food was prepared for distribution in the 'servery' on the orlop deck immediately above. The cook was expected 'to dress and deliver out the victual, he has his store of quarter-cans, small cans, platters, spoons, lanthorns, etc. and to give his account of the remainder'.[27] The concentration of skeletons in the galley no doubt included the cooks, and with them was a large number of wooden plates, bowls and tableware. One of the cooks had roughly cut his name and occupation 'Ny Coep cook' on a wooden bowl, and 'Ny Cop' on a wooden tankard, as if his name may have been Cooper.[28]

The feeding schedule each day was fixed for every ship, so we know that on Sunday 19 July the crew of the *Mary Rose* was served with two meals, 'dinner' in the late morning, and 'supper' normally around 6pm. Each man received 1lb of bread or eight biscuits 'well baked and dried', each biscuit weighing 2oz, with one gallon of beer, and with some beef and fish.[29]

Remnants of food found in the *Mary Rose* reflect some of the ship's victuals for the week, including mainly cod, and bones of pig/pork and cattle/beef. There was some cereal grain, mainly rye, but no trace of biscuits that would have left appreciable quantities of bran.[30]

It was the Purser who ensured that the ship was adequately supplied with food, drink and equipment by using the ship's cash to buy from suppliers, which records show ensured that the cook had victuals for everyone. This included fresh bread, beer, powdered beef, fresh beef, bacon, white herring, stockfish (fish split open and sun dried), butter and cheese, and overall reflected a restricted but fairly healthy diet, though more vegetables and fruit would have improved it enormously. The beer was stored in heavy barrels mainly in the hold where many casks were found. He also bought other necessities, ranging from fuel logs for the galley ovens to candles for the lanterns.

It has been suggested that a chest found on the orlop deck containing gold and silver coins was the Purser's property and that the money was part of the ship's cash.[31] This is not credible as he was a senior official with considerable responsibilities, and cash to purchase supplies would have been kept in a secure place in the officers' accommodation in the sterncastle and certainly not in a personal chest. A more likely chest for the Purser was found on the upper gun deck, beneath the sterncastle in sector U9, where it could have fallen from higher up, and contained personal possessions, and also a wooden box with scales and four weights to check the value of gold coins.

The Purser was assisted by a Quartermaster who oversaw the stowage of ballast and supplies in the hold, coiling cables, checking steerage, keeping time by the watch glasses. 'The Quarter-Masters to have the charge of the hold for stowing, romaging and trimming the ship in the hold, and of their squadrons, for the Watch, and for fishing'.[32]

From at least the fifteenth century the crews of naval ships worked in a system of 'watches' that were probably similar to the four-hour duty periods of later times because it was a practical division of the day. The watch periods were sounded by the ringing of a 'watch bell' at the start of each period, a 'watch bell' being recorded on the *Regent* in 1495.[33] The small brass bell that fell outside the sterncastle of the *Mary Rose*, and had remained with the ship since she was built in 1510–12, was evidently the ship's 'watch bell'. Its inscription says that it was cast in Mechelen, near Antwerp in 1510.[34] Parts of four, possibly five, sandglasses that measured the time, probably in hours or half hours, were also found, two in the debris of the collapsed sterncastle.[35]

The watch duty periods presumably commenced at noon when

sightings were made of the sun at its highest point determined the time. We do not know what the periods were then called, but later they were known as the Afternoon watch from noon to 4pm, followed by the First Dog watch from 4pm to 6pm, the Second Dog watch from 6pm to 8pm, the First watch from 8pm to midnight, the Middle watch from midnight to 4am, the Morning watch from 4am to 8am, and the Forenoon watch from 8am to noon. The men were also probably divided into the larboard (port) and starboard watches, and each was subdivided into divisions with each man having a dedicated station, such as the 'topmen' who managed the sails on each mast, the 'fore-castlemen' in the forward end of the ship, the 'afterguard' in the stern-castle, and 'waisters' in the waist amidships, each division being super-vised by a senior person.

The crew of the *Mary Rose* was definitely divided into 'messes', each of four men who sat and ate together, as was described in a contempo-rary manuscript: 'The Wednesday dinner and supper is allowed for four men one mess of fish and one pound of cheese.'[36] John Smith described the arrangement as 'The next is to mess them four to a mess, and then give every mess a quarter can of beer, and a biscuit of bread to stay their stomachs till the kettle be boiled, that they may first go to prayer, and then to supper, and at six o'clock a psalm, say a prayer.'[37] We do not know if prayers were part of the daily routine in the *Mary Rose*, and although priests were not part of a ship's complement, later naval prac-tice suggests that this was likely.

It was the main body of sailors on board, trained to follow the proce-dures, who got the ship under way at high tide around 6pm, following Admiral Lisle's order to sail, probably by hoisting a flag on his flagship.

Setting sail required teamwork and skill, which fortunately can be reconstructed from the specialised names given to the anchoring and rigging fittings in the *Mary Rose*. A flavour of the procedure was given in the entertaining book by Captain John Smith in 1627 following his long seafaring career in which he was noteworthy for having explored the east coast of America around Jamestown, Virginia, and for devel-oping a close relationship with the native Pocahontas who saved his life.[38] Everyone had to go to their appointed stations in the ship:

> The Captain or the Master commands the Boatswain to call up the company; the Master being chief of the starboard watch doth call one, and his Mate on the larboard [port side] doth call another, and so forward till they be divided into two parts. Then each man is to choose his mate, consort or comrade; and then divide them into squadrons according to your number and burthen of your ship as you see occasion. These are to take their turns at the helm, trim sails,

pump, and do all duties each half, or each squadron for eight glasses, or four hours, which is a Watch. But care would be had that there be not two comrades upon one watch, because they may have the more room in their cabins to rest. And as the Captain and Master's Mates, gunners, carpenters, quartermasters, trumpeters etc. are to be abaft the [main] mast, so the Boatswain and all the youngsters or common sailors under his command is to be before the mast.[39]

Older and less agile 'deckmen' handled the rigging and mooring ropes at deck level, including turning the capstan to lift the mooring cable and anchor, while the fitter and stronger 'topmen' climbed the masts to handle the yards and sails. Each group of 'topmen' had a 'captain of the top' as well as a 'captain of the crosstrees' to ensure that teams were coordinated. One can almost hear the orders being shouted in John Smith's lively description only eighty years after the loss of the *Mary Rose* as some men pulled in the cable to raise the anchor while others on the horizontal timber yards dropped the sails:

> The Master and company being aboard, he commands them to get the sails to the yards, and about your gear, or work on all hands, stretch forward your main halliards [the rope used to hoist and lower sails]; bring your cable to the capstan; Boatswain fetch an anchor aboard, break ground or weigh anchor. Heave ahead, men into the tops, men upon the yards; come is the anchor; a 'Pike', that is to heave the hawse of the ship right over the anchor; what, is the anchor away? Yea. Let fall your fore-sail. 'Tally', that is haul off the sheets [the main sails]; who is at the helm there? Coil your [anchor] cables in small sakes; haul the cat [secure the anchor to the ship's side], a 'bitter', belay, loose fast your anchor with your shank-painter, stow the [ship's] boat; set the land, how it bears by the compass, that we may the better know thereby to keep an account and direct our course; let fall your main sail; every man say his private prayer for a bon voyage; out with your sprit-sail; on with your bonnits and 'drablers' [extra sails used in light winds]; steer steady and keep your course.[40]

In the *Mary Rose* the anchor cable was initially shortened by pulling it in by turning the capstan until the ship's bow was almost above the anchor on the seabed, its position marked by an anchor buoy. This would be the 'bower' anchor, one of the pair of primary anchors, backed up in the *Mary Rose* by the other bower anchor and by two 'sheet' anchors, two 'destrelles' (probably what were later called 'stream' anchors), and one smaller 'kedge' anchor that would be used on other occasions.[41] One bower and the sheet anchor lay on each side

Gold coins from a personal chest on the orlop deck of the *Mary Rose*.

of the ship's bow, each with its own cable that entered the ship through a separate hawse hole just above the upper gun deck, as shown on the Anthony Roll picture. The bower was so named because it was the most forward anchor in the ship at the bow, and the 'best bower', the one most used, was presumably on the port side.[42] The starboard side one (seen in use on the Anthony Roll) was only used occasionally when a mooring position had to be fixed as there was a danger when using both at the same time that the cables became twisted together as the ship turned with the tides and currents. The sheet anchors were the spares just aft of the bower as shown in the Anthony Roll.

The smaller kedge anchors were usually stowed in the ship's large boat ready to be tied to a cable and dropped at a new mooring position so that the crew in the great ship could haul on the cable and pull the vessel to a new position. The kedge cables passed through a pair of round 'cat-holes' in the *Mary Rose*, one on each side of the stern above a gunport as shown on the Anthony Roll picture of the ship, and in pictures of later ships. Their use was described by John Smith: 'cat holes are over the [gun] ports, right with the capstan as they can so heave the ship astern by a cable or a hawser called a stern-fast'. He added that the Boatswain's mate had 'command of the long-boat for the setting forth the anchors, weighing or fetching home an anchor, warping, towing or mooring'.[43]

Three wrought iron anchors were found in the mud outside the collapsed bow of the *Mary Rose*. The two largest, perhaps her bowers, were 4.34 metres and 4.6 metres long with an original span between their spade-like flukes of 2.12 metres and 2.4 metres. The third, a little smaller, had a length of 3.79 metres and a span of two metres, so may have been a sheet anchor. This means that one more anchor has yet to be discovered.

The probable method of anchoring the *Mary Rose* required the anchor cable to enter the bow through a hawse hole at the upper gun deck. Initially it was made fast to 'bitts' just aft of the foremast. Later the cable was turned on a capstan to lift the anchor, and the cable was fed down through hatches to a cable locker on the orlop deck.

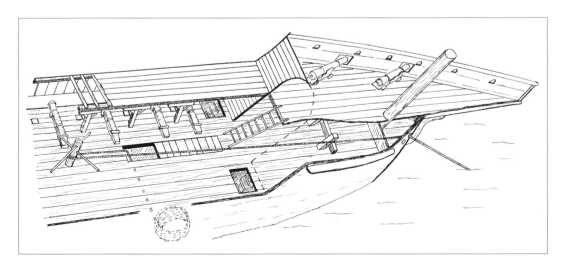

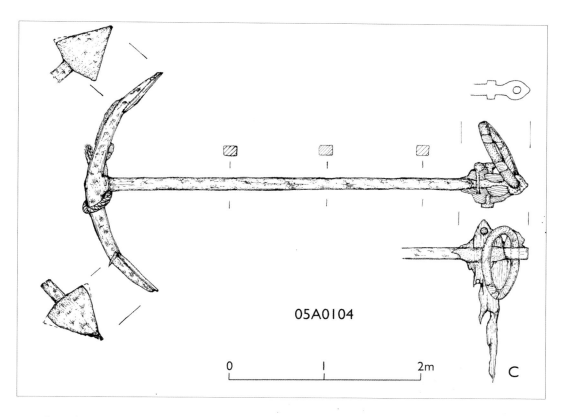

05A0104

0                    1                    2m

C

A fourth and much larger anchor found on the upper gun deck has been interpreted as a 'spare' in the ship, but this cannot be true as the sheet anchors were the spares. Anyway, the waist area was so encumbered with guns and other equipment, as well as covered by side roofs, that there was no space for an extra anchor there. It was probably lost from one of the salvage ships in 1545 or 1546.

The deckmen initially uncoiled the anchor cable from its securing around the massive timber 'riding bitts', upright posts joined by a horizontal bar just aft of the foremast on the upper gun deck. These 'bitts' were referred to in a letter of 1545,[44] but they have not survived though traces of their support fixings may remain in the sides of the main gun deck beams. The anchor cable was then coiled a few times around the capstan further aft, and the men began to heave on the capstan bars to turn it and so lift the anchor from the seabed. As the cable was pulled through the hawsehole at the bow, shown on the Anthony Roll, men are presumed to have cleaned off weed and mud in what was called the 'manger', a low-sided boarded compartment immediately inside the bow. Yet more men pulled the end of the cable from the capstan and fed it down through hatches in the upper and main gun decks to a 'cable locker' storage area on the orlop deck where it was found neatly coiled and ready for use when the ship came to a mooring.

Surviving traces of the rope by which this anchor was held to the side of the ship. *(Mary Rose Trust)*

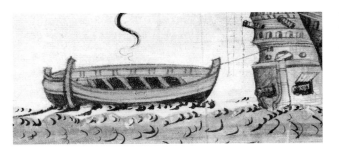

The large ship's boat of the *Mary Rose* that was towed astern, is shown on the Anthony Roll. *(Pepys Library, Magdalene College, Cambridge)*

The main capstan in the *Mary Rose* has not survived, though its fittings to secure it to the sides of main deck beams may survive. In later ships the capstan was usually situated just aft of the main mast, but this may not have happened in the *Mary Rose* as the upper gun deck beams there seem too light to take the stresses. The capstan may have existed in the waist where it would help manage the 'jeers' of the *Mary Rose*, lifting the timber yards and sails on the foremast, as in later ships. The deck beams there are more substantial, and this location is suggested by a reference in a document to the *Mary Rose* to her having had a 'capstan gun with two chambers', as if the capstan had a small gun mounted on top.[45]

Mooring cables were found stowed on the starboard side of the orlop deck in the forward Boatswain's store, and in a cable locker. Each area was three metres square, and it was filled with the coil of tarred cable up to the underside of the deck above. It is not yet clear how the cables were entered into the stores.

A third coil, found in the large general store further aft on the orlop deck, seems not have had a protective coating of tar so was of inferior quality and therefore was probably not in use. It reflects the recurring complaints of poor quality cables supplied to naval ships, such as when Thomas Howard was Lord Admiral and wrote to the King from the *Mary Rose* in May 1513 saying that the wind had blown 'so strainably that we have been forced to lay out shot [i.e. 'sheet'] anchors and have broken many anchors and cables. Your new cables are the worst stuff that ever man saw, at my coming to Hampton [Southampton] I will send you an ensample'.[46]

Once the anchor was lifted out of the sea it had to be 'catted, fished and stowed'. 'Cathooks' and 'fishhooks' are listed among the fittings in the *Mary Rose* in 1514 as well as 'davets with two sheaves' at the fore-castle, and 'davits with two sheaves of the destrell' anchors. These terms show that the top of the anchor was pulled up out of the sea by an iron 'cathook' hanging on a rope from a timber 'davit' angled out over the water like a crane. The top of the anchor was then tied to a timber on the ship's side. As davits were not then permanent fixtures, it seems likely that they were taken from the stores when needed. A timber that may have been a davit was found loose in the forward part of the main gun deck where it could have fallen down the hatches from the upper gun deck. It was a shaft 2.46 metres long and about thirty centimetres square in section, and was originally clad with iron reinforcing bands. Its lower end had a timber tenon as if to slot into the ship's side, and its upper end is forked with a hole for the central pin of a pulley wheel.

As soon as the top of the anchor was tied, 'catted', to the ship's side, its lower end was lifted and secured, 'fished', horizontally by rope to the ship's side. Amazingly part of the 'fish' rope that tied the anchor to the ship's side has survived in the concretion build-up around an anchor.[47]

On the order to 'make sail' the topmen sitting astride each yard or horizontal spar untied the lashings and dropped the furled sails. Ships then did not have the safety of footropes hanging along the yards, for, surprisingly, these did not come into use until the seventeenth century. Consequently, falling to the deck was always possible, which may explain the trauma to the legs of some of the crew.

As the foresail and mainsail were dropped, the men on the deck below took hold of the rope braces to pull the yards around so that the sails caught the wind. Ropes and pulley-blocks that enabled this to happen were found loose in and around the ship, and on the forward side of the sterncastle was a pulley fixing for a rope called a 'sheet' that enabled the crew to pull aft the lower corner of the main sail. Further forward on the starboard side were holes for the rope 'tack' that enabled them to pull the lower corner of the mainsail forward.[48]

A silver model of a three-masted carrack, known as the Schlusselfelder Nef, made in Nuremburg about 1503, is remarkable in

Anchor cable from the *Mary Rose*, found stored on the orlop deck.

A forked timber with
an internal sheave
found in the ship
might have been a
possible davit used to
help raise an anchor.
The sheave was not
found. *(Mary Rose
Trust)*

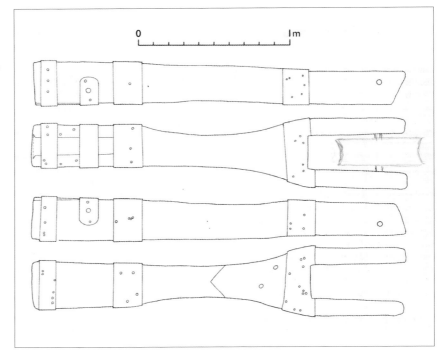

showing a carrack warship getting underway and preparing for battle
in a situation similar to that facing the *Mary Rose* on 19 July 1545.[49] The
anchor is raised but not yet 'fished' horizontally, the foresail is already
set and billowing in the wind as sailors climb up a rope ladder on the
rigging to release other sails. Sailors sit astride the main yard untying
the ropes that held up the main sail, and others are on the mizzen yard
doing likewise. Similar views are also seen on the 1540's 'Embarkation
at Dover in 1520' painting.[50]

Normally, it might take the crew an hour to get a great ship
underway, even though the Master often rehearsed the crew in the
skills of sailing, turning and coming to anchor. But in this case they had
to prepare for battle as well, and there was no room for error with the
King and his court watching from the shore.

As the wind was light that afternoon it is likely that the Master of the
*Mary Rose* decided to lace extra canvas, the 'bonnets', to the lower
edges of the foresail and mainsail. The 1514 inventory lists the main sail
as having two 'bonnets', three bonnets for the foresail and one on the
bowsprit.[51] This extra sail area was to have terminal consequences for
the ship when the gust of wind caught her only hours later.

At high tide, about 6pm, the *Mary Rose* was slowly heading towards
the entrance to Portsmouth harbour with the Pilot, also known as the
'Lodesman', in charge of the men at the helm steering her out through
Portsmouth Narrows and safely passing the great tongue of Spitsand

that projected out into the Solent. The Cowdray picture shows this happening as each ship towed her large boat to take up positions in the Solent. The Pilot was one of the most senior officers on board, and his cabin would have been in the sterncastle close to the Captain's and Master's quarters, which explains why most of the navigation instruments from the ship were found in the collapsed debris of the sterncastle. They included two gimballed compasses, sounding leads for checking the depth of the sea, dividers for working with charts, two roughly carved wooden sticks on which charts were rolled, a log reel on which a line was originally wound to check the ship's speed, and sand glasses to tell the time. He may have been assisted by a junior navigating officer who had quarters in a tiny cabin at the forward end of the main gun deck, judging from the boxed gimballed compass that was in his elm chest, and the box of dividers on the deck there.

As 'battle stations' was called, Lord Admiral Lisle encountered a problem. Instead of facing the enemy's great warships, which were at anchor about four miles away off St Helen's Head beyond the east end of the Isle of Wight, he was confronted by the dreaded highly manoeuvrable French rowing galleys, each with a deadly basilisk gun that could seriously damage the English carracks. Admiral d'Annebault was evidently not planning a conventional attack in which the major sailing warships opposed each other. Lisle had to think quickly how best to respond as the stage was set for a naval battle that would decide the fate of England.

Normally the fleet would sail in three divisions, with the Lord Admiral leading in the central Battle division, a Vice-Admiral, in this case Sir George Carew who had just been appointed, would lead the Van division to one side, and extra vessels, including the rowing and sailing galleasses and the highly manoeuvrable rowing pinnaces, on the Wing ready to help any of the great ships that were in difficulty. Judging from where the *Mary Rose* sank and from the Cowdray picture it seems that the Van division, led by Carew, lay to the north of the Battle division, and the galleasses and pinnaces of the Wing division were southwards near the Isle of Wight.

Preparations for action required the Master Carpenter and his team of carpenter's mates to be ready to repair any damage to the ship with 'nails, clinches, roove and clinch-nails, pikes, splates, rudder-irons, pump-nails, scupper nails, and leather, saws, files, hatchets and such like, and ever ready for caulking, breaming, stopping leaks, fishing or splicing the masts or yards as occasion requireth'.[52] Their cabin was on the main gun deck and through the sliding door entrance were wooden bunks with mattresses for three men. Part of the preparation was for one or two carpenters to be stationed in a storage area on the orlop deck, judging from the variety of tools found there. This matched the later practice when carpenters were sent to a deck just below the waterline to repair any damage caused by enemy gunfire.[53] In the *Mary Rose* such damage may have been reported to the 'Yeoman of the Strykes' who presumably supervised the repair of damage sustained in battle.

*Chapter Nine*

# THE FRENCH ADMIRAL ATTACKS

Admiral Lisle led his fleet out of the harbour in two groups, the first of forty vessels, 'favoured by the land breeze, came out from Portsmouth with great promptitude and in such good order that one might say they awaited with assurance the advance of our force to give it battle', wrote Martin du Bellay. 'But the Admiral [d'Annebault], advancing against them with the rest of the galleys, the remainder of their fleet came out of the harbour to oppose them.'

English warships exit from Portsmouth harbour to attack the French fleet, as shown on the Cowdray picture. *(Society of Antiquaries)*

Lisle may have been taking advantage of the double-high tides two hours apart that evening. The first at 18.17 was followed by a short ebb that carried most of the English fleet into the Solent, after which a short tidal inflow restricted the remaining ships until the second high tide occurred at 20.17. This was just after sunset at 19.54. Admiral Lisle had no problem with his fleet setting sail in the night as he had done that before. They anchored in the Solent to await sunrise at 04.24 on Monday, 30 July, ready for action.[1]

Battle stations had been sounded on board the English ships, probably by the usual trumpet call, followed by the crew and soldiers scrambling to their allotted positions. An undated 'Stations List' that defined the muster locations for officers and soldiers for the *Henry Grace a Dieu* probably reflects the positions in large warships generally, though the numbers of men would vary. The eight 'principal men', the officers who included the Admiral, Captain and Master, were situated at the forward end of the 'second deck' in the sterncastle with forty soldiers; sixty soldiers were positioned on the uppermost 'third deck' of the sterncastle, plus four at the helm; one hundred soldiers were stationed in the forecastle; one hundred and twenty in the waist; and eighty by the main sheets (ropes) and main capstan on the upper gun deck beneath the sterncastle.[2] This final location is exactly where the main concentration of soldiers was found in the *Mary Rose*.

Other soldiers situated in the crow's-nest 'tops' on the masts could fire their small anti-personnel guns, and throw containers of lime and arrows carrying gunpowder down onto the decks of the enemy. Six men were in the foremast top, twelve in the mainmast top; six in the lower mizzenmast top; two more in the upper mizzenmast top and two men in the bonaventure top. Finally, forty men were located in the ship's main boat, twenty more in the middle-sized cockboat, and ten in the small jollyboat.[3] These ships' boats gave extra flexibility to boarding, which is why the Cowdray engraving shows them being towed out into the Solent by their parent vessels.

Admiral Lisle was aware of the immediate threat from the French galleys who were looking for weaknesses in the defences of the English ships, and were probably scattered like bees around a honeypot. As Van der Delft described: 'The English fleet at once set sail to encounter the French, and on approaching them kept up a cannonade against the galleys.'[4]

The English had good reason to be worried about the vulnerability of their great ships when facing the galleys, as was graphically confirmed by the archaeologist Alexzandra Hildred when she plotted the arcs of fire of guns in the *Mary Rose*. She found significant areas that were lightly defended in the 'quarters', the 'corners', of the ship,

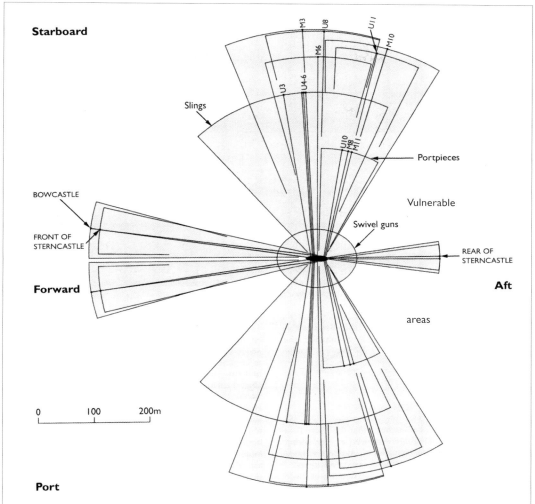

Gunfire arcs of the *Mary Rose* show that the ship's 'quarters' were poorly defended, and, as all large guns were in fixed positions, it was the ship that had to be manoeuvred to fire at the enemy. The mix of gun types meant that a variety of shot could be fired at different ranges, and although most shot found would kill and maim men, or make holes in enemy ships, very few shot were found that could damage sails and rigging. *(Mary Rose Trust)*

especially at the stern. Although covered by guns on the forward and after faces of the sterncastle, and on the after face of the forecastle, some guns had to fire through the rigging and lower sails which was likely to cause damage. John Smith referred to this as a problem, albeit in a muddled way: 'The fighting sails, which is only the fore-sail, the main and fore top sails, because the rest should not be fired nor spoiled; besides they would be troublesome to handle, hinder our sights and using our arms; he makes ready to close fights fore and aft'.[5]

The first indication that the *Mary Rose* had been sunk is in a letter written later that evening by the King's Secretary, Sir William Paget, in Portsmouth to Sir John Russell, Lord Privy Seal, who was in Bodmin,

Cornwall. Paget lamented the unhappy loss of the *Mary Rose* 'with such rashness and negligence cast away'. However, the French did not get away unscathed in this encounter, for Paget understood that seventeen galleys had come forward to fight, but one of them was sunk before they retired.[6]

Edward Hall remarked that after arriving with his fleet off St Helen's Point, Admiral d'Annebault:

sent sixteen galleys daily to the very haven of Portsmouth. The English navy lying in the haven, made them pressed and set out towards them, and still the one shot at the other ... but in their setting forward, a goodly ship of England called the *Mary Rose*, was by too much folly, drowned in the midst of the haven, for she was laden with much ordnance, and the [gun]ports left open, which were very low, and the great ordnance unbreached, so that when the ship should turn, the water entered and suddenly she sank. In her was Sir George Carew, knight, Captain of the said ship, and four hundred men, and much ordnance.[7]

Four days after the disaster the Imperial Ambassador, Francis van der Delft, handed a sealed letter, addressed to the Emperor, to his own courier in which he described the disaster in greater detail:

Towards evening, through misfortune and carelessness, the ship of Vice-Admiral George Carew foundered, and all hands on board, to the number of about 500, were drowned, with the exception of about five and twenty or thirty servants, sailors and the like, who escaped. I made enquiries of one of the survivors, a Fleming, how the ship perished, and he told me that the disaster was caused by their not having closed the lowest row of gun ports on one side of the ship. Having fired the guns on that side, the ship was turning, in order to fire from the other, when the wind caught her sails so strongly as to heel her over, and plunge her open gunports beneath the water, which flooded and sank her. They say, however, that they can recover the ship and guns.[8]

Bellay believed that the loss of the *Mary Rose* was caused by French gunfire: 'The *Mary Rose*, one of their principal ships, was sunk by cannon shot ('*a coups de canon*'), and of the five or six hundred men who were in her only thirty-five were saved'.[9]

Taking all the evidence together it seems that around 7pm the *Mary Rose* was engaged in a fight with a French galley while sailing northwards. As she approached the shoals of Spitsand, she prepared to turn

Survivors being rescued and the corpses of drowned sailors and soldiers from the *Mary Rose* being collected after her sinking are shown on the Cowdray picture. *(Society of Antiquaries)*

eastward (starboard), to avoid running aground and became a fixed target for the enemy. Her Pilot would have warned the sailing Master and Vice-Admiral Carew of the approaching danger, which could explain why a sounding line lay on the upper gun deck in the waist as if a sailor had been checking the reducing depth of water.

The manoeuvre that she was about to carry out was called 'wearing', turning eastward towards the French from a northerly course to a southerly one. This required the skilled action of her crew who had to haul yards and sails around to catch the wind, and needed a fair amount of sea-room. Wearing was quite complicated, for as the rudder was turned, the mizzen and main sails had to be positioned so as to allow the wind to fill only the foresails and bowsprit to turn the ship. Having turned, the main and mizzen sails were positioned to allow the wind to fill them and carry the ship southwards. It was as if the ship was rotating on a pivot point in the centre of the vessel. In later times this manoeuvre began when the order was shouted to 'Stand by to wear the ship!' which meant that gunports should have been closed. But in 1545 a sudden and unexpected gust of wind apparently interrupted the manoeuvre with devastating results. Judging from her heeled angle on the seabed the wind was from the west.

Van der Delft stated that the *Mary Rose* had already fired her guns at the French ship, which explains why a wrought iron breech-loading port piece on the main gun deck (in sector M8) was only half reloaded when the ship sank. Its stone shot had been placed in the barrel, but its cartridge, an iron breech chamber filled with gunpowder, was found

A bronze muzzle-loaded gun from the *Mary Rose*. These had to be pulled inboard for loading. *(Mary Rose Trust)*

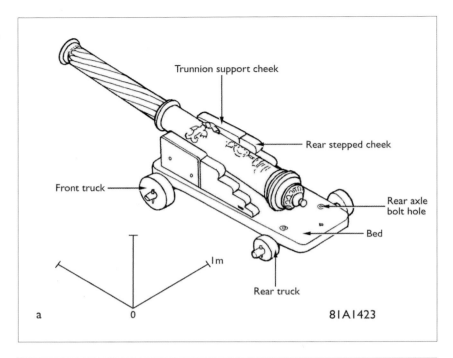

Trunnion support cheek

Rear stepped cheek

Front truck

Rear axle bolt hole

Bed

Rear truck

I m

a          0          81A1423

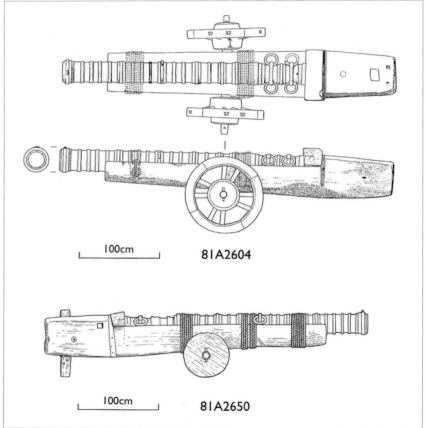

100cm          81A2604

An iron breech-loaded gun from the *Mary Rose*. These were loaded from inboard, so did not require pulling inboard. *(Mary Rose Trust)*

100cm          81A2650

still lying on the deck waiting to be put into place. The gun had a range of roughly 200-300 metres, indicating the approximate distance of the French galley. The range also accords with signs that the ship's archers had been firing arrows at the enemy and needed replacements from the archery store on the orlop deck.[10]

Rescue boats quickly reached the survivors, including the man waving his arms from the 'top' on the main mast as shown on the Cowdray engraving. Others collected floating corpses. Admiral Lisle had to put this terrible disaster aside in favour of continuing the battle until darkness descended. Around 8pm Admiral d'Annebault withdrew his galleys to his anchorage off St Helen's Point. His delight at the sinking of the *Mary Rose* was dashed by the news on his return that his own flagship 'the *Maitresse*, the best and principal ship of our fleet and on which he had resolved to fight, had run aground' wrote Bellay. 'And there was little hope but to save the crew and the King's money which was in her for payment of the fleet.' Bellay believed that this disaster was caused by the ship running aground while coming out of the French port of Honfleur. The keel was displaced, which caused her to leak 'so badly that they could scarce get rid of the water by pumping'. Before Admiral d'Annebault returned from the galley fight, 'Seigneur de la Mileraye, Vice-Admiral of France, had already unloaded and sent her [the *Maitresse*] into [Honfleur] harbour for repair.' As Admiral d'Annebault had no option but to make the Venetian galley *Contarina* his third flagship, he may have entertained doubts about the expedition, as did the French diplomat, Jean de Monluc, who later recalled in his memoirs, 'I had a bad feeling about our campaign'.[11]

Dawn that Monday morning revealed the French galleys at anchor,

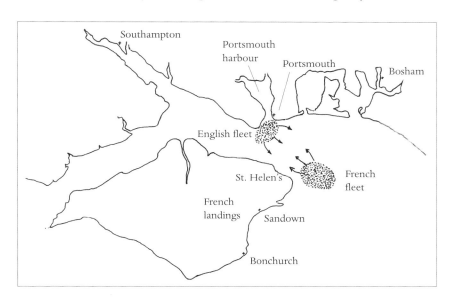

Disposition of the English and French warships during the battle in 1545.

English carracks
(right) and French
galleys in the battle
in the Solent in 1545,
seen in the Cowdray
picture. *(Society of
Antiquaries)*

forward of the large enemy battle fleet of carracks. Behind them were
about two hundred transport vessels filled with thousands of soldiers,
supplies, and five hundred horses waiting to invade the Isle of Wight.
The soldiers were bored, and cramped while they waited for the order
to land, but before that could happen Admiral d'Annebault wanted to
force Admiral Lisle into a full-scale battle. Unless he could defeat the
English fleet, he was worried that Admiral Lisle could disrupt the flow
of supplies from France to the proposed French camps on the Isle of
Wight, and could starve them out.

The last thing that d'Annebault did on that Sunday evening was to
assemble his leading officers and issue fighting instructions for the next
day. So on that Monday morning his carracks manoeuvred into three
squadrons as the English had done, with himself in command of the
centre, accompanied by thirty picked vessels. 'The Seigneur de
Boutiers, sailing by the side of this squadron on the right wing', which
from the French position meant to the north, was 'accompanied by a
like number of ships', wrote Bellay. Baron de Curton on the left wing
led a similar force to the south, 'and, having considered the advantageous position of the enemy, [d'Annebault] ordered the galleys to take
up a position in the morning where they could maintain a hot
cannonade with the enemy and during the engagement retire towards
our fighting line in order to, if possible, draw on a general engagement
and entice them [the English] outside the narrows'.

The French executed this fleet order

very daringly … but the changeable weather so varied the danger
that one could not judge in so short a space of time to which side
fortune had shown herself the more favourable, ourselves or our

enemies, for in the morning, favoured by the sea, which was calm, without wind or strong current, our galleys were able to manoeuvre at their pleasure and to the disadvantage of the enemy.

The English, meanwhile,

> not being able to move for want of wind, remained exposed to the fire of our artillery, which had greater power on the ships than they had on it, the ships being higher out of the water and more bulky; added to which, our galleys, by using their oars, could retire out of danger and gain the advantage. In this manner fortune favoured our arms for more than an hour.[12]

This stage in the battle is depicted on the Cowdray engraving.

Van der Delft viewed all of this from his vantage ashore on Southsea Common, and noted that the English had difficulty in manoeuvring into battle formation in the absence of wind: 'The English were determined to give battle as soon as they get their ships together and the wind is favourable'.[13]

Admiral Lisle realised that d'Annebault was trying to tempt his ships to follow the galleys, but with fewer warships he needed to be cautious. The French had similar carracks to the English but these remained moored off St Helen's Point, leaving the dangerous highly manoeuvrable galleys alone to lead the action, each with a heavy forward-firing gun. Lisle's own armed rowing pinnaces were hardly a match for the French galleys, and the loss of the *Mary Rose* had left an important gap in his fleet. He also knew that the French aim was to land their army to seize the Isle of Wight or Portsmouth, but as long as he could keep his fleet intact d'Annebault would not dare land his troops. Lisle showed a brilliant understanding of naval tactics, and in these circumstances showed that winning a naval battle was not always about destroying an enemy, but also about stopping a superior force succeeding. If he could avoid an all-out fight and let the enemy run down its supplies, d'Annebault would have to give up and return home, tail between his legs.

This type of response was to serve the English successfully again in 1588 when the Spanish sent its great Armada and ended up having to sail home, leaving many of its fleet wrecked on the rocks of western Ireland, and again in 1690 at the Battle of Beachy Head in the English Channel when the French again tried to invade England. In the latter case the commanding admiral, Lord Torrington, had to explain to Parliament why he did not fully engage with the enemy, and it was accepted that maintaining a fleet in defence of the nation was a better outcome than fighting a superior force and possibly losing. This tactic has remained British defensive policy to today.

Under normal circumstances Lord Admiral Lisle's previous battle manoeuvres off Le Havre and his fighting instructions issued in August showed that he would normally expect his fleet to mirror the disposition of the French fleet, with his three squadrons to be 'half a cable [300ft] length between every of the ships'.[14] Consequently, if he had to engage with the French carracks he would lead the Battle squadron on the *Henry Grace a Dieu* to d'Annebault's flagship in the middle of the Solent, and 'our vice-admiral shall seek to board their vice-admiral, and every captain shall choose his equal.' Had the *Mary Rose* not been sunk, Sir George Carew would have led the Van squadron against the northern French squadron, specifically engaging the flagship of Seigneur de Boutiers.

The battle that Monday was described by Bellay:

> The *Great Harry* [i.e. The *Henry Grace a Dieu*] which carried their Admiral, was so damaged that had it not been aided and supported by the neighbouring ships it would have come to a like end [as the *Mary Rose*]. They would have sustained still more notable losses had not the weather turned in their favour, which not only freed them from this peril, but also enabled them to attack us, by the rise of a land [northerly] wind, which bore them with the tide full sail against our galleys [high tide occurred at 13.11 hours]. So sudden was this change that our men scarcely had time or opportunity to turn their prows; for during the calm I mentioned, and the heat of the engagement, the galleys were so hotly attacked, the ships coming down on them so suddenly and at such speed, that unavoidably they would have struck them below the water line and sent them to the bottom had they not, by the presence of mind of the commanders, and the address and experience of the sailors and convicts [the rowers of the galleys], been turned with a will and quickly. By this means our men, having turned their prows by the smartness of their rowing and the management of their sails, in less than an hour got out of range and began to row more gently and slacken their way so to entice the enemy, as they had been ordered, outside the sandbanks and dangers of the place above mentioned.[15]

It was during this battle that the Captain of one of the French galleys 'was so hurt, by reason of a shot [of] the *Great Harry* [*Henry Grace a Dieu*], that he [later] died at New Haven [Le Havre] and there is buried'.[16]

Admiral Lisle had let loose his fast small galleasses and pinnaces, armed with several guns including, for a few, one big one which fired forward.[17] Bellay described what followed:

> There was a special kind of ship used by our enemy, in shape longer than broad, and much narrower than the [French] galleys, the better to contend with the currents which are usual in this sea, to which the men are accustomed, that, with these vessels they compete with the galleys in swiftness, and are called "ramberges." Some of these boats were lying within this shelter, and with incredible speed followed our ships astern and grievously annoyed them with their artillery fire, because ours, having no stern artillery, were obliged to turn on them and so expose themselves to obvious destruction, for, while thus turning to fight, the enemy had time to board them [under] full sail and run them down. However, the Prior of Capua, the brother to Pierre Strosse, unable to stand this indignity any longer, and trusting to the smartness of his galley in manoeuvring, began to turn on one of them, which, being ahead of the others, nearly took one of our galleys athwart hawse [i.e. at the bow], but this ship, by being shorter, turned first and made its way straight again towards its squadron, after which neither it nor the others were able to follow.[18]

Van der Delft's view ashore was that: 'On Monday the firing on both sides went on nearly all day, and could be plainly witnessed from here. Some people say that at nightfall the English did some damage to a French galley.'[19] After the calm of that day the weather changed and the anchored fleets had to ride out a westerly gale that night.

Admiral d'Annebault's frustration grew as Lisle continued to refuse to have his great carracks fight the French carracks. After attacking the French galleys Lisle simply withdrew the English fleet to safety near the entrance to Portsmouth harbour. The French admiral 'would have given the signal to begin the action' wrote Bellay,

> had he not seen the enemy retire from the pursuit [of the French galleys] and retrace their course towards their fort, where they knew they could wait in safety till we, trusting to our strength, should rashly come and seek them to our disadvantage, for he divined their intention of not following our galleys till they could do so without risk, hoping to lead us on to the sandbanks and shallows. In the encounter we lost a few galley slaves and a small number of fighting men taken prisoners, but of men of mark not one.[20]

He was here referring to the unfortunate Spanish rowers who were chained to the benches in the French galleys.

Bellay continued:

The French fleet at anchor off the east end of the Isle of Wight, as shown in the Cowdray picture. *(Society of Antiquaries)*

The Admiral [d'Annebault], having grasped the enemy's plan of remaining near Portsmouth he resolved to try to draw them out by other means … He was of the opinion that by landing, wasting and burning his [King Henry's] country [the Isle of Wight] in his sight, and slaying his men almost within his reach, indignation at such an injury, compassion for the blood and death of his subjects, and the wasting and burning of his country, would move him to such an extent that he would dispatch his fleet to their assistance, especially as they were but two cannon-shot distant, unless he wished to incur the wrath of his subjects on seeing themselves unaided in any way by the presence of their sovereign, which would result in a conspiracy and rebellion throughout his dominions.

King Henry viewed the matter entirely differently, having already called up reinforcements to be ferried to the Isle of Wight.

Admiral d'Annebault ordered some French troops to land on the east coast of the island, and

to keep the enemy's forces separated, a simultaneous descent was made in three different places. On one side the Seigneur Pierre Strossi was bidden to land below a little fort where the enemy had mounted some guns with which they assailed our galleys in flank, and within which a number of Island infantry had retired. These, seeing the boldness of our men, abandoned the fort and fled southward to the shelter of a copse. Our men pursued and killed some of them, and burned the surrounding habitations.

About a century later Sir John Oglander, who knew the Isle of Wight very well, wrote an account of the battle in which he identified the places from clues that still survived and were in local memory. He concluded that the galley commander, Pierre Strosse, had landed at St Helen's where there was then a 'little fort'.[21]

Bellay continued:

In another place there landed the Seigneur de Tais, general of the foot soldiers, and with him the Baron de la Garde, commander of the galleys. Meeting with no opposition, they pressed on to reconnoitre and spy out the country, but they had not gone far before they came across some companies of footmen, who by hidden ways, and screened by the wood, had assembled in the most advantageous spots to give us battle. These, confident of their position, showed a bold front to our men and wounded some of them. Amongst others the Seigneur de Moneins had his right hand pierced by an arrow, but the rest of our men, marching in array, made them abandon their position and retire precipitately by the same way they had come, where we could only follow them in loose order and in single file.

Oglander believed that this occurred at Bonchurch where

we had there most of the Companies of Hampshire, where Captain Fischer, being a fat gentleman and not able to make his retreat up the hill (for they put our men to rout), cried out "£100 for a horse," but in that confusion no horse could be gotten for a kingdom. Whether he was taken prisoner (which was most likely and that he died at sea) or what became of him we could never hear, although search was made here and inquiry in France.[22]

Belay described the third landing: 'In another place there landed two captains of the galleys, Marsay and Pierrebon, who were both wounded in a fight with an English band that had assembled' to oppose their landing. Oglander placed this landing near Sandham, now part of Sandown on the south-east coast of the Isle of Wight.

Everyone ashore at Portsmouth and on Southsea Common was anxious to know what was happening, and messengers continued to cross the Solent to keep the King and his Privy Council informed. Van der Delft saw the smoke from fires on the island, so took up his quill pen again:

On Tuesday [21 July] the French landed some men on the Isle of Wight, opposite this town [Portsmouth]. They set fire to four or five places, as we saw from here, and it is said that they burned ten or twelve small houses, after which they had several skirmishes with the English, who held the entrance to a strait, and who repelled the

Frenchmen twice with some loss. At length the number of Englishmen kept on increasing until they reached 3,000 or more, and the Frenchmen were obliged to fall back and take refuge in a small earthwork fort [presumably at St Helens]. A large force was sent against them, so that the English have now no fear whatever of the French, as there are now 8,000 English soldiers ready to resist their enterprise, and they say it will be easy to do so, as the island is covered with woods and hedges.[23]

Frustrated by the lack of serious action, some of the waiting French soldiers on board the anchored troop ships took matters into their own hands and landed on the eastern shore of the island, as du Bellay described:

Other fighting men … on board the ships and waiting the Admiral's order to disembark, saw the countryside ablaze and the shore undefended, landed unobserved and without permission at a place distant from their commander so as not to be prevented by him. These, landing without guide or commander, scattered over the country at will and with no plan of campaign, and having in sight of the enemy gained the top of a range of hills traversing the breadth of the Island, were assailed by horse and foot so briskly that some were killed and others captured, and the rest driven in disorder to the foot of the hill close to the shore, where thanks to our army and a hedge and ditch they came across they rallied and made a stand,

until their comrades arrived in hastily manned boats. 'This gave the men ashore such courage that they regained the hill, put the enemy to flight, and forced them to retreat inland to a stream which they crossed by a ridge, cutting it behind them for fear of our pursuit, and there made a stand awaiting reinforcement.' When Admiral d'Annebault heard of this he concluded 'that they, without officers, were only stragglers ("vagabonds") and so would receive no ill-treatment. He therefore bade the Seigneur de Tais to rescue them.'

The seven English nobles of the Privy Council worryingly watched from the shore and anxiously wrote to Admiral Lisle warning him that 'in sending forth his row vessels he should take heed lest the French galleys cut between them and home'.[24] They also summoned up extra weapons by writing to Anthony Anthony to send to Portsmouth by land 'with all diligence' five hundred bows, one thousand sheaf of arrows, one thousand bills, many bowstrings, gunpowder, two sacre guns, and six falcon and falconet guns 'if he can furnish so many'.[25]

Henry, 'perceiving the great navy of the Frenchmen … sent letters for men into Hampshire, Somersetshire, Wiltshire and diverse other places adjoining, which repaired to his presence in great numbers, well furnished with armour and victuals, and all things necessary, so that the Isle was garnished, and all the frontiers on the sea coast furnished with men in great number'.[26] However, the order for troops took time to reach some places, and as late as 24th of July the Under Chamberlain and the Sword Bearer of the Corporation of London were mustering men in St George's Fields to conduct them 'with an honest citizen appointed to assist from each ward until they arrived in Portsmouth'.[27]

Meanwhile, the Battle in the Solent had ground to a halt as Admiral d'Annebault did not know what to do. Admiral Lisle still refused to confront the French carracks, so, on that Tuesday evening, d'Annebault assembled his Pilots, Captains and senior seamen to discuss the possibility of attacking the entrance of Portsmouth harbour, 'representing to them', said Du Bellay 'our superiority both in number of our ships and the valour of our men, and pointing out what advantage such a victory would bring to the [French] King and country, a victory he was certain of if he could only get at the enemy'. Many officers and men were eager to fight but others pointed out the impossibility of undertaking it without certain loss. The entrance to Portsmouth harbour was a narrow channel where only four ships could sail abreast, and was easily defended by the English. 'One could only enter on a favourable wind and tide, and, when the said four ships should be obstructed, the current would carry those following upon them and shatter them.'[28] Others suggested that if they dropped their anchors at the harbour entrance they might make some progress. But the Pilots pointed out that cables could be cut, and even if they remained, the current would turn the ship around and bring the poorly defended 'sterns of our vessels towards the enemy instead of their bows or sides'. As such, this idea was also abandoned.

Admiral d'Annebault believed that the Pilots were making excuses and 'only by cowardice made things out worse than they really were'. He therefore decided to send three Pilots under cover of darkness that night to sound the depth of the channel, ascertain its width, and estimate the advantage that the interior of the inlet gave to the enemy. The extent of the survey went beyond just Portsmouth for the Privy Councillors soon heard from the Constable of the nearby town of Bosham that two French boats had been spotted making soundings in Chichester haven. As a result they alerted the Earl of Arundel to prepare its defences.[29]

In this hiatus Lisle wrote to the King seeking his advice: 'Being so near the fountain [i.e. the King] and would die of thirst, it were little joy of my life' by not having his advice. The ship's Masters, he wrote, say that the location of the French fleet anchored off St Helen's should enable them to ride out a gale, though, if the English approached under sail, the French would have to up-anchor and would be carried eastwards and might run aground on the Owers sandbank.[30]

The view from the shore was less clear, and Van der Delft reported that he had heard artillery firing on the Isle of Wight throughout Tuesday night, and was told of rumours that the French intended to land at another point. As neither the King nor his Privy Council had asked to see him to request assistance from the Emperor, he returned to his lodgings to complete his latest letter to the Queen-dowager, a relative of the Emperor Charles, observing that: 'It is certain that whilst the war lasts the Emperor's subjects will not be allowed to sail the seas without being robbed and spoiled by one side or the other. This is recognised already by some of the subjects here, as they complain of the French as much as they do of the English'.[31]

At dawn on Wednesday Admiral d'Annebault knew that he could no longer delay making a final decision on what to do. On their return his Pilots reported that the navigable channel into Portsmouth harbour was so narrow and winding that his warships could scarcely enter without a Pilot or without the certainty of being discovered. Therefore, he had only two options – to withdraw his fleet back home to Picardy and assist the army by preventing English supply ships from reaching Boulogne, or by seizing and fortifying the Isle of Wight.

Some of the French nobles, wrote Du Bellay, favoured fortifying the Isle of Wight so that

> having it in our power, we could easily make ourselves masters of Portsmouth, one of the finest English ports, and by that means put the enemy to incredible expense in having to maintain an army both by sea and land … Besides, we should be on the thoroughfare [the English Channel] to Spain and Flanders, which we could hold at our pleasure, and in time cultivate the Island and gather provisions for the support of the garrison the King would keep there.[32]

Others disagreed, especially the Seigneurs de Tais and de Remy who saw practical difficulties whilst building three forts simultaneously on the Isle of Wight, particularly as they had no port as a

> refuge against the rage and fury of the wind nor abundance of provisions, and the late season approaching, which is always rainy and windy, the ships would not be safe, nor would the soldiers left ashore be able to withstand the rigour of the weather, having no dwellings to shelter them, neither tents nor huts.

Faced with these problems d'Annebault reluctantly decided to defer the matter until the wishes of King Francis were known. Meanwhile, he decided to withdraw the entire fleet back home, even though he knew that the consequence of his failure to destroy the English navy and seize the Isle of Wight had left him open to recriminations from his King and the French people.

D'Annebault prepared to depart on Thursday, 23 July after collecting fresh water. 'The spot they found most handy to fill the casks was a place at the foot of a hill adjoining the shore of the Island, opposite Havre de Grace [Le Havre]', wrote Bellay. This was at Bonchurch where there was a well-known spring of fresh water. Bellay continued:

Having arrived there Chevalier d'Aux, a Provincal captain of the galleys raised in Normandy, not to be stopped from getting fresh water ... set a guard, and, having no confidence in his convict-master, placed him with a band of men who had followed him on his leaving in his galley and climbed to the top of a hill to overlook them better. Here he fell into an ambush of Englishmen, who made him run so briskly that his men ... were put to flight and deserted him. At this moment the Chevalier was struck in the knee by an arrow, which made him stumble, and on rising he was struck on the head by a bill, which are arms carried by the English, so severely that it beat his helmet from his head and made him stumble a second time, when another blow dashed out his brains, which was a great loss to the King's service, for he was a right valiant and experienced gentleman. While some of the enemy were occupied in stripping him of his armour, the rest pursued our men, who did not recover themselves or stop till they got to the shore. On seeing this, the Admiral sent the Seigneur de Tais to rally them and make them hold out in some neighbouring dwellings so as not to throw into disorder those who were getting the water. On his arrival, a number of good and tried soldiers he had brought with him and others who formed the escort to the water carriers, formed up and marched straight at the enemy and drove them back to the hill, by which means they received no further loss ... The Prior of Capua was assailed in another place, but he was so well attended ... that after he had put more than thirty to the edge of the sword he put the rest to flight.[33]

Lisle had no idea that d'Annebault was planning to withdraw, and at about 9am, Van der Delft met the Privy Council to discuss matters further. 'I reminded them that when I spoke to the King [on Saturday 18 July] there was no knowledge of the coming of the enemy.' Also, 'I pointed out firmly that the war was being waged solely for

Boulogne.' After the meeting 'I took my leave, and returned to my lodgings to draft this letter, as they are sending off their couriers, and mine must accompany him in order to ensure his passage, the ports being closed.'[34]

Fears that the French still intended a major landing of troops were reinforced when the Privy Council received an anxious letter from 'the captain of the Isle of Wight' warning that the French will attempt to capture Sandown Castle and land horses there.[35]

That these fears were unfounded came apparent to Van der Delft on Thursday 23 July:

> The French flagship, however, with the whole fleet drew away, of which the King [Henry] sent me word. The wind has continued throughout in favour of the French, who they say have with them 500 light horse. The English assert here that they have sunk one of the French galleys, and that the Chevalier d'Aux of Provence was killed on landing in the Isle of Wight.[36]

The French fleet set sail eastwards leaving Admiral d'Annebault 'as a rear guard with his galleys to withstand the enemy should they sally out', wrote du Bellay,

> So favourable was the wind on the departure of our fleet that it arrived at "Valseau," 14 leagues [forty-two miles] from the Isle of Wight, before the galleys could come up with the ships. This place, being level and open, presented such a good opportunity for landing that a great number of our men took the occasion to go ashore, which they did in the absence of their commander without order or guidance. Straggling some distance from the shore towards a village, which appeared deserted, they assailed it, thinking to obtain booty, but they were awaited by the enemy near a stream which was pretty deep by reason of the ebb tide. These, seeing part of our men had passed over some planks, suddenly issued from a little fort where they had lain in ambush, and, after breaking the bridge to hinder the others from crossing charged those on their side so vigorously that they were compelled to take safety in flight. In re-crossing the bridge, however, some of our men were carried away by the stream and drowned, while others, who knew how to swim, strove against the force of the water and saved themselves, thanks to their comrades on the other side of the stream who supported them with arquebus fire. Meanwhile, the Admiral arrived and repulsed the enemy with artillery fire and made them evacuate the fort, and by this means retired our men.[37]

The location of this landing is indicated by a letter from Stephen Vaughan, the King's financial agent in Antwerp, dated 26 July, to Lord Cobham. He says that the previous night a boat from England had brought news 'that the French King's galleys were arrived at "Sutherey" besides Arundel. If it be true, I trust that both those that came with them shall be well beaten and their galleys remain ours.'[38] The nearest port to Arundel was Littlehampton, though Shoreham is usually favoured by historians. However, the forty-two miles from the Isle of Wight mentioned by du Bellay coincides with the then fishing village of Brighton, which was depicted by Anthony Anthony on a chart that is dated July 1545. Some historians have suggested that this picture refers to the French attack on the village in 1514, but this is clearly incorrect as the artist would have been too young and such a picture would have been pointless. In any case, one of the illustrated ships flies the flag of the admiral of France in 1545. Moreover, the design of the carracks is as they were in the 1540s.[39] This attack may have caused the loss of some guns from a ship of around that time, which were found at Brighton Marina.

As the French retired homeward Emperor Charles continued trying to forge peace between England and France, and Henry even received an offer of mediation from the Protestants in Europe. The King's Secretary, Paget, thanked them and replied that as the French King had invaded England with all of his power by sea, with thirty thousand men, he evidently meant not to make peace. In any case, King Henry's honour might be touched if he consented to any mediation.[40]

By now the French fleet was straggled out along the English coast, and at 10am on Saturday Edward Gage in the port of Seaford, east of Brighton, was panicked to see that: 'At sunrise came twelve score [i.e. 240] sails of French ships into Seaford bay and at 10 o'clock landed men there. There are six galleys and above 20,000 men, if every ship carry his full freight; wherefore all Kent must repair hither for their repulse.' He immediately wrote to the Justices of Kent for urgent help, ending his letter: 'Haste, haste, haste, post haste, for thy life, haste.' That same day Edward's father, Sir John Gage, and Sir Edmund Peckham wrote to Lord Cobham that 'about 10 of the clock the French navy landed in Sussex within four miles of my house [Firle Place, inland from Seaford], and I think not the contrary but my house is burnt already'.[41]

At Portsmouth the Privy Council relaxed and began to order troops back to their homes. They wrote to the Duke of Norfolk and to the Earl of Hertford telling them that the 'conductors' of two thousand men from London must return them, and that other men from Worcestershire must return also 'which upon an error were coming forward'.[42] At their meeting next day, attended by Lord Admiral Lisle who had come ashore specially for the occasion, they agreed to send letters requiring the men from Hampshire and Sussex to be sent home, and on 27 July they sent a letter to a Mr Bellingham ordering him to dismiss men from the Isle of Wight.[43]

In Cornwall, in response to Paget's urgent demand for extra ships to join the King's navy, Lord Russell encountered difficulties because of a lack of mariners.[44] In fact, the Mayor of Saltash, a small Cornish town a little inland from Plymouth on the estuary of the River Tamar, had written to Russell saying that he had been unable to send ships because fifteen mariners were already in the King's service and more were being taken to Portsmouth by a Mr Wyndeham.[45]

Meanwhile, at sea Admiral d'Annebault knew that he would receive an uncomfortable welcome back home in France as he confronted criticism for his lack of success. This had been the most expensive sea engagement of the reign of King Francis I, and had left France almost bankrupt. The criticism began on the day that his fleet dropped anchor at Dieppe on 28 July, as was explained by Jean de Saint-Maurice, the Imperial Ambassador to France, who told Francisco de los Cobos, the sixty-eight-year-old Secretary to Emperor Charles V: 'The French fleet has retired from the Isle of Wight, having been unable to seize the harbour, and is now at Dieppe, whence it is said that an attack will be made against Boulogne, or another descent attempted upon England itself'.[46]

Two days later d'Annebault moved his fleet closer to Boulogne to block supplies from England, as Lord Poynings in Boulogne told King Henry:

> Their whole army upon the sea, 200 sails, drew hitherwards [Boulogne] and brought their galleys into a little bay before "Paulled," where they set the Admiral of France on land to communicate with Mons. du Bies and others about finishing their fortress and making another upon the hill where the Master of the Horse lay [Sir Anthony Browne]. The same day they sought a great skirmish at our hands, and were, as before, forced to retire with loss.[47]

Admiral Lisle had successfully beaten off the French attacks and remained in command of the Channel, though the *Mary Rose* had been lost. In spite of his success the Privy Council feared that the French might attack again, so the country remained on alert and warnings were sent out ordering coastal defences to be strengthened and beacons and other landmarks to be removed. It was time for Lord Admiral Lisle to seek revenge on his terms.

*Chapter Ten*

# ADMIRAL LISLE'S REVENGE

As soon as it was clear that the French Admiral d'Annebault was not going to return to the Solent, Lord Admiral Lisle led his fleet eastwards from Portsmouth to attack the French, partly to protect the Channel crossing of supplies between England and Boulogne, and partly as retribution. He issued two sets of fleet battle instructions to ensure that when he found them his Captains would form the usual three battle squadrons to attack. But with no sign of the French he seems to have returned to Portsmouth where he spent two weeks carrying out repairs. He reported to Paget, the King's Secretary, that the list of ships' Captains remained unchanged, except 'such as be gone sick and one that is dead', referring to Lokyer of the *Guard*. Curiously, there is no mention of the death of Sir George Carew or of the loss of the *Mary Rose*. However, he did mention that James Baker and the other shipwrights had checked the *Jennet*, the *Newe Bark* and 'the bark with salt', but they were not going to be ready for service within a month's time 'for the upper overlop [deck] of the *Newe Bark* must be clean taken down and … their overlopps [decks] be so near together that men could not row in them'.[1]

Eventually, the long awaited, but depleted, ships from south-west England reached Portsmouth, far too late to be of use.[2] Sir John Russell wrote to the Privy Council from Exeter explaining that some had returned home, their crews pretending that they lacked victuals and grain. In reality, they intended other adventures pertaining to pillage and robbery. As it was, he had transfered guns from the returned ships to other vessels and land defences, adding that any crew who absconded would be punished.[3]

Russell was well aware of the potential defensive importance of the western ships as he had been Lord High Admiral (1540–42) prior to Lord Lisle. He had also been knighted earlier in 1522 after losing an eye in the naval attack on Morlaix, Brittany. He had authority to commandeer the ships after being created Baron Russell in 1538/9 and appointed as President of the Council of the West, and, in 1539, as Steward of Cornwall.

Meanwhile, back in France the Emperor's sixty-eight-year-old Secretary, Francesco de los Cobos, heard from the Imperial Ambassador to France, Jean de Saint Mauris that: 'The [French] Admiral is at present with the fleet in Boulogne roads, between Calais, Boulogne and Dover, thus preventing [English] succour from reaching Boulogne. Up till the time of his [the Admiral's] coming thither the English had always had free entrance to, and exit from, Boulogne both by land and sea.'[4]

However, Admiral d'Annebault's arrival was greeted with anger and dismay from the people of France, and he quickly found himself, along with Captain de la Garde, facing serious criticism from the galley commander Piero Strozzi for the failure of the campaign. Strozzi accused La Garde of cowardice because, among other things, on Saturday 25 of July, when the English navy was out of port but not yet in battle order, it was only after much dispute that La Garde, the Lord Prior of Capua and San Piero, agreed to attack the English.[5] Stung by this criticism, d'Annebault decided to return to attack Admiral Lisle's fleet. Lord Poynings, in Boulogne saw d'Annebault's departure and sent an urgent message to the Lord Deputy of Calais asking him to inform him if he 'hear where the French navy is become'.[6]

Lisle became aware of d'Annebault's search for him when three French galleys unexpectedly appeared off St Helen's Point and tried to capture a boat from Rye to obtain information. The boat managed to escape, though the galleys followed her 'almost against Saint Helens Haven' where the English warships the *Mistress*, *Ann Gallant*, *Greyhound* and *Fawcon* came to the rescue and 'canvassed them away again'.[7] The French galleys seized a Dutch trading ship for information, but this too was rescued by the English, though not before her Master had told the French that Lisle's fleet was at sea.

The arrival of d'Annebault's fleet off Rye later that day sparked news that was rushed to the Privy Council meeting at Petworth in Sussex, home of the Percy family, who immediately informed Lord Admiral Lisle in Portsmouth asking him to put to sea. News was also sent to the Lord Warden of the Cinque Ports and to Sir Thomas Seymour, declaring that the Lord Admiral had departed to seek the enemy off Rye, and that a battle was expected within two days. It was requested that men and boats be made ready to defend the coast. Similar letters were sent to Lord La Warre, Mr Comptroller and to the justices of Sussex.[8]

It is not hard to imagine the urgent flurry of messages through the efficient court postal system of couriers and riders for Lisle received the letters from the Privy Council at 7pm that same day while he was in the *Henry Grace a Dieu*. Even though it was evening Lisle got his fleet of one hundred and twenty fighting ships underway, replying that no news could be more welcome.[9] At 3am on 12 August, he wrote to the King confirming that his fleet was under sail, carried by a wind from the west-north-west, but 'blowing very little'.

The two fleets met off Shoreham three days later, on the 15 August, and at 10am Lisle wrote to Henry VIII, 'The enemy and we have sight of one another, striving who shall get the advantage of the wind. Their galleys row fast for it, and our Wing does their best'. The French gained the advantage, but seemed reluctant to fight in spite of the light wind that favoured the galleys.[10]

About noon, d'Annebault's galleys attacked but were repelled by 'The *Mistress*, the *Anne Gallant*, the *Greyhound*, with all your Highness's shallops and rowing pieces, did their parts right well, but especially the *Mistress* and the *Anne Gallant* did so handle the galleys.' They used their guns so well that the English 'great ships', the carracks, had little to do. The result was that the French 'galleys were well beaten and repulsed'. Lisle anchored his fleet to show that he was not afraid and the French Admiral merely shot off two warning pieces as if meaning to do likewise.

D'Annebault did not press his advantage, which surprised Lisle who wrote that 'not a ship was struck, and all they did was break three oars in the *Mistress*; and yet they bestowed among us 200 cannon shot'. It was night before their fleet came near and both armies anchored within a league (about three miles) of each other. Lisle had his fleet under sail by daybreak, but during the night d'Annebault had set sail so that in the morning 'our good neighbours were not to be found'. Throughout the engagement the English managed to sink a foyst ('fuste'), a long narrow galley with two masts carrying lateen sails, with eighteen to twenty oars and a crew of about one hundred. They also destroyed the poop of another galley.[11]

The unexpected sudden departure of the French puzzled not only Lisle but also the Imperial Ambassadors to England and France. The explanation was subsequently revealed by du Bellay who said that when La Garde attacked, his galleys were not properly supported by other ships, and when the wind increased that night, they were in danger of sinking. La Garde managed to save them by his great skill, and although firing continued until dark, little damage was done to either side. Bellay said that the French saw a number of dead bodies and much floating wreckage though this seems to have been an exaggeration. They had apparently damaged two of the English ships before their galleys withdrew hoping to tempt the English to follow towards the French battle fleet. Lisle was not tempted by the tactic that d'Annebault had previously and unsuccessfully used in the Solent. As the wind changed, the Strozzi brothers who were in the galleys took matters into their own hands because, they claimed, of the cowardice of Captain de la Garde.[12]

All the time this was happening, Lisle's fleet was carried east by the flood tide. He ordered it to anchor off Beachy Head to stop the ebb carrying it back again, and sent small boats after the French to find out where they were going. On their return they reported that the enemy had sailed east as if to go to the Dover strait, and that they had departed in no order leaving five miles between their foremost and hindmost ships. Lisle particularly noted this disorder when he wrote to Gage, realising that the lack of discipline among the French meant they would not fight.[13]

Lisle wanted to follow that evening and take his fleet to Dover, but the weather changed on the night of 17–18 August blowing a gale from the north-east. He was still at anchor off Beachy Head two days later which gave him the opportunity to check some of his ships. In partic-ular, he found that the *Mistress* was unable to keep the seas without losing her masts and tackle overboard. Her mainmast was loose, and the cross trestles of the foremast and main mast were broken. He sent her back to Portsmouth for repair, and, as soon as the wind allowed, he decided to send the Master Carpenter who made her to Portsmouth and report the state of the ship to the King. Moreover, he said: 'Sundry of this fleet are ill appointed with anchors and cables, especially the merchants and strangers.'[14]

The big question was, had the French fleet sailed home or was d'Annebault preparing for further action? Lisle dispatched a vessel to capture a French fishing boat off the coast between Dieppe and Fecamp, from which he learnt that d'Annebault had returned to Le Havre. But, had he given up? After all, the weather was fair, his fleet had victuals for two months and was receiving weekly supplies from Dieppe, Le Havre and Fecamp.

D'Annebault had gone ashore to see King Francis at Arkes, a league (three miles) from Dieppe, and it seemed unlikely that he would set sail again that year. Lisle was heartened to hear from the poor captured fishermen that there was never a journey so costly to France as this armada had been, 'nor more shame spoken of amongst themselves'. The ordinary folk in the French countryside were angry with d'Annebault's lack of success, for it had left them famished 'through the furnishing of them'.[15]

Lisle sent Thomas Hardyng in the *Fawcon*, and a bark from the West Country, to the French coast to find out for themselves what was happening. His view was that if the French fleet 'be retired into harbour or drawn to any road upon their own coast', they would not fight, 'for a more commodious day for their advantage they shall never see again'. Their demeanour was shameful.[16]

On his return Thomas Hardyng reported that he had heard that the French fleet of two hundred ships was anchored at the mouth of the Seine. A captured Master and merchant of a Flemish vessel told him that on Monday last the French Admiral and a number of gentlemen had landed at Le Havre, but there was no rejoicing among the French. Their fleet then dispersed to the ports of Honfleur, Hafleur, Le Havre and Dieppe. A great number of the men who landed were sick. Consequently, the French were not able to return to sea for the lack of both victual and men, and would 'rather be hanged than go forth again'.

The common people of France were upset that their King had achieved nothing except great cost. Fourteen of the galleys rode at anchor between 'Hartflete' and Le Havre, four had been sent to Rouen, and five or six were at Dieppe. Lisle was delighted to hear this and longed for weather 'in which to annoy the King's enemies'.[17] He had already planned a revenge attack, one that the French would not forget. However, forward movement was stymied as food supplies had become dangerously low, leaving scarcely any drink, and if supply vessels did not arrive soon 'a good many of this fleet may happen to drink water' he wrote to Lord St John.[18] Thereafter ordered his fleet to lift anchors and sail to the Solent.

Lisle's revenge happened just over a week later. On 2 September, he set sail from Portsmouth with about forty armed ships. It is not clear why he chose to attack the peaceful town of Treport in Normandy for it had not been involved in any of the previous battles, yet on his arrival he landed six thousand troops with orders to massacre the men and women and burn the town, including its abbey and thirty ships in its harbour. It was a terrible revenge that is remembered in the town's history to this day. Lisle lost only fourteen men, and returned to Portsmouth about three days later.[19]

This shocked King Francis who immediately sent M. de Neves, M. D'Aumale and M. de Boissy to Treport, who found the English had already left. The Imperial Ambassador in Paris reported that 'The English now dominated the sea, as the French fleet is broken up. They talk of commissioning at once 40 armed ships to protect the [French] coast until a truce or a peace be concluded. As to the galleys, the season condemns them to stay in the corner of a harbour to serve as food for rats.'[20]

Back at Portsmouth, Lisle found his fleet blighted by an outbreak of plague in thirteen of his thirty-four ships, which stopped any hope that he may have entertained in carrying out further retribution against the French. He and Seymour quickly reported the outbreak to the Lord Chamberlain and the newly established Council of the Admiralty, stating that nobody was willing to enter the infected vessels. Lisle could only muster healthy men to serve in unaffected vessels, but even those fell sick, and some died 'when they have come to receive their money, with the marks of plague'.[21]

King Francis had lost the Battle of the Solent by underestimating the strength, commitment, discipline and organisation of the English navy and the tactical skill of Lord Admiral Lisle. This contrasted with the loose discipline of the French under Admiral d'Annebault, the bitter rivalry from the Strozzi brothers, and the lack of a will to fight even when the French dominated the situation. Lisle did not respond as d'Annebault expected, and as a result was unable to bring his great carracks into action. The Imperial Ambassador to France soon heard at his residence in Paris that the Strozzi brothers had even taken their complaints to King Francis personally:

> Ten days ago, in the presence of the King, Paulin and the Strozzis had a dispute arising out of Polin [La Garde] having said that the Strozzis had charged him with neglect of his duty against the English at sea … The Strozzis declared that they had not imputed the blame especially to Polin, but they said that several good opportunities had been missed during the voyage of effecting notable exploits against the enemy. In support of their assertion they drew up a written statement of the events of the voyage, describing in detail the opportunities that had presented themselves. The King finally told them, however, that he wished them [i.e., the Strozzis and Polin] to remain friends as he held them all as good servants of his own, and everything that had been done in the voyage had been by his own special orders, given for sundry reasons.

The Imperial Ambassador ended: 'Thus, Sire, the Admiral of France was exonerated from the fault imputed to him by everybody, namely that he had conducted the expedition extremely badly, which has made him very unpopular with the French.'[22]

Peace between England and France was signed on 7 June 1546 with the Treaty of Ardres, otherwise known as the Treaty of Camp. Instead of casting blame on his Admiral, King Francis made d'Annebault a signatory, and in response Henry VIII made Lord Admiral Lisle a signatory. At last the two Admirals met. Thus ended the most costly and bloody naval war of the reign of both kings. The English had repelled the might of the French navy, but also had gained a healthy respect for their enemy's galleys. It was agreed that Henry would keep Boulogne until 1554 when he would return it on payment by the French of his 'expenses', which included building fortifications against the enemy. The total cost was to be two million ecuse in gold payable at Calais within fifteen days after Michaelmas in 1554. This rubbed salt into the wound as Henry chose the feast of St Michael the Archangel, 10 or 11 October on the old Julian calendar, as if to underline his success over the French. St Michael was the English patron saint of the sea, maritime lands, ships and boatmen.

In gratitude for the English success a solemn *Te Deum* was sung in St Paul's Cathedral in London, and on 20 August 1546 Admiral d'Annebault sailed up the River Thames with twelve galleys on a state visit as a French Ambassador to finalise the peace agreement. He landed at Tower Wharf, by the Tower of London, and was received with great pomp and ceremony, and was entertained at Hampton Court where he met King Henry VIII. Before he departed on 30 August, he solemnly swore in the name of his King to perform the articles of peace.[23]

Lord Admiral Lisle remained puzzled by d'Annebault's lack of commitment to engage the English fleet in an all-out battle or to invade the Isle of Wight. When the two men privately met during the treaty negotiations at Guines, near the then English town of Calais, Lisle found Admiral d'Annebault 'a right proper man, and very gentle and well spoken, and very fine in his apparel'.[24] He then asked d'Annebault about the great naval battles in which they had been engaged as 'the French Admiral and I walked together in the field'. Surprisingly, d'Annibault denied that a battle had taken place, and merely:

spoke of his great desire to serve my Master [King Henry VIII], and of their army last year upon the sea, ascribed to God that there was no battle, else had been the greatest occasion of men that was this many years. I answered that our army was not in number of ships to be compared with theirs, and they had besides an army of galleys sufficient to fight an army of ships, and yet we sought the battle. He said there was no need to speak of the good will of both sides to serve their Masters [Kings Henry and Francis], but God preserved us for a better purpose, and now we were met for an honourable peace. I said that I had less hope of it since our meeting, when I saw their demands so great and their offers so meagre. He said God might work in our Masters' hearts, whose affection for each other was such that once friends they would never be foes again. He trusted someday to see the King [Henry] and declare his desire to serve his Majesty, whose goodly ships were such that our Masters could together fight all princes Christian upon the seas. I showed him that the King was better furnished this year [1546], having made 8 or 10 new galleasses that shot six or eight cannons a-piece, beside sundry light vessels, as swift with oars as their [French] galleys, shooting the demi-culverin in the prow.

At this point the French Admiral changed the subject, 'He [d'Annebault] seemed as though he scant heard it, asking me whether I would see Mon[sieur] Ganaple's hawks fly the myllan [a French word for 'kite']. Having shown us this sport he took leave'.[25]

The two kings died less than a year later, King Henry on 28 January 1547 and Francis 31 March, after which English history fundamentally changed. The loss of the *Mary Rose* showed that warfare at sea had changed, and that by 1545 her design was outdated and dangerous. England was about to embark on an era of maritime history that would lead her to explore the world, and in time this would be in partnership with her old foe, Scotland. The British and French navies would again meet in battle 145 years later, in 1690, also off Beachy Head, and the French would again retire without success. And yet again, most famously, 115 years after that, in 1805, off Trafalgar, where under a new Admiral, Nelson, the French were defeated. Throughout all those years the remains of the *Mary Rose* lay entombed in the seabed awaiting discovery and answers. She would eventually embark on a new and very different voyage of timeless adventure when, in the twentieth century, her watch bell was rung once again, bringing the great ship back to life in an amazing new museum.

*Chapter Eleven*

# SALVAGE

Jacques Francis, a young Portuguese speaking black man from West Africa is the first person that we know of to see the sunken *Mary Rose* when in 1546 he led a team of Venetian divers employed to salvage the ship. Initially, Charles Brandon, Earl of Suffolk, was given responsibility for organising this immediately after the disaster, but he died on 22 August 1545 at Guildford, and progress thereafter was limited. Brandon believed that raising the ship was possible, and reported so to the King. This put him at odds with Lord Admiral Lisle who was anxious not to be caught out if the French returned. Curiously, it was the proximity of the wreck to the extensive naval facilities at Portsmouth that created the problem, for it meant that Lisle had to divert equipment and men from the defence of the port at a time of great danger.

Only twelve days after the disaster Brandon wrote to Sir William Paget, Secretary of State to the King, outlining his plan to raise the ship. His message was simple: he would set men to work, even though he found the defence of Portsmouth against the French 'So far out of order, for here have we nothing in a-readiness, neither pick-axes [nor] mattocks.'[1] The next day he told Paget that he had just met two Venetian salvage experts, Piero de Andreasi and Simone de Marini, who offered to raise the ship. Ever opportunists, they had quickly worked out how to bring her up, and presented Brandon with a shopping list of equipment:

2 of the greatest hulks that may be gotten.
The hulk that rideth within the haven.
4 of the greatest hoys [a type of boat] within the haven.
5 of the greatest cables that may be had.
10 great hawsers.
10 new capstans with 20 pulleys.
50 pulleys bound with iron.

5 dozen ballast baskets.

40 lb of tallow.

30 Venetian mariners, and one Venetian carpenter.

60 English mariners to attend upon them.

A great quantity of cordage of all sorts.

With Brandon's approval events moved forward rapidly, and later that day he told Paget that two empty hulk ships with cables and pulleys had been provided by the Lord Admiral, together with lifting cables. They were the old vessels, *Jesus* and the *Sampson*, and with them the salvors felt confident that the *Mary Rose* would be raised as 'speedily done as may be for the serving of the tides'.

Lisle's concern that this would weaken the port's defences were stated bluntly in a letter to Paget on Sunday, 2 August: 'We must forbear three [*sic*] of the greatest hulks of the fleet till the thing is done, which must be emptied of all her victuals, ordnance and ballast during the business, which will be a great weakening to the Navy if anything in the meantime shall happen'.

Initially, the Venetians were to cut away the mess of rigging, sails and yards from which the sails were hung, and then they would tie cables to the three most substantial masts, the foremast, mainmast and mizzenmast, and attach them to a hulk lying alongside. This would allow them to heave the sunken ship upright from her angle of 60 degrees to starboard. Then they were to drag great cables under the *Mary Rose* with the ends attached to capstans on each hulk. When the ship was cradled on the cables they would allow the rising tide to lift the ship, and would then tow her, submerged, towards the shallows, probably to nearby Spitsand, until she ran aground. At low tide they would repeat the process, and tighten the lifting cables by turning the capstans so that as the tide rose, the *Mary Rose* would again be lifted and towed to even shallower water. This would be repeated again and again until eventually the *Mary Rose* was in water shallow enough at low tide to be visible. Her open gunports would then be blocked and the water inside her pumped out until she floated on her own.

The first stage of clearing the ship went well on the Monday and Tuesday as the divers cut away her sails, yards and rigging, and on Wednesday Brandon reported to Paget that they were now ashore and drying. Three cables had also been tied to the masts ready to pull the ship upright on Thursday, 6 August, 'and that done, they propose to discharge her of water, ordnance and all other things with as much diligence as is possible, and by little and little to bring her nearer to the shore'.

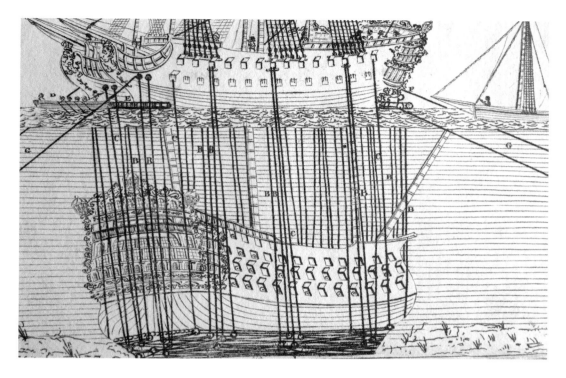

The problems began with Admiral Lisle's written complaint to Paget on that Thursday that saving the *Mary Rose* 'hath so charged all the King's majesty's shipwrights with making engines for the same, that they had no leisure to attend any other things since his majesty's departure hence, which I beseech you to signify into his highness'. That same day the ship would not yield to being pulled upright, which we now know was because she was sinking deep into the clay seabed. On Friday, 7 August Brandon and Lisle discussed the lack of progress over lunch, though they remained cautiously optimistic as Brandon wrote to Paget: 'My Lord Admiral … had a good hope of the weighing upright of the *Mary Rose* this afternoon or tomorrow.'

However, catastrophe then struck. As the salvors heaved the masts they heard a loud crack and a cable ran loose. The foremast had snapped. The Venetians immediately went to see the Lord Admiral who, on 9 August, wrote to Paget to explain that 'they desire to prove another way, which is to drag her as she lieth until she come into the shallow ground, and so set her upright, and to this they ask six days' proof'. The Lord Admiral was in a real tangle about whether or not he should continue to spare the hulks, but after careful consideration he agreed. Nothing more is heard of the efforts to raise the ship, and it seems that the Venetians simply gave up. On 8 December the Privy Council agreed to pay 'Petre de Andreas and Symone de Maryne, Venetians, 40 marks sterling, to be divided betwixt them by way of the

The method used to try to lift the *Royal George* on a rising tide in 1782, with ropes beneath her hull, was the same as was attempted to raise the *Mary Rose* two centuries earlier.

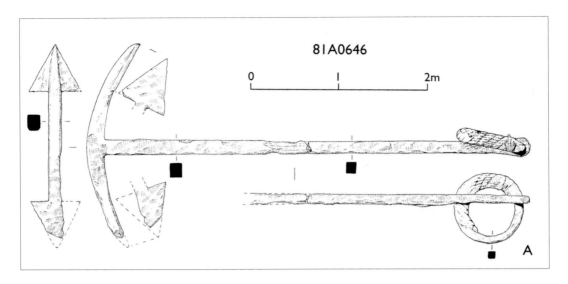

81A0646

0                    |                    2m

A

A large anchor from above the waist of the *Mary Rose* was possibly lost from a salvage ship in 1545. (*Mary Rose Trust*)

King's majesty's reward for their pains taken about the weighing of the *Mary Rose*.' The Privy Council also provided twenty-two casks of beer for the salvage men.

After the *Mary Rose* was raised in 1982, archaeologists discovered two of the salvor's cables under her hull almost amidships, which means that they were well advanced towards lifting her. As the stern was more deeply buried in the mud than the bow, the Venetians had clearly pulled the cables under her bow and dragged them aft to the middle of the ship. They also seem to have abandoned an enormous anchor that had been used to hold one of the lifting hulks. It was found lying on top of an iron gun in the ship's waist just forward of the sterncastle, with its thick cable trailing forward to the forecastle. This has been interpreted as a 'spare' in the ship as it was thought to have stowed on the upper gun deck in the waist, but this must be incorrect as the sheet anchors were the ship's spares, and were ready to be deployed at the bow. Moreover, there was insufficient room for it as the waist only measured 14 metres long by 9.5 metres wide and already accommodated eight guns, the main mast, the pump and possibly a capstan, the main hatch and at least two more hatches at its forward end. In addition, the waist was largely covered by a protective roof, on which the ship's jolly boat, mentioned in the 1514 inventory, was probably stowed ready for it to be swung outboard into the sea. In this very restricted deck space the ship's crew, the gunners, the archers and the soldiers who were waiting under the sterncastle ready to board an enemy vessel, were expected to go about their duties!

The winter gales of 1545–6 eroded deep scourpits on either side of the ship as currents swirled around the wreck, causing the *Mary Rose* to settle even deeper into the mud. Her interior filled with fine silt that settled on her decks and in her cabins, gently burying the remains of the crew, their possessions, and the ship's equipment. By the summer of 1546 it was clear that raising her was out of the question, and that any further effort must concentrate on salvaging items of value, particularly the guns.

In 1546 another Venetian salvor, Piero Paolo Corsi, known to the English as Peter Pawle, was commissioned to save the guns. His head diver was the young black man Jacques Frances, about twenty years old. Frances was a slave probably from the tiny tropical island of Arguin, off Mauritania, in West Africa, where the Portuguese had established a fort and traded slaves. We know that Francis spoke Portuguese because of a dispute, not related to the *Mary Rose*, between Corsi and Domenico Erizzo, an Italian merchant living in England who represented a partnership of merchants. Peter Pawle was a shady character who the merchants accused of stealing valuables when he salvaged their ship after it had caught fire near Southampton in July 1546. This dispute ended up before a judge in the High Court of Admiralty in London where Jacques Francis agreed to give evidence on behalf of Corsi. The merchants objected as they felt that Francis was 'an infidel', 'a morisco' and a 'Blackemore' who was 'not christened' so 'no credit nor faith ought to be given to his sayings'. The judges dismissed this intolerance and admitted Francis's expert evidence. Sadly, we do not know the outcome.

Corsi salvaged the *Mary Rose* intermittently from 1546 until 1549 and managed to recover some guns, for which he was paid £20 in 1547 and £50 in 1549. But then it was discovered that he had fiddled his reports, for in September 1549, he was arrested for taking 'certain of his stuff out of the sea' in Portsmouth and was imprisoned in the Tower of London by the Duke of Somerset. Pawle seems to have privately sold salvaged goods from the *Mary Rose*. We do not know the outcome of this matter, except that he was 'to be examined by Mr. Wootten'. This brought the salvage of the ship to an end.

By 1549 the starboard side of the ship was deeply buried and would be preserved, but the exposed port side, the castles and bow structure of the *Mary Rose* had become infested with the wood boring mollusc *Teredo*, also known as the 'shipworm'. In time this so weakened the ship that eventually the bow and the forecastle collapsed, as did the port side of the hull and much of the sterncastle. Excavation of the bow in 2004–5 revealed the collapsed stempost and slabs of decking and other structures, but only the stempost was raised. The extra structures would only have added to the enormous pile of timbers from the ship already in the queue for conservation. They will be raised one day. The final reckoning by September 1552 was that the salvage operations had cost £559 8s 7d, and that the value of the guns remaining on the ship was £1,723.

We can judge how many years it took for the exposed parts of the *Mary Rose* to be destroyed by erosion and marine life, because a record exists of the decay of the warship *Royal George* which was sunk nearby in the Solent in 1782 with a similar list and in a similar environment. A Mr Ancell reported in 1817 that thirty-five years after the *Royal George* sank there had been considerable decay to the vessel resulting in the fore and stern castles having collapsed. The port side as low down as the upper deck had entirely gone, and the oak planking amidships was very much eaten by worms revealing beams and framing beneath. He reported that:

> The wreck has a beautiful appearance, when about a fathom [6ft] above the deck, being covered with small weeds, interspersed with shells, star-fish, and a species of the polypus, lying on a thin greasy, grey sediment, about an eight of an inch thick … All below the upper deck, is a perfect solid mass of fine black mud. When suspended over the larboard [port] side of the ship, she appears a rude mass of timber, lying in all directions, and I have every reason to believe the after part is fallen in.[2]

When the salvage expert, John Deane, examined the *Royal George* fifty-two years after her sinking, 'He found her one huge indescribable mass of old timber, stores, and materials confusedly mixed and intermingled with mud, clay, sand, etc.' By 1840, six years after that, parts of the wreck apparently stood thirty-three feet above the seabed, for the stem and stern were reported to be perfectly above the level of the lower deck, and the whole starboard side stood to nearly the same level, 'the larboard [port] side having fallen over; whilst the fragments of the upper deck, whose fastenings have been eaten away by the worms, lay in a confused mass over all'. A mound of silt and debris had built up around the wreck, which in August 1840 was up to fourteen-feet high.

We can infer from this that by 1600 parts of the *Mary Rose* were still visible and that she was a hazard to shipping, but by 1640 probably little of her upstanding structure was to be seen. This could explain Sir William Monson's report in 1623 that 'Part of the ribs of this ship I have seen with my own eyes', suggesting that he had seen salvaged bits of hull structure rather than having dived on her.[3] All of this erosion of the upper part of the sterncastle would explain why a few of the human bones found in that part of the ship were eroded before they fell to the upper gun deck.

Fragile textile clothing, paper and string in the personal chests of the more senior members of the crew, as well as food and drink in the casks gradually disappeared and small iron objects simply corroded to nothing, even when deeply buried in mud. However, many other items from the lower parts of the ship survived superbly well due to the wet silt that excluded oxygen. In particular, wood, leather and bronze remained almost as fresh as they were in 1545. The bones of the dead crew were also in an excellent condition, the articulated parts of some skeletons being held together by leather clothing, with foot bones in shoes and boots, and ribs and spines sometimes protected by leather jerkins. The silt also had an amazing ability to preserve some organic materials, including at least one semi-decomposed brain inside a human skull. Slowly, ever so slowly, the ship and her contents adjusted to the buried natural environment of the seabed, though from time to time the currents exposed the eroded upper ends of her timbers.

As the ship lay heeled over on her starboard side, it was only the buried parts of that side which survived, as Prince Charles, the future King of a then united Britain, found four centuries later when he dived beneath the waves and explored the wreck for himself. Her journey through time was not without incident for the ship and threatened her survival. In 1836 five local fisherman trawling across the area caught their precious nets on some of her slightly projecting hull timbers. On 10 June they employed Henry Abbinett and his diver to release them, and 'on Abbinett's man going down, he discovered it to be a piece of old wood, he disentangled their lines and came up'. He wore a diving suit of the type invented by John and Charles Deane, one of whom, by chance, was nearby salvaging the wreck of the *Royal George*, sunk in 1782. The fishermen invited John Deane and his colleague William Edwards to investigate the obstruction in case it was of value.[4]

Deane's diving suit was of waterproof India rubber, rather like a modern diver's dry suit, and he was weighed down by lead shoes and weights hanging from a belt around his waist. His head was inside a round metal helmet that had two small, thick, glass windows, one for each eye. Fresh air was pumped down to the helmet through a hose from a boat on the surface, giving him enough time on the seabed to use a pole with a hook on the end to find objects and tie a rope around them so that they could be lifted.

Deane saw 'some more old timber' sticking out of the seabed and spotted a gun that proved to be of exceptional quality, a brass twenty-four-pounder from the reign of Henry VIII. Since it was naval property, he reported it to the Admiralty and was paid £220 19s 0d so that it could be preserved at the Royal Military Repository at Woolwich. Then he found two more bronze guns, a forty-two-pounder and an eighteen-pounder, as well as an iron gun on a wooden carriage and part of yet another iron gun. He noted that the iron guns were strangely primitive and were 'constructed of thin iron bars' and were loaded with stone shot, whereas the bronze guns, were more conventional and were decorated with the royal coat of arms. They were all found, said Deane, 'resting on some wreck, which was so completely buried in the sand that the diver could find nothing to which he could affix a rope'. Fascinated by these discoveries Sir Frederick Maitland, Admiral Superintendent of Portsmouth Dockyard, delved into historical records and quickly identified the wreck as the *Mary Rose*.

John Deane and the fishermen had signed a salvage contract in which they agreed to share any salvage income equally, but when the valuable guns were found, the fishermen wanted to take total control. This is so typical of what often happens when valuable wrecks are salvaged, that one well-known modern wreck hunter had a T-shirt printed with the words 'Treasure spells Trouble!'

Abinett and John Deane applied to Admiral Maitland to arbitrate. The fishermen wanted to become sole salvors, because they claimed to have found some of the guns. Moreover, they did not trust Deane who was withholding paying them their half of the salvage award on the lame excuse that he was waiting for the permission of the Board of Ordnance before doing so. Deane told the Admiralty that the angry fishermen were using 'a great deal of unpleasant language ... for not paying them half the value of the gun'. Eventually a salvage settlement was agreed, but just as they thought that this drama was settled, Henry Abbinett decided to make a claim on his own behalf. He wrote to the Admiralty claiming his right to salvage the wreck, and considered Deane to be an interloper.

This dispute, fortunately for us, created a mass of correspondence and reports, with the result that we know a lot of detail about what was found. The Admiralty rejected Abbinett's claim, but accepted the agreement between the fishermen and Deane. Future salvage rights were given exclusively to Deane as long as he shared equally the value of the guns that they had jointly recovered. Thereafter, the fishermen would receive one-third of the value of any extra finds.

The discoveries excited a great deal of public interest through newspapers, and in 1836 Admiral Durham commissioned a poster with drawings of four guns, three from the *Mary Rose* and one from the *Royal George*. With an eye to publishing a future book John Deane also had watercolour drawings made of the guns and other finds, and, although the eventual publication never occurred, the drawings survive in Portsmouth City Museum. Other objects that he illustrated include parts of iron guns, rope, bronze sheaves from pulleys, and even human bones.

Meanwhile, three military officers, Major General Millar, Colonel Sir Alexander Dickson, and Major Dundas delved further into historical records and reported to the Admiralty: 'the *Mary Rose* was lost at Spithead and the ship was never weighed up [i.e. raised] ... It may fairly be presumed, therefore, if the wreck the guns were laying on could be dispersed to some degree, that more guns and other articles of an interesting character might be discovered and weighed'. Their prediction was realised almost 150 years later!

John Deane wisely stopped salvaging the *Mary Rose* in 1836, and allowed the acrimonious events to settle down for several years before recommencing salvage in his own right. He returned to the *Mary Rose* in 1840, armed with six old Admiralty gunpowder bombs that had been condemned and were given to him by the Ordnance Board. He also acquired casks of gunpowder to explode on the seabed and open up the wreck. Colonel C. W. Pasley of the Royal Engineers, who was salvaging the *Royal George* and *Edgar* nearby, joined Deane and described that:

Mr John Deane invariably descends himself, and our usual course is first to go down and survey, and select out the best situation to place the powder in, so as to have the most powerful effect in the destruction of the object. We then haul the Cask or Cylinder of powder down and secure it in the desired spot, and afterwards fire it with a

John Deane used the same diving equipment on the *Royal George* to salvage the *Mary Rose* in the 1830s.

quick fuze through an India rubber or leaden tube, and we find 50lbs or 60lbs of powder placed in a proper position, amazingly destructive under water.

Fuses like this were notoriously unreliable, so the Deane brothers and Colonel Pasley experimented with electrical firing from a 'Voltaic' battery. This too was successful, as the archaeologists around 1980 found when they mapped the distribution of fragments of the cast iron bombs. These showed that Deane had tried to open the central area of the wreck around the base of the main mast. It is from these fragments that one bomb, a hollow cast iron ball thirty-three centimetres (13in) in diameter, with a fuse hole 1.5 centimetres in diameter, has been reconstructed.

Deane did find fragments of hull structure and many objects which ended up for sale in local shops. A piece of timber about six inches square was sold for 5s, and an archer's bow was sold for £1 10s. These were popular, and to this day it is possible to buy wood from the ship, carved into chairs, tables, work boxes, walking sticks, sword sticks, riding crops, ink stands, guns, carved sailors and even book covers, each with a printed note showing that it is from the *Mary Rose*.

Deane managed to salvage four more bronze guns, nineteen parts of wrought iron guns, and eight 'warrior's bows'. The guns were mostly shipped to the Office of Ordnance at Woolwich in October 1840, and as a result they survive. The main structural timber found in 1840 was believed to be the lower part of the oak main mast, 'fifteen feet long [4.5m], and nearly as large as that of a 75 gun ship'. As there was no seventy-five-gun ship then, the writer was presumably referring to a seventy-four-gun ship, whose mast was normally thirty-seven inches (0.93m) in diameter. The main pump that lay adjacent to the mast was also found, but no details are given.

Salvage ended in 1840 and left a crucial legacy: a chart of the seabed on which the locations of the *Mary Rose*, the *Edgar* and the *Royal George* were marked. This was drawn in 1841 by Commander Sherringham of the Hydrographic Department of the Admiralty, and 120 years later, in 1966, an amateur diving historian examined that chart and rediscovered the location of the *Mary Rose*. The ship's long journey through time in the seabed would end, but not before she encountered even more amazing adventures.

*Chapter Twelve*

# DISCOVERY AND RAISING

The *Mary Rose* was rediscovered on 5 May 1971 by Alexander McKee, a diving historian and author with a passion for maritime stories. Living on Hayling Island near Portsmouth, in 1965 he decided to look for the wreck. It was his belief that the ship would illustrate how warship fighting methods changed from late-medieval anti-personnel fighting with small guns, bows and arrows, swords and pikes, to the use of heavy ship-smashing guns.

He called a meeting of local amateur divers, mostly from the Southsea Branch of the British Sub-Aqua Club, and under his direction they entered the world of archaeology and history where finding clues to the maritime past was far more important than discovering objects of intrinsic value. Known as 'Mad Mac's Marauders', from 1968 to 1971 they could be seen in their small boat bobbing around on the cold grey waters of the Solent searching the sea floor up to twenty metres below. McKee began by diving for the *Royal George*, sunk in 1782, whose site was known, in the belief that the *Mary Rose* was nearby. This proved to be incorrect. Then he and a volunteer, Margot Varese, chose another area where he thought that the *Mary Rose* might have sunk, and noticed nothing more than a low mound and a shallow hollow in the seabed. Could these have been caused by the action of currents around a buried wreck? But with no wreck to be seen in underwater visibility that was often less than a metre, McKee realised that his dream project would not be easily achieved.[1]

As his divers started bringing up objects for dating they encountered an unexpected complication: government officials applying the administrative 'red tape' of commercial salvage law. British law at that time did not recognise that historic sites could lie underwater, and salvage law, the Merchant Shipping Act 1894, was applied regardless of the age of objects recovered. This seriously discouraged the investigation of historic wrecks. The Act insisted that any finds that were unclaimed by their owners had to be sold and could not be given to museums. Furthermore, McKee was soon disappointed that archaeologists did not give him the enthusiastic support that he wanted, when it was obvious to him that the benefits of studying the remains of historic shipwrecks could add so much to our knowledge of the past. Archaeologists, however, were worried that if McKee did find the incredibly important *Mary Rose* then many of her treasures would probably end up having to be sold, and if a museum wanted them then it would have to buy them probably at auction and in competition with collectors, as this was the only means of establishing monetary value.

Bust of Alexander McKee, discoverer of the *Mary Rose*, in the Mary Rose museum.

Fortunately, the Ministry of Defence still owned the ship and fittings, though not the possessions of the men on board, and could claim its property and give it to museums if it so wished. It was at this stage that I first met Alex McKee, and found his enthusiasm and quality of research impressive. As a young professional archaeologist at the Guildhall Museum in the City of London, I had, by 1964, found and partly excavated two Roman vessels near London Bridge and had also encountered the murky byways of heritage and salvage law as government officials applied inappropriate legislation. Government lawyers had decided that as ships were originally designed to move they were simply large chattels in the same class as kitchen pots and pans. Therefore, they could not be protected by the same Ancient Monuments law that protected fixed historic sites and buildings on land. Moreover, museums were reluctant to collect artefacts from wrecks because they were not usually part of local history, and would occupy a disproportionate amount of limited storage space at a cost that most local museums could not support. Consequently, if the *Mary Rose* were to be found, her fate would be bleak. Historic shipwrecks in the 1960s were the Cinderellas of our heritage, unrecognised, unloved, unwanted, homeless and unprotected!

Following these revelations, in 1964 I approached a small group of archaeologists, maritime historians and amateur divers and we set up the Committee (later Council) for Nautical Archaeology (CNA), with George Naish, of the National Maritime Museum, as its Chairman and myself as Secretary. Our purpose was to campaign for a law to protect historic shipwrecks in British territorial waters and on land; and to monitor what was happening as diving groups sought underwater sites. Because of the potentially outstanding importance of the *Mary Rose* the CNA welcomed a suggestion from a diving naval officer, Lt. Cdr. Alan Bax, that he also search for the *Mary Rose* to enable the CNA to become involved in discussions on how the wreck might be protected. McKee and Bax initially worked separately in different parts of the Solent without success, but with the mediation of Joan du Plat Taylor, an archaeologist and member of the CNA, they soon agreed to combine their limited resources. Their first step was for Bax to enquire at the old naval archives of the Hydrographic Department in Taunton, in Devon, to see if they had a chart location for the *Mary Rose*. It was a long-shot, but perhaps the disagreements between salvors in the 1830s had resulted in the location of the site being recorded.

When McKee arrived at the offices on 10 May 1966, he was thrilled when the Hydrographer opened a drawer and slid out Commander Sherringham's chart dated 1841, with the location of the *Mary Rose* marked by a red cross on the edge of Spit Sand in six fathoms (11m) of water at low tide. The Admiralty had evidently expected further trouble from salvors in the future. The position was exactly at the hollow in the seabed where McKee had dived with Margot Varese in 1965. He generously wrote that 'without Bax's help we would never have obtained access to the chart, so we could hardly act dog-in-the-manger ... We should have to co-operate. CNA neatly solved the situation by making Mrs Rule Director of the project, with Bax and myself as representatives of S&TG [Scientific & Technical Group] and Southsea Branch [both of the British Sub-Aqua Club] respectively.' McKee remained Director of Excavations until 1978 when Margaret Rule took over.

Margaret Rule, a professional archaeologist and Curator of the Roman Palace Museum at Fishbourne near Chichester, had joined the team as a volunteer and had learned to dive so that she could take her archaeological and curatorial skills underwater. This would be crucial to the success of the project. Margaret also joined the Committee for Nautical Archaeology, and supported pressing the government to recognise in law the existence of historic wrecks and their need for protection, rather than be treated as piles of scrap to be salvaged.

McKee returned to the seabed hollow in May 1966, but was disappointed when all he saw was soft mud with slipper limpet shells and occasional pools of sand. He needed to look below the seabed, and so enlisted the help of a charming American scientist, Professor Harold Edgerton, or 'Doc' as he was fondly known, who was professor of electrical engineering at the Massachusetts Institute of Technology. His distinctive deep voice was reminiscent of Bing Crosby, and he had a relaxed way of speaking that masked his genius as an electronic wizard. He was a co-founder of the company EG&G Geophysical that had developed side-scan and profiling sonar that used sound waves to look through sand and mud below the seabed to view anomalies that could be wrecks. Doc generously agreed to help, and in 1967 and 1968 the survey boat could be seen passing over the site with his sonar equipment in tow as it sent sound pulses down through the water and into the seabed. The echoes, reflected back from buried features, were printed out on a continuous roll of paper, and showed a dark W-shaped feature in section buried under the hollow. It did not look like a ship, but nevertheless *something* lay there that might just be the *Mary Rose*. The only way to find out was to dig.

Before rushing ahead they did pause to consider the consequences of finding the wreck, for they knew that it would contain valuable artefacts, including more bronze guns, bows and arrows, and the personal possessions of the men on board. As they had no way of protecting the wreck from diving interlopers intent on stealing these historic treasures, or from a salvor bringing a ship to the wreck site and using a grab to drag up its unique antiquities for sale by auction, they had to think of another solution. They decided to establish themselves as a formal body, and so Alexander McKee, Margaret Rule, Alan Bax and Bill Majer formed the 'Mary Rose (1967) Committee', whose ambition was: 'To find, excavate, raise and preserve for all time such remains of the ship *Mary Rose* as may be of historical or archaeological interest.'

It seemed crazy to have set themselves such unrealistic aims, and to this day I am in utter awe that they and their successors achieved *all* of them. In hindsight, the ultimate success of raising the *Mary Rose* partly depended upon their not considering the project in its entirety, but rather as a series of stages each significant in its own right. Moreover, the project did not depend on government money, so they were free to do as they considered most appropriate. They not only needed funds to excavate and raise the ship, but also to preserve it all and create a new museum that would earn an indefinite revenue income from visitors. Had the total cost of the project been estimated at the outset then the hopes and dreams of McKee and his team would, I am sure, have been dashed.

So, how could the *Mary Rose* site be protected? The Mary Rose (1967) Committee decided in November 1967 to apply to the Crown Estate Commissioners, owner of the seabed, for a lease of 1,200 square feet (334sq m) of the site. This would reinforce the Committee's legal position as 'salvor in possession' of the wreck, and would help enable it to assert its rights of salvage under the Merchant Shipping Act 1894. They also kept the exact location of the wreck secret, and in the years that followed both Alex McKee and Margaret Rule jointly used sighting alignments to landmarks from the dive boat to fix their position.

They began by borrowing a crane-grab and water-jets operated from a moored vessel, and on 30 May 1970 discovered part of an old ship's plank, and two months later a sixteenth-century iron gun 2.28 metres long. They were in the debris field surrounding the *Mary Rose*, so it was only a matter of time before the ship herself was discovered.

Percy Ackland, an amateur diver on McKee's team, was the first to see the hull of the *Mary Rose*. On 5 May 1971 he was making an exploratory dive after winter gales, and was amazed to find that the seabed alluvium had been scoured away, exposing a line, twenty metres long, of the ends of blackened timber ribs projecting slightly out of the seabed. At first he saw a loose timber in the gloomy one-metre visibility.

I moved ahead and saw an indistinct dark object. I moved towards it. It looked like a frame. IT WAS A FRAME! Eroded at the top like a pyramid about two inches by ten inches. Six inches away was another one, and beyond that another. I moved along, noticing that they ran north to south. I found more frames – only this time with some planking attached. I touched it, half to reassure myself it was real and half to check the width of the planking which was about four inches. I swam along all the frames visible above the seabed. This **must** be the *Mary Rose*.

Exploratory excavation quickly confirmed the identification as other sixteenth-century objects were found, including a wooden comb, wooden dagger handles, another wrought iron gun and some human bones. As news of the discovery spread, people and organisations generously offered help, among them was John Barber, a local businessman, who donated the catamaran *Roger Grenville*, appropriately named after someone from a noble family who had died in the *Mary Rose*. This made diving possible between 1971 and 1979, with limited excavations that resulted in the wreck's outline being mapped, whilst ashore the Committee built up a body of supporters, including the Lord Mayor of Portsmouth and the Commander in Chief, Naval Home Command.

Meanwhile, the Committee for Nautical Archaeology successfully campaigned for a law to protect this and other historic wrecks. As a result, in 1973 Parliament passed the Protection of Wrecks Act, and the *Mary Rose* was one of the first historic wrecks in the UK territorial waters to be protected. Moreover, on 30 July 1974 HRH Prince Charles, who had a personal interest in archaeology, dived on the *Mary Rose* and examined her hull, giving royal support to this royal ship. In due course he became the Patron of the project.

By 1977 the test excavations had made it clear that the ship was lying heeled over at sixty degrees on her starboard side, and that much of that side had survived because it was buried in mud. In contrast, the port side had been eroded away long ago due to its exposure to erosion and marine creatures. This gave the plan of the wreck a strange oval outline, with, inside, the ends of the beams of four decks sticking upwards at an angle. In order to understand better what they could see, McKee decided to dig a trench across the forward end of the wreck. This not only revealed yet more sixteenth-century objects, including items of wood and leather, but also showed that the bow had been destroyed, though some of its collapsed timbers remained in the mud.

It was at this stage that the government's Receiver of Wreck, based in a box-like concrete office building far from the sea at Sunley House, overlooking busy High Holborn, in central London, became interested in the discoveries. According to salvage law as embodied in the

Merchant Shipping Act 1894, if the Mary Rose (1967) Committee wanted to keep any of the personal possessions of the crew, then the Receiver of Wreck was determined that it had to buy them at auction as this was the only way of establishing their monetary value. Margaret Rule and Alex McKee were equally determined not to go down that route, and dug their heels in, refusing to reply to letters of demand that items with no known owner must be handed over for sale. I too was in dispute with the Receiver at that time over another historic wreck, refusing to comply, and was amused to hear from the frustrated Receiver of Wreck official, in his private capacity a very likable person, that he found the *Mary Rose* team, and especially Margaret Rule, particularly intransigent when dealing with the salvage law. 'Don't they realise', he said with exasperation, 'that we have the right to send in our Customs officers to seize the possessions of the crew of the *Mary Rose*, and put them up for sale?' But he also knew that if that raid on Southsea Castle Museum, where objects from the ship were on temporary display, did take place, then the adverse publicity would be massive. This resulted in a stand-off that continued for many years as other archaeologists and even museums took the same attitude, until it was amicably resolved by new government policies.

By 1976 it was known that roughly a third of the *Mary Rose* had survived, so it was time for the Mary Rose (1967) Committee to decide what to do about her future. There were three options: to rebury the wreck and leave it alone; to excavate it fully to recover the artefacts but leave the ship in the seabed; or to excavate and raise the ship for preservation in a new museum. Help came from a crucial new source, Richard Harrison, Director of Portsmouth Museums, who was appointed Chairman of the Mary Rose (1967) Committee and urged the need for a long-term plan. After much discussion it was decided to excavate the inside of the ship over three years, and in 1978 they established a Steering Committee to oversee the work, but deferred a decision on what to do with the ship. They also agreed to create a more secure administrative framework by establishing the charitable Mary Rose Trust, so that, hopefully, in due course the Ministry of Defence would transfer by deed of gift all of its property in the wreck to the Trust, including the ship, guns, stores and equipment.

Undertaking a major underwater archaeological excavation on this scale in the open sea was without precedent anywhere in the world. It required a substantial management team that could raise large sums of money, employ staff, deal with huge quantities of fragile waterlogged objects, ensure safety throughout the operation, and control a diving operation using large numbers of volunteers who required careful supervision. They would need to rent workshops and offices, find a salvage ship and provide food, toilets and accommodation for staff and volunteers. Key staff would have to be appointed to manage the equipment, diving, the excavation, cataloguing objects, recording the ship's structure, on shore create a laboratory in which to conserve and store objects, and in the end find a museum in which to display the collection and tell the ship's story. Their aim was to apply the principles of excavation on land to this underwater site.

The appointment of someone to head up the project as Archaeological Director was crucial, and it was agreed that Margaret Rule was the ideal candidate. She had experience of excavation on land, had managed a museum, knew the site and history of the *Mary Rose*, and had learnt to dive. Moreover, she had the utter determination to succeed. By the end of 1979 a highly skilled team had been assembled, with the underwater work being led by Jon Adams, Andrew Fielding, Barry Andrian, Christopher Dobbs and Alexzandra Hildred. There was also a team ashore to handle the finds and documentation, with Andrew Elkerton the cornerstone of the increasingly complex computer-based archive.

Portsmouth City Council provided amazing support for the project, and generously purchased the salvage vessel *Sleipner* that in 1961 had raised the Swedish warship *Vasa*, sunk in 1628, from Stockholm Harbour. She was moored on site by April 1979, whilst on shore wet stores for waterlogged ship's timbers and other finds were established in Portsmouth Naval Base. The City Council and Whitbreads generously provided office accommodation mainly in Old Portsmouth, the quaint historic heart of the port, and the conservation of precious and delicate objects was made possible by Portsmouth City Museum.

Excavation began in earnest in 1979, with working hours usually from 6am to 8pm, supervised by staff who worked two days onboard *Sleipner*, leaving every third day for rest ashore. Margaret Rule kept up a break-neck pace of control on site, coupled with meetings and fundraising arrangements with essential support from Andrew Fielding and Jon Adams who were her Deputy Directors. There were usually six supervisors, including Christopher Dobbs and Alexzandra Hildred, who were to take even more leading positions as the project developed, managing up to forty-five volunteers at any one time. Some volunteers started by staying for a short period, but were sucked into the project and stayed much longer. As the enormity of the task unfolded, so the skills of everyone increased, but in spite of a strict diver safety management programme one volunteer tragically died whilst taken ill underwater. It is a credit to everyone concerned that throughout the entire operation there were no other serious accidents.

The success of the project depended upon all of the volunteers understanding that the aim of the excavation was to find information on which archaeologists and historians could reconstruct the story of the ship and her complement of men, and that the monetary worth of objects was irrelevant. This meant that their task was to record the structure of the ship and the location of objects in the vessel for subsequent analysis. After briefings by supervisors the volunteers excavated the ship deck by deck, recording everything in each sector or compartment as if they were entering the rooms of a house. At the end of each dive the volunteers filled in a 'Dive Log' form in which they described, preferably with sketches, what they had done and found, including with measurements. Objects raised to the surface were given numbers and the details of where they were found were recorded. The layers of sediment in the ship were found to be a crucial record of the history of the wreck. The lowest layer was of fine silt that had gently washed into the cabins and on to the decks whilst the ship was intact. Then, as the vessel began to break up and collapse months or years later, less fine silts were able to get inside and overlie the fine silt. All of this was recorded in the four main excavation records: the Dive Log, the Trench Book, the Supervisor's Book, and the Site Director's Book. Plans of parts of the decks and other areas of the ship supplemented this detailed record.

The digging was carried out gently by hand and trowel, and by using air lifts, a kind of underwater vacuum cleaner made from long plastic drain pipes into the bottom of which air was pumped. As the bubbles rose they sucked up water and silt and discharged them down current away from the excavation.

Andrew Fielding took charge of recording the ship, numbering each timber with a nailed tag. Because of the low visibility underwater this was difficult, but was vastly improved when Sonardyne International Ltd loaned the Trust a Partridge Rangemeter which gave an accuracy of plus or minus ten centimetres. The positions of thousands of objects in the ship was recorded in three metre-long sectors defined by the deck beams, and more precisely by Nick Rule, Margaret's son, a computer expert who devised a location system based on fixed points.

Objects were placed in bags and boxes on the seabed and lifted by crane to the deck of *Sleipner* where they were given numbers, cleaned, recorded and related to the Dive Logs before going ashore for storage and conservation.

By 1982 the ship was almost empty, and on 14 January at a meeting of specialists called by Margaret Rule in the Civic Offices of Portsmouth, the Mary Rose Trust considered whether or not to raise the ship. I was among those attending because of my experience in excavating Roman and medieval wrecks in London, and investigating later ships sunk off Sussex. It was unanimously recommend that the ship should be raised for preservation in a museum. The decision was not made lightly, for nothing like had been done before by a charitable trust, and there was no museum to receive the ship. Indeed, the only partly comparable project, the raising of the early seventeenth century Swedish warship *Vasa* from the depths of sheltered Stockholm Harbour, had been carried out by the Swedish government with almost unlimited resources and funds, and she became part of the Swedish National Maritime Museum. In the end I suspected that Margaret and her colleagues had already made up their minds, and simply needed to show that they had consulted others. What is now clear from experience gained from the discovery of many early ships and boats worldwide, is that it is necessary to raise their remains for recording, regardless of size. It is simply not possible to record the construction of a vessel on site. Even in the decades following the raising of the *Mary Rose* there are still important details that have not yet been found, let alone investigated, such as fittings in the deck beams for the 'bitts' and the capstan.

Preserving the ship ashore required the creation of a Mary Rose Museum, and that museum would need to become a business that generated its own income from visitors. The Mary Rose Project mushroomed, and it was a courageous board of Trustees that agreed to take this on. They are the unsung heroes in the project as they took ultimate responsibility for the risks.

With the decision made, the Trustees needed a practical plan as the ship was very large and very fragile. Underwater she weighed only forty-five tons due to buoyancy, but out of water she would weigh 272 tons. She also lay at an angle of 60 degrees, so it was necessary to support her fragile starboard side which could easily collapse under its own weight.

They engaged John Reid, an engineer, to coordinate various consultants and already in 1978 had held a seminar to examine the options. Several proposals were considered, and the final plan seemed simple enough, but as they would be working in the open sea, success depended on having the right weather, which could not be guaranteed. The scheme was to raise the ship in one large piece whilst suspended from cables attached to a metal Underwater Lifting Frame, but this required archaeologists to dig tunnels in the mud beneath the ship, and to drill over one hundred and fifty holes through the hull to attach steel eyebolts for the suspension wires. A crane would then lift the Frame, still underwater with the ship suspended below, and gently lower it onto a large cushioned Cradle placed on the seabed nearby. The crane would then lift the Cradle and ship together out of the water and lower it onto a barge, which would then be towed into Portsmouth

Dockyard, where the ship would be placed in No.3 Dock, alongside HMS *Victory*. With this scheme agreed the Trustees then took the momentous decision to proceed and in 1980 the Mary Rose Trust established a Hull Salvage Recovery Team, with Wendell Lewis as the Project Manager.

A team of professional divers, led by Jonathan Adams and Christopher Underwood, began to dig tunnels beneath the ship and drill holes through the hull and fix the eyebolts. They also removed partitions, deck planks, brick ovens and gravel ballast, and installed internal stiffening braces whilst removing deposits from outside the ship. Divers from the Royal Engineers took charge of the heavy engineering aspects under Captain Jonathan Brannam, whilst Howard Doris Ltd kindly loaned their salvage ship *Tog Mor* to carry out the lifts.

The Underwater Lifting Frame was positioned over the hull on 16 June, 1982, with hydraulic jacks at each of its four legs positioned on the seabed outside the ship. On 29 September the Cradle was lowered to the seabed alongside, and at this point anxiety set in for some of the Royal Engineers were called away for service in the Falkland Islands War. The project was perilously close to the autumn gales that were expected in October, so work continued night and day. At midnight on 30 September jacking up the *Mary Rose* began, and three hours later Christopher Dobbs, swimming alongside, reported that she had at last lifted free from the seabed that had been her home since 1545. On 9 October the Underwater Lifting Frame (ULF) with the *Mary Rose* suspended below was carried sideways and gently lowered onto the Cradle, and it was at this point that they encountered the first technical problem. One of the four ULF legs was found to be bent and could not be properly fitted into position. After some adjustments the final lift of the Cradle took place on 11 October, just after 8am. An hour later *Mary Rose* broke the surface amid great public excitement and hooting from numerous vessels moored nearby, and overseen by notables, including Prince Charles who was by now Patron of the Mary Rose Trust. The BBC-TV was broadcasting the event globally live, and recorded the heart-stopping drama as one leg of the ULF collapsed. A tubular pin had sheared, causing part of the frame to collapse. But the drop stopped just above the fragile ship so, fortunately, no damage was done. It dramatically demonstrated how close the project was to the edge of untried engineering technology.

The *Mary Rose* was gently lowered onto the barge *TOW1*, and Wendell Lewis proudly signalled the Port Admiral of Portsmouth Naval Dockyard 'for permission to enter the harbour after a rather long commission of 437 years'. That evening, 11 October 1982, she was towed to a mooring in Portsmouth Harbour and arrived at almost

10pm. They had beaten the autumnal gales! Subsequently, on 8 December, she was transferred to a smaller barge and entered No. 83 Dry Dock, alongside HMS *Victory*. Throughout the entire operation she was sprayed with water to keep her timbers wet otherwise they would begin to split and shrink as they dried.

As early as 1978 plans for a temporary Mary Rose Museum were being drawn up, so by the time the ship was in the dock, a plastic spandrel roof was soon in place covering the vessel. But it was not until 4 October 1983 that she was opened to the public for the first time, and viewing was made easier when later the barge carrying the cradle was removed and the ship was rotated nearly upright. Meanwhile, an exhibition of many of the treasures found in her was opened by Prince Charles on 9 July in No. 5 Boathouse, close to the Victory Gate of the Dockyard.

In the years that followed the Mary Rose Museum remained one of the top visitor attractions in Britain bringing in much needed cash for the huge amount of conservation work to continue under the direction of Mark Jones. Thousands of objects were recorded by Peter Crossman, whilst the computer based archive was developed by Andrew Elkerton.

The care of the ship by the conservation team was crucial, and from the beginning the Mary Rose was sprayed daily with chilled fresh water under low lighting so as to reduce any growth of bacteria. Eventually she was sprayed daily with the synthetic hydroscopic wax Polyethylene glycol to replace the water and bulk out any degraded wood cells with the much more solid 'wax'. Then she would be allowed to dry out, and the glycol would solidify and so reduce shrinkage and distortion to the timbers. Deck planks that had been dismantled were gradually returned to the hull, though there is still much of the ship's internal structure waiting to be conserved and reassembled, including the partitions, stanchions and cabins. Consequently, it will be many years before the ship is completely restored.

Between 2003 and 2009 the Mary Rose Trust assembled a team of specialists to publish the preliminary results of the researches in five volumes.[2] These were financed mainly by the Mary Rose Trust, the Heritage Lottery Fund and Hampshire County Council. They are academic reference books that made available to everyone, scholars and the public alike, what had been discovered. The first two volumes were completed by myself with many contributors, one volume dealing with the history of the ship, including the excavation and raising, and the second describing and reconstructing the ship, with excellent detailed drawings and contributions by Douglas McElvogue. The third volume, led by Alexzandra Hildred, discusses the ship's guns and the other weapons found on board; and the fourth volume, edited by Julie Gardiner who was also the major contributor, details all other objects, including the human remains, and received the prestigious Keith Muckleroy Award in 2006 for the quality of its contribution to nautical archaeology. Finally, the fifth volume, by Mark Jones, describes the conservation of the ship and the objects. Dr. Julie Gardiner, from the archaeological company Wessex Archaeology, was General Editor for the entire series.

The final result was the publication of over 2,300 pages of information with contributions from about one hundred authors. They were supplemented by additional books and articles published by the historians Professors David Loades and Charles Knighton who found previously unknown documents that helped us understand the story of the ship, by Ann Stirland on the human remains, and by Douglas McElvogue on his view of what the ship looked like in 1545.[3]

The volumes enable anyone with relevant specialist knowledge to add to the research in future years. For example, a huge number of Tudor documents relating to the ship are listed in the published State Papers of Henry VIII and still need to be transcribed so the full value of the information that they contain can be understood. Even as late as 2007, when the volumes were in their final stages of publication, Charles Knighton found a crucial document in the archives of Hatfield House that not only proved that the sterncastle had at least two decks, something that had been disputed for many years, but also described which guns were on those decks. Then, in 2011 David Potter published an assessment of the French archives, fortunately in English, which added a new dimension to our understanding of the place of the *Mary Rose* in European history,[4] and in 2017 Charles Knighton and David Loades published further archive records that help clarify the use of the ship in 1545.

The *Mary Rose* is a very British project, started by skilled amateurs with nothing more than a dream that captured the imagination of the nation. Alexander McKee and Margaret Rule received national recognition with an OBE and CBE, for their unparalleled contribution, for without their vision and drive the *Mary Rose* would still be resting on the seabed. But very many others have been involved and are the unsung heroes who made possible every phase of the work – turning raw archaeological and historical data into 'history'.

One of the results of this work was the preparation of a series of reconstruction drawings of the *Mary Rose* in 2009 – just in time for the Mary Rose Trust to receive a huge grant from the Heritage Lottery Fund towards the £35 million needed for a new museum. This grant application, masterminded by Rear Admiral John Lippiett, the then

Preserving the *Mary Rose* involved evaporating 100 tonnes of water from the ship to dry her out.

Chief Executive of the Mary Rose Trust, enabled the story of the ship to move into the twenty-first century, in a new museum building designed by Wilkinson Eyre. The new exhibition, designed by Chris Brandon, himself an archaeologist of Pringle Brandon, was opened in 2013. It is a curious coincidence that Sir Charles Brandon, who was initially responsible for trying to salvage the *Mary Rose* in 1545, should have been succeeded by another Brandon to help tell the ship's story over four centuries later.

After seventeen years of spraying the vessel with water and chemicals to preserve her, the sprays were finally turned off in 2013, allowing the *Mary Rose* to begin the long process of drying out. By 2015 about 100 tons of water had evaporated from her timbers, enabling the waterproof barriers around the ship to be removed. In 2016 visitors at long last saw the *Mary Rose* properly, and so fulfilled the dreams of Alexander McKee, Margaret Rule and their team. Alexander McKee did see the ship raised, but, sadly, died before the final museum was opened, and Margaret Rule was present at the opening ceremony when the ship's bell was rung for the final time. It is appropriate that in 2014 John Lippiett, together with Mark Jones who supervised the conservation, received MBE awards for their huge contributions to the project.

It might have seemed that the story of the *Mary Rose* was over, whereas in some ways it is just beginning. There was then no clear answer to who was responsible for her sinking, but with a wealth of information now available it has been at last possible to reconstruct what happened and find out who was involved in far greater detail. Importantly, a personality has begun to emerge from the dimly lit halls of history showing who caused the disaster, but in order to find that person, it is necessary to step back in time, reconstructing what the ship looked like and what happened on board in her final moments on that Sunday evening of 19 July 1545.

*Chapter Thirteen*

# RECONSTRUCTING THE
# *MARY ROSE*

The first step in finding out what caused the sinking of the *Mary Rose* is to reconstruct what the ship looked like in 1545, how she was used and discover her sea-worthiness. This is not as simple as it might seem because only a third of the ship was found buried in the preserving seabed mud, but by good fortune, this includes much of her starboard side with parts of four decks. It is helpful therefore to envision her as a floating castle with many of the facilities that her officers and soldiers would have expected on land, combined with the characteristics that apply to any vessel: her shape and construction that gave her capacity and strength, and her methods of armament, propulsion, steering and anchoring that determined her performance. All of this is reflected in the distribution of her weight and in her draught as she had to balance two opposing natural forces acting on the ship – gravity that wanted to sink her, and buoyancy that wanted to push her out of the water.

## Her Shape

As far as her shape is concerned, the only known contemporary picture of the *Mary Rose* is on the Anthony Roll that was given by Anthony Anthony to the King in 1546, so the vessel was probably pictured just before she sank in 1545.[1] This shows that she was a type of vessel known as a 'carrack', one of the most common large European ships at that time. The picture should be fairly accurate as Anthony Anthony was a clerk in the Ordnance Office who supplied naval ships with their armaments, though he does show her as having three main gun decks instead of the two that actually existed. Similarly, his view of the stern does not match with his rendering of the side of the sterncastle. In other respects, such as the ship correctly having four masts, the picture seems reliable and matches the remains of the vessel.

Fortunately, we can assess the accuracy of the Anthony Anthony

The Embarkation of King Henry VIII's court at Dover in 1520, as seen about 1540. *(Royal Collection Trust, Her Majesty Queen Elizabeth II)*

picture of the *Mary Rose* by comparing it not only with the remains of the ship, but also with a different picture by another artist depicting the King's ships of around that time. This is a painting that supposedly shows the 'Embarkation of King Henry VIII at Dover in 1520', an event in which the *Mary Rose* was involved, guarding the fleet as it carried the King and his court across the Dover Straits to Calais to meet the French king at the Field of the Cloth of Gold.[2] However, it was painted around 1540 and shows ships as they were then and not as they were in 1520. The largest warships in that painting have main and upper gun decks, squared sterns and slender main masts, all features that relate to the *Mary Rose* after her rebuild around 1536. But the painting is not perfect, for although the artist included technical details of the hull and rigging, such as the parrel fittings that enabled the horizontal timber to be raised and lowered on the masts, and men to climb the rigging to set sail, he mistakenly showed the two mizzen masts as having square sails instead of fore-and-aft sprit sails, and he exaggerated the inward curve of the sides of the ships above the waterline.

### Longitudinal Plane of Symmetry

Fundamental to reconstructing of the *Mary Rose* is finding the fore and aft centre-line of the vessel that the Tudor shipwrights used to build her, because each half had to be a mirror image of the other to provide the vessel with balance and stability. That centre-line, termed 'the longitudinal plane of symmetry', ran along the middle of the ship from stem to stern as if the ship has been vertically cut in half, longitudinally.

The remains of the ship show that the keel, the surviving sternpost, and the middle of the central hatches of the orlop deck and main decks all followed the centre-line, so we know the plane of symmetry up to four metres above the keel. By projecting this up even higher through the less complete upper gun and the castle decks, based on the fact that all of the discovered decks lay about two metres above each other, it is possible to find the shape of the upper part of the vessel at each deck level.

### Castles

Very little of the castles remain, as only the forward starboard corner of the sterncastle and a corner timber of the forecastle have survived, so there was an initial uncertainty as to how many decks were in the castles. At first it was thought that each castle had only one deck, and that the forecastle lay inboard of the bow, as shown in the Cowdray House picture of the battle scene made for Sir Anthony Browne. But this interpretation had to change when it was realised that this was unlike the Anthony Roll picture of the ship and did not provide enough accommodation. In addition, the Cowdray engraving was made about thirty years after the event, when galleon-type ships with smaller inboard castles had superseded carracks.

The importance of the discovery of the Hatfield House letter, probably from 1545, cannot be over-estimated for it confirms that the sterncastle had at least two decks, but even this did not solve the problem of insufficient accommodation space for about 500 men. It was therefore necessary to review the contemporary pictorial evidence, starting with the Anthony Roll which showed that the *Mary Rose*, and her slightly smaller but similar sister ship *Peter Pomegranate*, had three decks in their sterncastles. Pictures of ships on the 'Embarkation' painting by a different artist also showed three decks, and, as such, solved the accommodation problem, showing that there was sufficient space for everyone.[2]

Although almost the entire forecastle had been destroyed, its surviving angled corner timber fixed the position of the inboard face of the forecastle, also known as the 'cubbridge head'. This timber and the inboard face of the forecastle are shown on the Anthony Roll, together with the top of the arched-opening in the face whose position had to fit between the companionway hatches at the forward end of the waist on the upper gun deck.

## Inboard Ship's Fittings

With the outline shape of each deck established, it was then possible to add in the known internal partitions, stanchions, cabins, hatchways, stairways and guns that were found on the starboard side, and conjecture that they extended across to the port side to ensure symmetry and stability. This was fortunately helped by the survival of some guns and parts of cabins of the port side which had collapsed down to the starboard side.

## Distortion of the Ship

It soon became apparent that the ship had suffered some distortion from burial during the four centuries that she lay in the seabed. The upper part of her starboard side had been squeezed in slightly by the pressure of the seabed mud which made the castle decks a little narrower than they were originally, and therefore not always able to accommodate all of the guns that we know were there. This might explain why the shape of the ship's bottom is somewhat different on each side of the keel, though, judging from other excavated historic ships, the difference may also be partly due to the shipwrights not having constructed the shape of the hull exactly the same on each side.

Comparing the sterns of several large warships by two artists confirms that the *Mary Rose* had at least three decks in her castles. The *Mary Rose* (left) and *Peter Pomegranate* (upper right) by Anthony Anthony, and an unnamed ship (lower right) by another artist in the embarkation picture. *(Pepys Library, Magdalene College, Cambridge & Royal Collection Trust, Her Majesty Queen Elizabeth II)*

The forward end of the keel was also slightly bent to starboard, probably due to the weight of the forecastle collapsing to that side, which made her bow appear wider than it should be. As a result, the conservators could not physically fit the upper gun deck planks against the ship's starboard side, though by straightening the keel on the drawing, that end of the ship became narrower and the deck planks fitted.

## Armament

The guns were all situated above the waterline, and, in general the heaviest guns firing anti-ship shot were on the main and upper gun decks, with the smaller guns firing mostly anti-personnel shot high up in the castles and in the crow's-nest tops on the masts. This is not an absolute pattern, but it kept the centre of gravity of the ship fairly low.

## Propulsion

The ship was propelled only by sail, and, although none of the records describe the shape of the sails, it is because they had a practical function that we can use pictures of other carracks to show that originally they comprised square sails on the bowsprit, foremast and main mast to drive the ship forward, and lateen fore-and-aft sails on the two mizzen masts to give the ship direction. Both mizzen masts in the *Mary Rose*, according to the Anthony Roll, apparently also had a topsail, presumably square, which was unusual before 1600.

Although the main mast was missing, its position is given by its socket or 'step' in the timber keelson in the ship's bottom almost amid-ships, and by the large deadeyes on the ship's side used to hold the lower ends of the rope shrouds that supported the mast. Furthermore, the survival of the smaller deadeyes for the rope shrouds that supported the mizzen mast on the ship's side gave the position of that mast. What was thought to be the lower part of the main mast was actually found by Deane in 1840 and was reported to be of oak,[3] but as the masts of the *Sovereign* and *Regent* were recorded to be of straighter-grained spruce, it is possible that it was also of spruce. This means that only the precise locations of the foremast and the bonaventure mizzen mast remain uncertain, though the Anthony Roll picture shows approximately where they were.

There was a stability relationship between the size of a sailing ship's hull and the dimensions of her masts, yards and sails, but it was not until 1627 that English documents began to describe how those dimensions were calculated.[4] At that time, the length of the main mast of a large ship was 2.4 times the ship's beam, so if this formula was being applied in the 1530s when the ship was rebuilt and the beam of the *Mary Rose* was 37.4 feet (11.4m), this would make her mast 89.76 feet (27.35m) long. Moreover, as the diameter of the mast would also be one inch per three feet of its length, its diameter would be 29.92 inches (76cm). Fortunately, the step or slot for the tenon of the main mast of the *Mary Rose* has survived and is 27.5 inches (69cm) long, and the keelson timber that supported the mast at that point is 32.5 inches (82cm) wide. This means that the diameter of the base of the main mast was between 27.5 inches and 32.5 inches (69–83cm), which exactly fits the independent calculation of 29.92 inches (76cm) based on the 1627 rule. So it would seem likely that the traditional rule was applied to the *Mary Rose* during her rebuild. Assuming that this is true, we can now use the formula to calculate the dimensions of all masts and yards, with the exception of the bonaventure mizzen, which had become obsolete before 1627 (see Appendix A).

## Steering

No trace of how the ship was steered was found, as only the lower half of the rudder has survived. The Anthony Roll simply shows that its tiller passed inboard onto the upper gun deck, so we can only assume that she was steered by the earliest known type used in ocean-going ships, the whipstaff. This was a vertical lever attached to the inboard end of the tiller, and was operated by the helmsmen at a higher level in the sterncastle by pulling the lever sideways.

## Anchoring

The Anthony Roll of 1546 and the List of ship's equipment of 1514 show that the *Mary Rose* had two anchors on each side of the bow, each with its own hawse hole for its mooring cable. The forward ones, the 'bower' anchors, were used for daily mooring as shown on the Anthony Roll, and the 'sheet' anchors, one of which is shown on the Anthony Roll as suspended on loops of rope hanging from the underside of the forecastle, was simply the ship's spares to be used should the bowers fail or if the ship needed an extra mooring in stormy weather. Such a situation is mentioned in a letter written by Admiral Sir Thomas Howard in the *Mary Rose* to the King on 18 May 1513, when he described how contrary winds had 'blown so strainably that we have been forced to lay out shot [i.e. sheet] anchors and have broken many anchors and cables'.[5] This matches the discovery of anchors outside the bow of the *Mary Rose* and three coils of anchor cable on her orlop deck, which, together with the documentary record of her mooring fittings, enable us to reconstruct how she was anchored.

In later warships the main anchor cables inside the vessel while at anchor were looped around timber posts known as 'bitts' that were normally situated just aft of the foremast on the upper gun deck. 'Bitts' also existed in the *Mary Rose* according to the Hatfield House letter of c. 1545: 'no more [or]dnance laid at the luff without the taking away of 2 kn[ees] and the spoiling of the clamps that beareth the bits…'.[6] These strong upright wooden pillars were presumably bolted to the main and upper gun deck beams with a cross-timber linking them. Although the 'bitts' themselves have not survived, the bolt holes in the deck beams may still be found.

The tarred cables for the bower and sheet anchors were found, one of which was seven centimetres thick and was stowed in its own three metres square plank-lined cable locker compartment in sector O5 on the orlop deck. This was close to another coiled anchor cable, six centimetres thick, that was stowed in the Boatswain's store, just forward of this in sector O3. Its position suggests infrequent use, as if it was for the sheet anchor. These two coils were originally matched by similar coils on the port side but had been eroded away. Exactly how they were put into the orlop deck stores remains unclear.

A third coil of cable, twelve centimetres thick, was also found further aft in the general storage area of the orlop deck in sector O9, as if it was not tarred and had been stowed out of the way because it was of poor quality. This echoes complaints to the King by Lord Admiral Thomas Howard, on 18 May 1513 about the poor quality of the cables supplied to the fleet: 'Your new cables are of the worst stuff that ever man saw.'

As the names of the anchors and their fittings in 1514 are mostly the same as in warships of later date, it seems that the process of anchoring was similar to that used subsequently. When the ship was moored, the location of the anchor on the seabed was marked by a buoy attached to a buoy-rope. On the order to raise the anchor, the inboard part of the cable was released from the 'bitts' and coiled around the capstan on the upper gun deck. The capstan was the turned by men pushing the capstan's bars and the cable was pulled inboard through hawse holes in the ship's bow, presumably passing initially through a 'manger' compartment where it was cleaned of weed and other debris. The end of the cable was then fed down through hatches in the upper and main gun decks to the cable lockers on the orlop deck below.

The *Mary Rose* also had a small kedge anchor, listed on the 1514 inventory, which was used to move the ship from one mooring position to another in harbour or on a river. In the early seventeenth century this anchor was normally stowed in the ship's great boat and was dropped at a new mooring position, as presumably occurred in 1545. It was held by a relatively light cable, a 'stern-fast', that extended into the ship through a small 'cat hole' in the stern. This certainly happened in the *Mary Rose* for two 'cat holes' are shown in the stern of the *Mary Rose* on the Anthony Roll picture, lying on each side of the tiller on the upper gun deck, above the sternchaser gunports on the main gun deck.

## Capstans

Although no capstans or their turning bars have been found, there is no doubt that the *Mary Rose* had two or three capstans. One capstan is reported to have had a small gun mounted on its top, so was presumably located on the upper gun deck either in the ship's waist or, as was normal in later warships, beneath the sterncastle immediately aft of the main mast so that the gun could fire at enemy borders through the entrance to the waist. She may also have had a 'jeers' capstan to operate the jeers, mentioned in the 1514 inventory, that raised and lowered the sails on the foremast.

### Stowing the anchors

The 1514 inventory of the fittings of the *Mary Rose* include iron and brass sheaves 'for the cattes' and a sheave 'in the davits'. There were also to 'cat hooks' and 'fish hooks', all of which make it clear how the crew secured the bower and sheet anchors horizontally to the sides of the bow as shown on the Anthony Roll, a process known as being 'catted' and 'fished'. Firstly, each anchor had to be 'catted', that is lifted by a rope hanging from the end of a timber davit acting as a crane jib on the side of the vessel near the bow. Such a davit may have been found in sector O4. It was a forked timber 2.47 metres long on the end of a shaft about thirty centimetres square that was originally reinforced with iron bands, its forked end having a slot twenty-two centimetres

One-third of the *Mary Rose* has survived, mostly on her starboard side because that part was buried in mud. The exposed port side had eroded away. As she was on her side, parts remained of her hold, orlop deck, main gun deck, upper gun deck, and the lower sterncastle deck. (*Mary Rose Trust*)

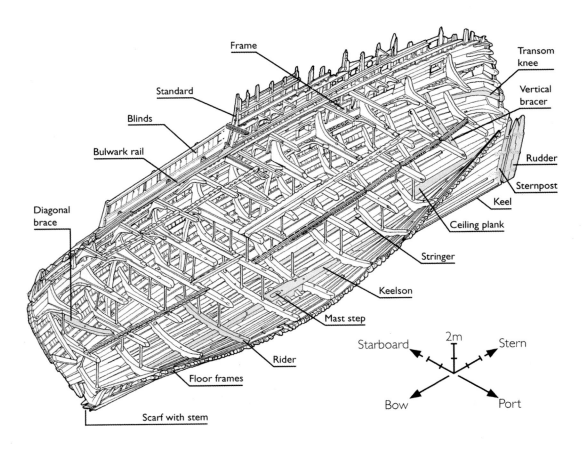

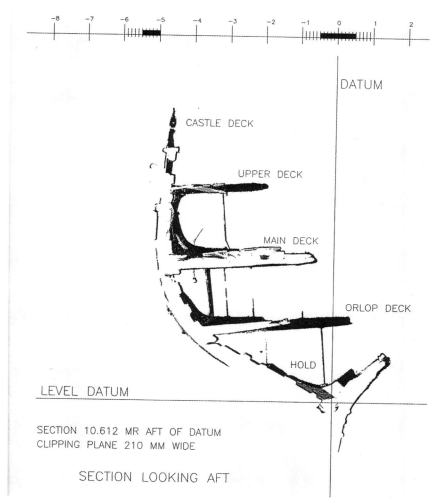

SECTION 10.612 MR AFT OF DATUM
CLIPPING PLANE 210 MM WIDE

SECTION LOOKING AFT

Recording the remains of the *Mary Rose* depended on scanning her structure in plan, elevation and section as here. *(Mary Rose Trust)*

wide for a pulley wheel. The other end is shaped for attachment presumably to the side of the ship.[7]

Then each anchor was 'fished', which means that the lower end with its flukes was pulled up aft so that it hung horizontally and was held by a rope from a 'fish-hook' tied to the ship's side. One of the anchors found by the *Mary Rose* is remarkable because the iron concretion around its lower end preserves the shape of some of the rope by which it was 'fished'.

## Distribution of Men and Objects

Establishing where many of the men and the ship's equipment were at the time of the sinking was made possible by the archaeologists who carefully recorded their location. Each deck was divided into three metre-long sectors, defined by the spacing of the deck beams, so that the forward end of the orlop deck, for example, was sector O1, followed by sector O2, until at the stern where there was sector O10. The hold sectors were given 'H' numbers, the main gun deck had 'M' numbers, the upper gun deck had 'U' numbers, and the sterncastle had 'C' numbers. The scourpits outside the ship were also labelled 'SS' on the starboard side and 'PS' on the port side.

When the sinking ship struck the seabed it jolted many things out of position, though the largest and heaviest objects are unlikely to have moved far from where they were kept or in use. Nevertheless, some did fall through hatches to the deck below. Smaller and lighter objects had drifted around the interior of the ship to some extent, carried by currents that flowed inside the vessel. That flow can be judged by the distribution of the fuel logs, each about a metre long, that were originally stored beside the galley ovens in sectors H4-5 in the hold and in the servery on the orlop deck immediately above. This showed that most of them remained in the areas where they were stored, with relatively few having drifted to nearby parts of the ship.[8] A similar restricted distribution seems to have applied to the personal chests that appear to have been stored in a now missing port-side compartment in sector M9 on the main gun deck opposite the carpenters' cabin.

### Skeletons

The sectors used by archaeologists to record the positions of objects in the *Mary Rose* during the excavation. The bow is on the left. *(Mary Rose Trust)*

The position of the Fairly Complete Skeletons (FCS), where bones from the same individual were found mostly clustered in the same sector, are assumed to reflect where they died and are matched by concentrations of clothing and personal possessions. Most of them below the main gun deck were probably 'deck men' involved in the

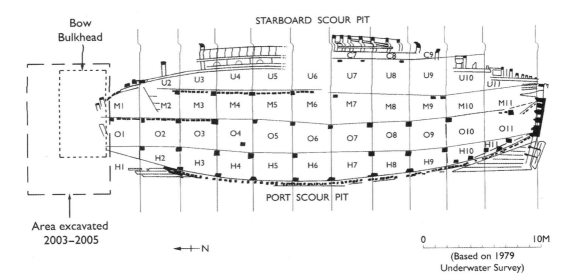

Bow
Bulkhead

STARBOARD SCOUR PIT

PORT SCOUR PIT

Area excavated
2003–2005

←—N

0                                    10M

(Based on 1979
Underwater Survey)

maintenance of the ship, rather than the 'top men' who climbed the masts, which explains why most of the shoes found on board were slip-ons instead of the more secure varieties that were held by straps.

The main group of soldiers was partly stationed on the upper gun deck in the *Mary Rose*, as set out in the Stations List for the *Henry Grace a Dieu*.[9] This list therefore probably reflects the general policy of where they were to be located in large warships, with small numbers of men in defensive locations in the sterncastle, ready to protect the officers and the steering helmsmen should she be boarded. Large numbers of men were in offensive locations, including the castles and in the waist, ready to attack and board an enemy vessel.

The soldiers on the upper gun deck beneath the sterncastle formed the greatest concentration of skeletons found in the *Mary Rose*. Other men are listed as being situated in the waist, and, although their remains had been washed away, they did leave parts of their equipment behind. This coincidence between the Stations List and the positions of groups of soldiers in the *Mary Rose* would explain why the ammunition used by the men in the crow's-nest 'tops' on the masts was absent from the excavated ship, because it too had been washed away.

Francis Van der Delft, Ambassador to the King of Spain, the Holy

Tree-ring dating of parts of the *Mary Rose* show that her hull was substantially modified, and that her bow and stern were completely rebuilt about 1536. *(Mary Rose Trust)*

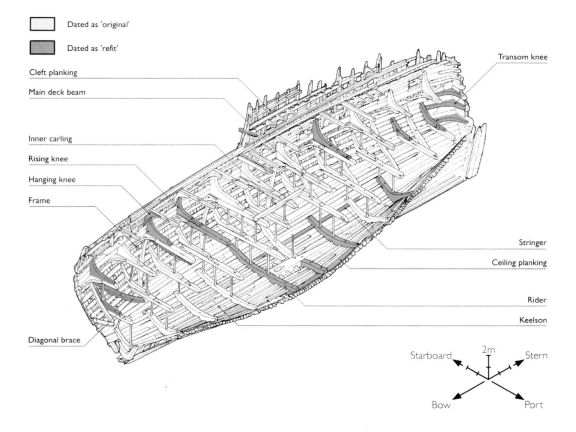

Dated as 'original'

Dated as 'refit'

Cleft planking

Main deck beam

Inner carling

Rising knee

Hanging knee

Frame

Diagonal brace

Transom knee

Stringer

Ceiling planking

Rider

Keelson

Starboard    2m    Stern

Bow    Port

Most of the many
leather shoes found
in the ship were of
slip-on type that
were most useful for
'deckmen' and
soldiers, rather than
'topmen' who
climbed the rigging
to set the sails.

Roman Emperor, who witnessed the loss of the *Mary Rose*, said that
just before the sinking, some of the guns had fired at an enemy ship.
This applies to at least one gun found at sector M8S on the main gun
deck as it was probably being reloaded when the ship sank. The shot
was in the gun but the cartridge was still on the deck. The other guns
were found loaded as if they had not been used or there had been
enough time before the sinking for them to be reloaded. Archers also
seem to have been firing arrows at the French galley, and at the
moment of sinking were apparently collecting replacements from the
archery store on the orlop deck. This all suggests that the enemy was
only about 200 metres away and had been attacked by the *Mary Rose*
about five minutes before she sank.

## Weight and Stability of the Ship

By modelling the lower part of her hull to establish likely waterlines,
we are able to work out how much of the sea was displaced by the hull.
This has yet to be done, but it will be on the basis that one cubic metre
of water weighs one tonne, so we are also able to weigh the ship and
her entire contents at each waterline and so put a cap on how much of
the ship can be reconstructed.

Initial calculations show that the total weight of the ship and her
contents was well in excess of the 700–800 tons that was the contemporary estimate. Thanks to the recovery of the ship, there are several
likely waterlines above her keel that can be converted to displacements
in the future. First, and most likely, is that on the day that she sank, her

waterline was later reported to be about only 16 inches below the lowest gunports.[10] This would set her waterline at about 5.5 metres above the bottom of her keel. Second, the waterline might have been at the widest part of the ship at about five metres above her keel, which is about a metre below her lowest gunports. She might also have had a waterline at 4.5 metres above the bottom of her keel, based on what was usual in later times, at about 1.5 metres below the lowest gunports. The actual waterline might be as shown in a photograph of the ship in the museum before conservation, which shows the surviving extent of the 'white stuff' that protected the underwater body of the ship from marine borers, but there is no level yet for this. Clearly, there is further work to be carried out on this issue.

For the ship to remain stable at each of these waterlines her centre of gravity had to remain as low as possible, and to help this she needed an appropriate weight of ballast. It is estimated that at least ninety-four tons of gravel ballast was found, which initial calculations show was not enough to make the ship stable.

Finally, we know that when she was heeled over by a strong gust of wind she was flooded through her open gunports. Thanks to the discovery of the ship we know that at the waterline of 5.5 metres she began to flood when the ship was at an angle of about 14 degrees, at the waterline of five metres she began to flood when the ship was at an angle of about 19 degrees, and at a waterline of 4.5 metres she began to flood at an angle of 23 degrees.

This leads us to question the strength of the wind that day, and what is reasonable. It looks as if the ship was normally sailing with closed gunports, but on the special occasion of the royal review on 19 July 1545 she was overloaded with guns to give a better impression of fire-power to the King, and therefore she had the higher waterline of 5.5 metres when she was caught up in the battle. So, by getting into these technological aspects we are able to delve into further detail of what went wrong and why the ship sank long ago with such an enormous loss of life. This helps us to identify who was responsible, and confirms a contemporary account that the ship was overloaded with guns when she went into battle.

*Chapter Fourteen*

# FINAL MOMENTS:
# THE CASTLES AND MASTS

The *Mary Rose* sank so quickly and unexpectedly that everyone on board had no time to leave their appointed positions whilst carrying out their duties. Consequently, a forensic examination of the ship, the men and their possessions, and the ship's equipment has the potential to show what happened, and why the disaster occurred. It is as if a three-dimensional photograph had been taken leaving us to examine every detail. We are able to check how the gunports were opened and closed, and consider why they were left open, remembering that the ship was responding to the attack by the French galley.

## Sterncastle

The command centre of the ship was presumably in the upper part of the sterncastle where Vice-Admiral Sir George Carew, the Master and Pilot, and the nobles and gentlemen were accommodated. They were

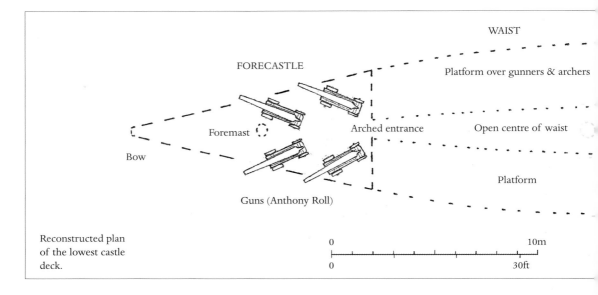

Reconstructed plan of the lowest castle deck.

guarded by soldiers who, in the event of the ship being boarded by an enemy, were positioned to defend the steering helm and the ropes that controlled some of the sails. Although most of the sterncastle is lost, enough clues have survived to enable the outlines of the decks to be reconstructed, together with traces of some of the people who were in the collapsed structure.

The names of decks in warships had not been standardised in 1545, which makes it difficult to interpret where the soldiers were assembled according to the Stations List for the *Henry Grace a Dieu*. The List presumably applied in general to other warships like the *Mary Rose*.

In the sterncastle:

*In the second deck for the main lifts, 20 [men].* This was at the forward end of the second deck of the sterncastle at the lifts for the main sail.

*In the said deck for the trin and the dryngs, 20 [men].* 'Trin' was derived from an Old English word for wheel, and 'dryngs' were halliard ropes to control sails. So, this refers to another part of the second deck of the sterncastle.

*To the stryks of the main sail, 8 principal men.* The 'stryks' were ropes, and the principal men were the Captain, Master, Pilot and nobles located high on the sterncastle.

*In the third deck to the topsail sheets, 40 [men].* This refers to the third deck of the sterncastle, and to the ropes that managed a topsail, probably at the mizzen mast.

*To the helm, 4 men.* This was at the after end of a sterncastle deck, behind the bonaventure mizzen where the helmsman operated the ship's tiller.

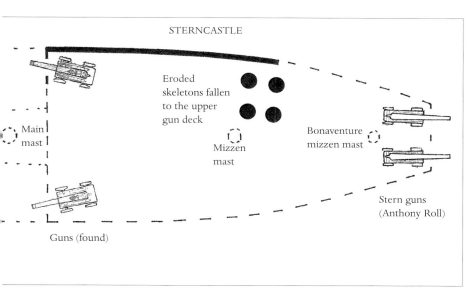

At least three decks in the castles, the lower, middle and upper, are shown on the Anthony Roll:

### Lower sterncastle deck

Many of the crew and soldiers seem to have had their accommodation on the lower sterncastle deck, where parts of its starboard side had survived two metres above the upper gun deck. The deck itself was originally about nine metres wide at its forward end which overlooked the ship's waist, narrowing to about 3.5 metres at the stern. The surviving side immediately above the deck had a one-metre high zone of overlapping planks, and above that was a horizontal timber gun rail that supported a row of 'decorative panels' with small curved gunport openings also about one metre apart, for anti-personnel guns. Each gunport was about thirty-five centimetres wide and twenty-five centimetres high, and the anti-personnel swivel guns fitted into Y-shaped swivel forks that were slotted into holes in the gun rail. These panels and gunports are shown on the Anthony Roll as extending along the entire side of the sterncastle and across the ship's stern, allowing the guns to have wide arcs of fire. The guns themselves were of wrought iron and were known as 'bases', and fired shot cast in lead with an internal iron dice. Three of the swivel guns from the sterncastle had fallen outboard showing that they were between 1.5 metres

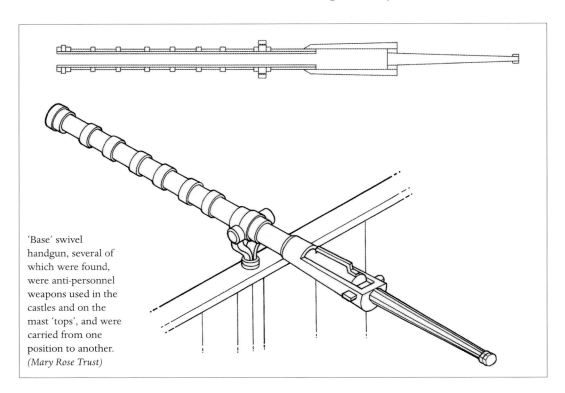

'Base' swivel handgun, several of which were found, were anti-personnel weapons used in the castles and on the mast 'tops', and were carried from one position to another. (*Mary Rose Trust*)

'Hailshot' iron anti-personnel guns were used in the castles. *(Mary Rose Trust)*

and 2.75 metres long, and had a bore of about five centimetres. There was space for about nineteen guns along the starboard side, and about six across the stern.[1] As the *Mary Rose* was listed as having thirty 'bases' in 1546, which was not nearly enough for all the swivel gun positions in the ship, it is evident that men carried the guns around the ship to where they were needed and simply slotted them into the existing holes in the gun rail.

Two much larger and heavy forward firing anti-ship bronze culverin guns on wooden carriages projected through square gunports in the forward face of the sterncastle, known as the 'barbican', on the lower sterncastle deck to give more distant firepower. One gun was still in

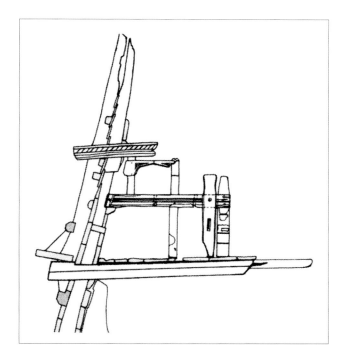

The lower part of the sterncastle, overlooking the waist of the *Mary Rose*, had two unglazed windows each with a swivel gun position. Below the windows was a wall of overlapping planks. *(Mary Rose Trust)*

position on its wooden carriage on the starboard side, its port side counterpart having been found by Deane in 1836–40. These guns are mentioned in the Hatfield House letter: 'and at the barbican head likewise forward over two culverins'. The Anthony Roll shows that the same deck also had two large sternchase guns that would have been mounted on carriages, though these had no survived.

### Middle sterncastle deck

The middle sterncastle deck lay two metres above the lower strencastle deck and was slightly narrower due to the inward sloping side of the sterncastle. This deck had not survived, but judging from the Anthony Roll its sides also probably had a zone of overlapping planks beneath another row of swivel gun openings in 'decorative panels'. Two larger forward-firing sakers were at gunports in its forward face overlooking the ship's waist, according to the Hatfield House letter: 'and the decks over the same [the lower sterncastle deck] shooting likewise forward over 2 sakers'. The Anthony Roll shows that it also had two sternchaser guns. This deck was probably occupied by some of the officers and gentlemen, such as the Master, the Pilot and the Surgeon and their servants, and would have been divided into cabins. Navigation instruments from the Pilot's equipment had fallen to the upper gun deck and included two gimballed compasses, one in a chest and the other loose. The ship's watch bell was probably also located here. The whipstaff helm could have been situated aft of the bonaventure mizzen mast, which, if correct, meant that the helmsmen could not see where the ship was going and had to respond to orders from the Master and Pilot.

### Upper sterncastle deck

The upper sterncastle deck presumably housed the ship's Captain, Sir George Carew, and other noblemen and gentlemen that included Roger Granville, together with their servants, where they had a commanding view of the ship and the battle. The Anthony Roll shows that the side of the sterncastle above this deck was flat and had painted diagonal stripes in alternating colours of red and yellow, and above that had a chequered pattern. It had no windows in its sides, but in its square stern were two sternchaser guns projecting out of gunports, and between them was a square window. The outligger pole, holding the rope to support the bonaventure mizzen mast, projected from the stern from the roof over this cabin, and curiously, the Anthony Roll shows a rope ladder hanging from it about ten metres down to the sea. The Hatfield House letter seems to say that at the forward end of this deck were two forward firing sakers: 'and the **decks** [plural] over the same [the Lower sterncastle deck] shooting likewise forward over 2 sakers'.[2]

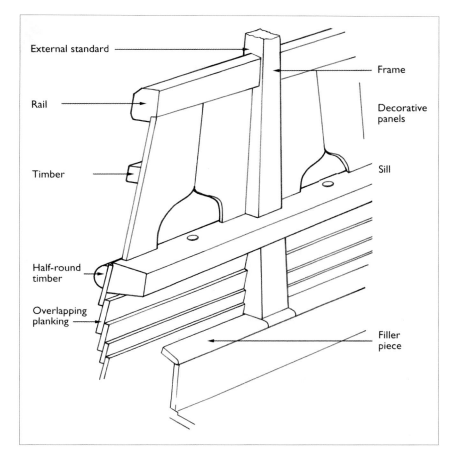

External standard

Rail

Timber

Half-round
timber

Overlapping
planking

Frame

Decorative
panels

Sill

Filler
piece

Many of the 'decorative panels' from the castles were found loose in the ship. They have small gunports, and tenons that match slots in a sterncastle beam. *(Mary Rose Trust)*

Traces of the high-status men who occupied the upper part of the sterncastle were found in the collapsed remains on the upper gun deck, including four pear-shaped bright red silk buttons and fragments of a silk costume with a human spine. These may be the remains of a nobleman, possibly Sir George Carew or Roger Granville, because dress laws, known as the 'Sumptuary Laws' at the time of Henry VIII, as set out in the Acts of Apparel of 1510, 1514 and 1515, decreed that only a knight or sons of a Lord were entitled to dress in a garment of silk: 'None shall wear ... velvet in gowns, cloaks, coats, or upper garments, or embroidery with silk, or hose of silk ... except ... knights [and] all above that rank, and their heirs apparent.'[3] DNA analysis of the human bones may one day identify the man.

Four skeletons had been exposed to erosion, so probably fell from high up in the sterncastle, three of whom were probably sailors or gunners, judging from the stressed state of their muscles. Two were in their twenties [FCS 42, 45] and one in his thirties [FCS 46], whereas a fourth man [FCS 53], also in his twenties, had 'gracile' bones and therefore could have been a servant.

The forecastle of the *Mary Rose* with the red 'figurehead' of the Tudor rose. *(Pepys Library, Magdalene College, Cambridge)*

The officers would have eaten supper before the ship set sail, their diet and tableware being distinctly different from that of the crew. Sir George Carew used pewter tableware with his initials 'GC' stamped on twenty-eight items that were stored in the servery on the orlop deck, though a few had fallen into the hold. Other tableware belonged to men of status, including flagons, plates, saucers, dishes, a bowl, spoons, a tankard, flasks for condiments and a wooden peppermill. We only know them by their initials of 'R' or 'BWE' on a pewter wine measure, the Surgeon with the initials 'WE', 'HB' was on a pewter saucer, 'GI' was on a bowl, and 'GA' on a plate.

Food that they were due to eat was also found in the servery on the orlop deck and in the galley in the hold. Some cattle bones were white instead of the usual brown of salted beef found in barrels, showing that they had gone through a different food preparation process and were probably cooked as fresh prime cuts of meat. Also, there were two haunches of venison from an adult fallow deer, and part of a cockerel that would have graced the officers' table. Part of a cattle skull, the only one to be found in the ship, was in the galley, suggesting that it provided high-status tongue or cheek. They would, of course, have been dressed with pepper and hop flavourings, which were also found.

This high-status cooked food could have been the unused remains of the meal with Henry VIII that Sir George Carew's servants had brought back from the flagship to grace the officers table together with wine, represented by the pewter wine measure and by a small oak cask from the stern of the orlop deck in sector O10 that contained two

Stairs enabled men to enter the forecastle from the waist of a warship, seen in the Embarkation painting. The *Mary Rose* may have been provided with a similar access on her upper gun deck, though this has eroded away. *(Royal Collection Trust, Her Majesty Queen Elizabeth II)*

grape skins, presumably the residue of wine. This would have been served with sweetmeats and fruit after a main meal. The fruit was represented by the discovery of a basket with plum or greengage stones, and stones of cherries, and traces of grapes or raisins and an apple, again mostly associated with baskets as if that is how they were stored. Finally, hazelnuts and walnuts were occasionally found around the ship, as if they were snack food, but they would have been harvested in the autumn of 1544 as July was too early for the crops in 1545.

These finds hint at the finer food on offer to the higher-status men on board, though much of their food was dissolved by the sea, or had floated away and was consumed by marine life. One has only to look at a Tudor cookery book to see that there was a huge variety of food available ranging from eggs, butter, vinegar, spinach, cheese, parsley, milk, onions, rabbet, lemon to almonds and, of course, peas. The table on which the food was served was probably collapsible with trestles, as was recorded in the Captain's cabin of the *Sovereign*. A fine folding trestle was found on the main gun deck of the *Mary Rose* in sector M6 and was for a table standing about a metre high.[4]

### Top or Poop sterncastle deck

The Anthony Roll shows that the uppermost cabins were roofed over by what may have been called a 'poop deck' that enabled the crew to manage the sails on the mizzen masts. An eroded winch had fallen over the side of the ship from the sterncastle and may have been used to hoist the sail on one of the mizzen masts.[5] The Anthony Roll also shows that this roof was covered in anti-boarding netting, which would have made managing the sails impossible unless it was only a temporary measure. The netting was shown as being supported by a tent-like framework with a central ridge pole held upright by five flagpoles flying the flag of England, alternating with royal ensigns.

## Forecastle

The Stations List of the *Henry Grace a Dieu* placed one hundred soldiers in the forecastle, and if the situation also existed in the *Mary Rose*, the men would have dropped down onto the deck of an enemy ship from their oversailing ship's bow.

The three or four decks in the forecastle were triangular in shape with the sharp end over the bow, and the inboard end was marked by a surviving corner timber at eight metres from the stempost. At battle stations, the forecastle must have been crowded with waiting soldiers.

### Lower forecastle deck

Access from the waist to the sterncastle was through an arched opening that is often seen in pictures of carracks and the top of which is shown in the *Mary Rose* on the Anthony Roll. The 'Embarkation' picture shows that a flight of steps led up from the waist through this opening to the lower forecastle deck.

The lower forecastle deck had two forward-firing 'sling' guns mounted on carriages in its sides, and these are both depicted in the Anthony Roll and mentioned in the Hatfield House letter: 'she hath right over the luff [the forward end of the ship] two whole slings lying forwards over quarterwise …'. The Anthony Roll also seems to show that the sides of the forecastle at this level had the usual overlapping planks and above them a row of arched gunports for swivel guns probably in a row of decorative panels, as in the sterncastle. These extended across the inboard face of the forecastle, and were bases on forked swivel mountings, judging from three which had fallen out of the ship.

### Middle forecastle deck

Similar swivel guns were positioned in the sides of the middle forecastle deck where the Anthony Roll shows a row of small gunports above a zone of diagonal painted planking in red and yellow. These gunports extended across the inboard face of the sterncastle above two large guns pointing aft through square gunports.

### Upper forecastle deck

There were no swivel guns in the sides of the upper forecastle deck, but instead a zone possibly of overlapping planks above diagonally painted stripes in red and yellow, and two aft-firing guns overlooking the waist, with a window between them.

## Top forecastle deck

The roof over the top of the forecastle could have been considered as a fourth deck as it supported a small cabin with ports in its sides for swivel guns, and a window in its inboard side overlooking the ship's waist. Flag poles stood at each corner of the cabin, with two more with the cross of St George near the forward end. The sharp forward end of the forecastle supported a carved, red painted 'figurehead' of a Tudor rose, which was found, although in an eroded condition.[6]

## Masts

Crows-nest 'tops' on the four masts of the *Mary Rose* were designed to hold several men who fired guns and threw other materials down onto the decks of the enemy vessel. A small decorative 'top' that was not large enough to carry men, was found in the *Mary Rose*, and was a miniature of the pictures on the Anthony Roll and on the 'Embarkation' painting which show that they were circular with a flat platform and outward flared sides. The foremast, mizzen mast and

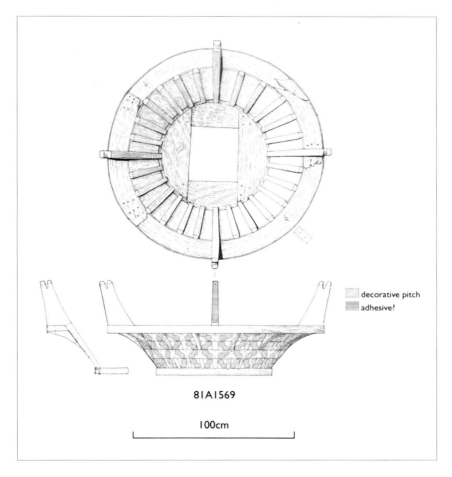

decorative pitch
adhesive?

81A1569

100cm

A small 'top' found stored in the *Mary Rose* was simply decorative as it was too small for use. (*Mary Rose Trust*)

bonaventure mizzen mast each had one top, and the mainmast had two tops with soldiers in the *Mary Rose* apportioned according to the size of each top. The Stations List for the *Henry Grace a Dieu* places six men in the fore top and twelve men in the main top. Six men were also in the main mizzen top, with two men in the little tops above, and two men were in the bonaventure mizzen mast top.

Only swivel iron gun 'top pieces' that fired the stone and lead shot are listed on the Anthony Roll. But as only three darts were found in the ship (in sector M10), the rest were presumably stored in the tops while at battle stations and were lost in the sinking. Each dart comprised an arrow with an incendiary substance, probably

A 'parrel' of wooden rollers that helped raise the horizontal 'yards' from which the sails were hung. This parrel was found in the ship's stores where it was awaiting repair.

A 'top' of an English warship from the Embarkation painting shows armed men with guns and spears ready to fire downwards and kill the enemy on other ships. *(Royal Collection Trust, Her Majesty Queen Elizabeth II)*

gunpowder, enclosed in cloth and covered with pitch, and pierced with wooden fuse pegs,[7] ready to be thrown down onto the enemy ship by the men on the tops.

The men in the tops of the *Mary Rose* threw 120 'lime pots' at the enemy crews to cause nasty burns and blindness, but as none of these were found in the ship, it seems as if they too were stored in the tops and were lost during the sinking.

*Chapter Fifteen*

# FINAL MOMENTS: SOLDIERS ON THE UPPER GUN DECK

The soldiers on the upper gun deck, aft of the main mast, formed the largest concentration of human skeletons in the ship. They died with their weapons whilst waiting to board the enemy galley.[1] Other soldiers were in the open waist between the castles but their remains had drifted away after the sinking, leaving behind weapons and other equipment, though skeletons of two archers had survived by having fallen down a hatch to the main gun deck below.

These men show a preparedness for military action on this, the highest continuous deck in the ship, which was then considered as three separate decks. Beneath the sterncastle it was known as

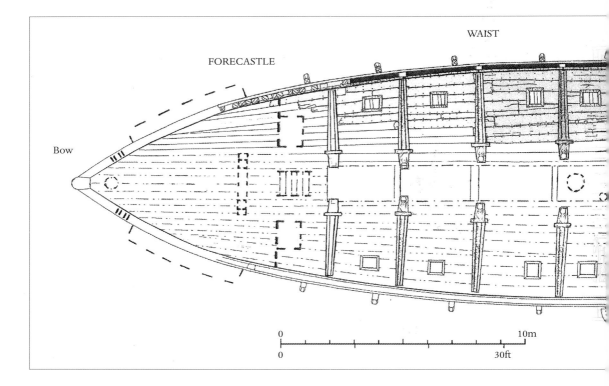

FORECASTLE

WAIST

Bow

0           10m

0           30ft

'the neder deck' of the somercastle, amidship it was 'the waist', and below the forecastle it was known as 'the upper lop', the 'overlop' or the 'neder deck on the forecastle'.

## Beneath the sterncastle

The upper gun deck stepped down twenty-seven centimetres from the waist to beneath the sterncastle where the deck beams were lighter. The forward wall of the sterncastle, known as the 'breast of the somer-castle' had two unglazed windows overlooking the starboard side of the waist, and in the sill of each window was a slot for a small anti-personnel swivel gun to repel boarders. Below the windows was over-lapping planking.

Projecting from a gunport at the forward end of the ship's side of the sterncastle was a large bronze muzzle-loaded 'culverin' on a wooden carriage. This was one of the ship's longest range broadside weapons for it could fire iron shot to roughly 600 metres, and some of the shot was found stored between adjacent ribs and planks. It was matched on the port side by a muzzle-loaded 'demi cannon', with a slightly shorter range of up to 500 metres, which had broken loose from its breeching ropes and had fallen to the starboard side.

There were at least twenty-five soldiers, armed with seventy-one spear-like bills and ten pikes, some of which were originally standing

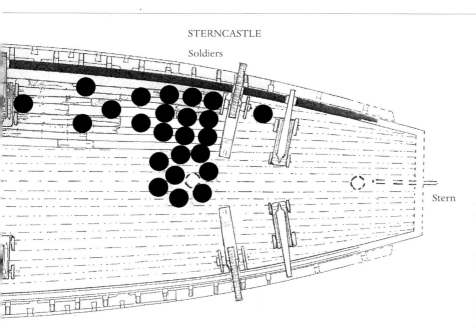

STERNCASTLE

Soldiers

Stern

Reconstructed plan of the upper gun deck of the *Mary Rose*, with the number of Fairly Complete Skeletons (FCS) that were found in each sector. The cluster of men under the sterncastle was mainly of armed soldiers waiting to board an enemy vessel.

upright, butt down against the starboard side of the ship, but had toppled over. With the men were also traces of what they were wearing, including chain mail armour, jerkins, and ankle boots but mostly slip-on shoes. There were also leather pouches in one of which was a comb, and two pocket sundials, the Tudor version of the modern wristwatch that had been mass produced in Nuremburg, Germany. As these were not otherwise found in England, the soldiers might well have included foreign mercenaries.

Most of the men were in their twenties, with only three aged between thirteen and eighteen (FCS 55, 56, 60), and one aged thirty–forty (FCS 44). Their heights ranged from 1.68 metres (5ft 6in) to 1.80 metres (5ft 11in), and their general health was good for the time, though their spines were often stressed from heaving heavy loads. One man had marked scoliosis, curvature of the spine, and others suffered from arthritis. A few also had bowed legs and other signs of rickets in their youth, and reflect a period of poor diet, perhaps in the famine of 1527–8. Many had caries in their teeth and abscesses in their jaws, and some had even lost teeth. One unfortunate man had four abscesses in his upper jaw and five in his lower jaw and must have been in considerable pain.

They may have seen the ship's main capstan behind the main mast, and further aft the lower part of the mizzen and bonaventure mizzen masts. Near the stern was a small gunport in the side of the sterncastle, whose iron gun was probably a 'fowler', judging from fragments that were found with the broken axle and wheel of its carriage. This gun fired shot at a range of roughly 150 metres, and a twenty-four stone shot found there fitted the gun, though some extra shot had been roughly shaped and therefore was hardly usable. Near the stern was another gun, perhaps a bronze demi-culverin that could fire iron shot up to about 500 metres, though only part of its carriage was found, and with it its ladle to load gunpowder and its shot rammer.

Naval policy then was evidently to mix varying types of gun on each deck, with different classes of shot that could be fired at various ranges. These were mostly round-shot to damage the hulls of enemy vessels, though a few examples of bar-shot were found to damage the enemy's rigging. Some short-range anti-personnel iron guns also existed to be used when an enemy vessel was almost alongside, the iron spikes of their swivel brackets able to be slotted into existing holes in timber beams.

The steering arrangement at the stern was probably by whipstaff, though this has not survived. The tiller at the top of the rudder extended inboard at this deck, but only the lower part of the rudder had survived. The Anthony Roll shows that a square window existed in the stern to enable the crew to check on the ship's great boat that was towed behind. The ship's kedge anchor was presumably carried in the boat, and its cable passed into the ship through a small round 'cat-hole' opening through the stern on each side of the tiller, its purpose, described by Captain John Smith in 1623, being 'to heave the ship astern by a cable or hawser called a stern-fast'.[2]

The living quarters for one hundred and eighty-four soldiers and two hundred mariners was most likely on the upper gun deck beneath the sterncastle, and on the lower sterncastle deck above, for traces of packing materials of moss, cereal chaff, bracken and hay, found in silt samples are thought to have derived from their mattress bedding.[3] The men would have been incredibly crowded together, for the deck area was only about eighteen metres long fore and aft, nine metres wide at the forward end, narrowing to about four metres wide at the stern. And it was dimly illuminated from the few gunports in the sides and the windows overlooking the waist. But as some sailors were always on duty they would not all require accommodation space at one time. As most of this deck area was destroyed by erosion, we know nothing about the layout of any cabins, hatches or partitions, other than that just over half-way towards the stern and just below the deck there was a timber drain, possibly a 'piss dale' or urinal, extending out through the ship's starboard side.

Of the total of about five hundred men carried by the ship, at least one hundred and seventy-nine are represented by parts of skeletons from the entire ship. A few of them were aged thirteen–eighteen, but 61 per cent were aged eighteen to thirty, 17 per cent were in their thirties, and only one was aged over forty. There were no women. One, possibly two, were children aged around ten to thirteen, who could have been servants or 'powder monkeys' who took gunpowder to the gunners, though where the gunpowder was stored is unknown.

For years it was believed that the soldiers and sailors of the *Mary Rose* were mainly English 'tars', but when Lynne Bell, a forensic scientist, studied the oxygen isotopes in the teeth of a random sample of skeletons, she discovered that between 33 per cent and 60 per cent of them had grown up in a warmer climate, so presumably came from the Mediterranean region.

This reflects Henry VIII's policy of hiring foreign mercenaries from Spain, Italy and Germany, employing them as bands of men, led by their 'Captain' who negotiated the terms of hire to anyone who would pay them. For example, in January 1545 Sir Philip Hobby was sent by the King to Falmouth, in Cornwall, to press six hundred Spanish soldiers into service and conduct them to Dover. They had been put ashore from nine ships bound for Spain and were in a terrible condition without work, 'dying daily from exposure and starvation', though the kindly people of Falmouth gave them lodging. The Emperor, Charles V, had no objection to this as he preferred that the Spaniards be on the English side rather than on the French. So, 'Having no money or victuals, [they] sued for service in the King's wars', and were accepted.

Having some Spaniards among the ship's compliment could explain why some Roman Catholic items were found, particularly prayer books and rosaries, and it raises questions about how committed the mercenaries were to service of the English King. Could a few have tried to sabotage this protestant warship by not closing the gunport lids immediately when ordered to do so? Or could it be that they simply did not understand orders in English? The growing Protestant beliefs in England and Germany, stirred up by Martin Luther, who had rejected Catholicism as it was, were so strong that it was only forty-three years later that the next King of Spain, Philip II waved farewell to his ill-fated Armada that was supposed to invade England and bring it and Henry VIII's protestant daughter, Queen Elizabeth, back under Catholic control.

It is to be expected that some of the skeletons of the sailors on the upper gun deck might have been the fitter men who served as 'topmen' climbing the rigging of the *Mary Rose*, but they were missing. This would explain why loose slip-on shoes worn by 'deckmen' were mostly found in the lower parts of the ship. The slip-ons would have been unsafe on those who climbed the rigging and sat astride the yards to set the sails.[4]

A few of the human remains from the ship generally have been studied in much more detail, as the bones take on an impression of any over-developed muscles used in stressful activities such as archery and heaving heavy guns. Ann Stirland found that the men were strong and robust and used their arms equally, though a few had suffered from rickets and malnutrition in their younger years. Horizontal bands or pits in 7 per cent of teeth enamel showed that growth in some had briefly stopped due to malnutrition or viral diseases such as measles or mumps in their youth. Others had pitting of their eye sockets and evidence of blood clots on some long bones, suggesting adolescent scurvy or anaemia. Otherwise, healed ribs in one or two men reflected respiratory disease, possibly tuberculosis.

There were surprisingly few bone fractures, suggesting that most were either soldiers or deckmen, one poor man having a severely strained ankle, perhaps caused by a bad fall onto the unstable deck of a ship. Another had a spiral fracture resulting from a twisting fall as if his leg was caught in the rigging. As his fracture had not been reset, it had healed in its fractured position. Very painful.

Fourteen cases of head injuries suggests that some were probably soldiers, with healed shallow depressions caused by being hit by a blunt instrument, and others had penetrating wounds from sharp missiles such as arrows. In one skull the angle of penetration on top of his head showed that the arrow had struck him with such force that had he not been wearing a helmet he would have been killed. This had not happened long before the ship sank as the wound was still healing, so he may have taken part in the battle against the French to seize Boulogne in 1544.

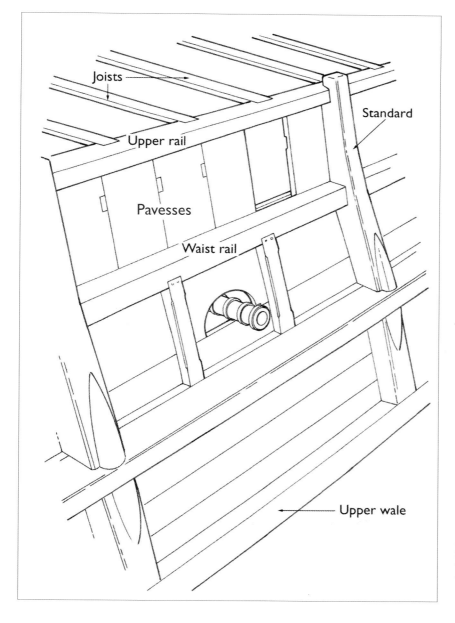

Reconstruction of the upper part of the side of the waist of the *Mary Rose*, with gunports and part of the roof that protected the gunners and archers. *(Mary Rose Trust)*

Injuries to the knee, elbow and the big toe of the foot were quite common, with five cases of hip fractures and dislocations. Given their physically stressed lifestyle as sailors and soldiers, it is not surprising that the men who passed the age of thirty developed osteoarthritis, particularly in the spine.

The archers were a distinct group of soldiers, for they were identified by their wrist guards and by having the rare condition called *os acromiale* where the tip of their shoulder blade had not united with rest as normally happens when aged by nineteen. Of the two hundred and seven shoulder blades found, 12.5 per cent had this anomaly. It was expected that in 1542 every man aged over twenty-four could use a longbow and could hit a target 200 metres away to be accepted into military service. Archers were important on board, for the Anthony Roll lists two hundred and fifty yew longbows, four hundred sheaves of arrows and six gross (eight hundred and sixty-four) bowstrings in the *Mary Rose*. Experiments with a replica longbow showed that it could be fired for a distance of up to 216 metres, so Ann Stirland concluded that 'the development of the pelvic muscles, as well as those on the thigh and buttock, all support the idea of a group of young men ... were using heavy war bows'.[5]

## The Waist

Just over fifteen metres long and nine-and-a-half metres wide, the waist had a massively constructed deck to support the four guns on each side, and in the centre of the deck was originally the main hatch that enabled supplies to be lowered to the storage areas below.

The four guns on wooden carriages on each side of the upper gun deck in the waist, were aimed out through small semi-circular gunports in the ship's two-metre high side. Only one gun, of iron, had survived, but Alexzandra Hildred thought that they were all medium-range weapons, 'fowlers' and 'slings', that fired shot up to 200–300 metres.

The battle Stations List for the *Henry Grace a Dieu* shows that this was where many soldiers waited to board an enemy vessel, though in the *Mary Rose* their bodies had been washed away, leaving behind longbows, arrows and arrow spacers, a wristguard, spear-like bills, swords, scabbards and kidney daggers, and a number of bills that increased towards the bow as if they were crowded there.

Other items in the waist included the main mast, about seventy centimetres in diameter, which stood at the after end just forward of the sterncastle, and beside it on the port side was the top of the main pump that removed bilge water from the bottom of the hold and discharged it into the sea on the starboard side through a timber drain, a 'dale', just below the upper deck planks.

On either side of the forward end of the waist was a hatch with, on the starboard side, one staircase that led down the aft wall of the forward cabin on the main gun deck below. It is presumed to have had a counterpart hatch on its port side. Although the upper gun deck in this area, and both hatches had been destroyed, it was clear that two archers had apparently fallen down the starboard staircase from the upper gun deck.

The soldiers had to avoid the presumed 'jeers' capstan which was used to raise and lower sails on the foremast, and space was needed for the anchor cables to reach the main capstan that in later times was traditionally placed just aft of the main mast.[6] The soliders also had to avoid four small hatches, each only fifty centimetres square, in the deck at the side of the waist, each above a heavy gun on the deck below. The primary purpose of the small hatches seems to have been to enable shouted communication between the gunners on the main gun deck with the men on the upper gun deck who pulled the ropes hanging down the outside of the ship to open and close the gunport lids.

A row of rectangular shields, known as 'pavesses', existed in the sides of the ship above the gunports, and are shown on the Anthony Roll as being painted with the red cross of St George on a white background, alternating with the Tudor colours of green and white. Fifteen pavesses were found still in position, each of poplar, and about forty-two centimetres wide by eighty centimetres high and four centimetres thick. Some were fixed, and others could be removed to enable archers and gunners to fire at the enemy.[7]

Most of this lay beneath a defensive roof or platform that protected the men from attack. It was a normal feature in carracks and was supported on joists and planks which were originally strong enough to support men. In the 'Embarkation' painting, King Henry VIII is shown standing proudly on such a roof with other members of his court. In the *Mary Rose* its collapsed timbers that lay on the deck with fragments of anti-boarding netting had caused many deaths as the ship stopped those men from reaching the surface of the sea to be rescued.

This was therefore a busy and heavily protected waist, with a sailor possibly standing at an opening in the pavasse shields (in sectors U4 and U5) at the moment of sinking as he took depth soundings while the ship headed towards Spitsand shoals only 300 metres away. His sounding lead, found lying on the deck, had a recess at the bottom for tallow to enable him to sample the seabed, and part of the string line lay in a wooden bowl nearby, and was tied with depth markers in leather, wool and madder, yellow wool, and red silk thread.

## Beneath the forecastle

Access beneath the forecastle from the waist was through the arched opening that is often seen in illustrations of carracks. It is likely to have had stairs leading up to the lowest forecastle deck, as in the 'Embarkation' painting, and shows how limited the space beneath the forecastle was. There was therefore no room for extra guns or men for it was occupied by the foremast, the angled bowsprit, anchor cables leading from the pairs of hawse holes at the bow, the 'manger' cleaning facility for the cables, and just aft of the foremast were the timber 'bitts' referred to in the Hatfield letter. In addition there was the lower end of the iron chain that held the grapnel hanging from the far end of the bowsprit, ready to be dropped onto an enemy ship's deck.

*Chapter Sixteen*

# FINAL MOMENTS:
# MAIN GUN DECK

Did the four young gunners, mentioned at the beginning of this book, who suffered a terrible death by drowning for not closing the lowest gunport in the ship on the main gun deck, justify the accusations of 'great negligence', 'so much folly' and 'carelessness'? Were they expert gunners, or simply men with little experience in how to close the lids in an emergency? The answer lay in whether or not there was a little hole through the ship's side above their gunport, for had there been a hole it would have carried a small rope through the hull to enable the gunners to raise and lower the lid. This could easily have been missed in more than twenty years since the *Mary Rose* was raised as similar holes exist in later warships, such as the Swedish warship *Vasa* of 1628 and in HMS *Victory* of about 1800. If the hole existed in the *Mary Rose* then the accusations may well have been justified, but if the hole did not exist then it proved that responsibility for operating the gunport lids was in the hands of other men. The search over the glistening, black, wet oak revealed no hole. The gunners were exonerated. So who was at fault?

The deaths of the four gunners was repeated among other crew members on the main gun deck, even though they may have believed that they were safe when firing their heavy bronze guns on a deck that was reinforced with oak planks seven centimetres thick and supported on massive oak beams. But they must have noticed that the bottom of their lowest gunport was dangerously close to the waterline, later said to be only sixteen inches, so the ship had to heel over only about fourteen degrees before the sea started to flood down the central hatches to the hold.

The gun crew's last view as the evening sunlight shone through the open port side gunports, was of wooden cabins along the sides of this main gun deck, interspersed with some of the ship's heaviest guns aimed through square gunports. The men would normally escape up a

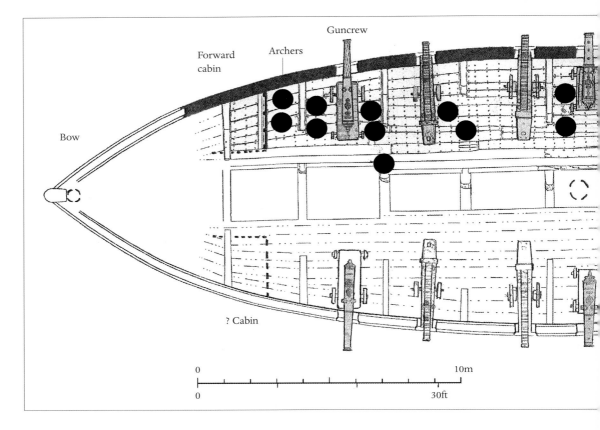

stairway on the sloping back of the forward cabin, but they had no chance to use it because two archers (FCS 82, 83), with archery equipment, had fallen from the upper gun deck and blocked their exit. The archers were in their twenties, one 1.68 metres tall and the other 1.82 metres, and one (FCS 83), in particular, provided the best evidence of an archer in the ship. He was found 'lying slightly tilted on his right side with his arms out, and his lower left leg drawn up' as if kneeling, with his foot still inside his leather shoe. On his right-hand side was a bundle of arrows. One of the archers may have been wearing the finest and most expensive wristguard found in the ship, its rounded form following the shape of the elephant's ivory tusk. Close by was his finger bone in a brass signet ring decorated with the letter 'K', perhaps representing his name.

The forward cabin, which archaeologists initially named the 'Pilot's Cabin' because it contained a few items of navigation equipment, was only two metres wide with planked walls, but had nobody in it. It contained a bunk for a single man, fastened to the side of the ship and supported by two legs on its inboard side. A personal chest lay on the deck and contained a gimballed compass in its wooden box, remnants of clothing, a silver coin in a decorated leather pouch, a knife sheath

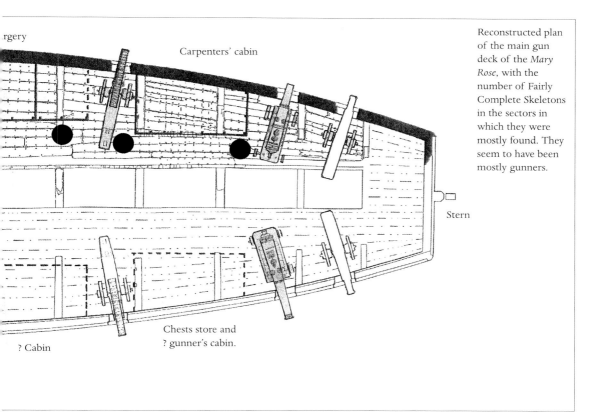

rgery

Carpenters' cabin

Reconstructed plan of the main gun deck of the *Mary Rose*, with the number of Fairly Complete Skeletons in the sectors in which they were mostly found. They seem to have been mostly gunners.

Stern

Chests store and ? gunner's cabin.

? Cabin

and an adze for carpentry. The gimbals kept the compass level as the ship rolled in rough seas, but as the box was fastened with iron nails the man it belonged to was probably ignorant of the effect of iron on the magnetic-compass needle. A professional Pilot would have known better. The only other navigation aid in the cabin was a little box containing two dividers and a sounding lead. One more item, initially thought to be a navigation aid, turned out to be a game board probably for chess or draughts. It seems, then, that the forward cabin was occupied by a junior officer, perhaps someone in charge of the forecastle, who may have aspired to become a Pilot one day, though he had much to learn with his flawed compass.

A short distance aft of the four gunners lay the Surgeon's sick bay cabins. His initials, probably WE, were engraved on several of his possessions, but his name cannot be traced as the Barber Surgeon's Company records for that time in the City of London do not survive. He had two adjacent cabins, each about two metres square, with walls of horizontal planks nailed to a timber framework, whose doors have yet to be found. His pharmacy and instruments were stored in the forward cabin, and the aft cabin was his treatment room where he worked by flickering lantern light as the cabins had no windows or ventilation, and only enough room for the patient, the Surgeon and his assistant.

Some of his equipment was locked away in a fine walnut chest stored in the pharmacy of the sick bay, and more instruments and medications were found lying on the deck as if they had fallen from shelves. He had an amazing collection, much having been shipped probably to London by Hanse merchants from Germany and Belgium, then centres of the pharmaceutical industry. Other things were from England, and a few special items were from much further away: a ceramic flask from Portugal, cork stoppers from Spain, peppercorns from Arabia and frankincense from India.

His tools reflect his range of duties, from removing ear wax to amputating the limbs of injured sailors and soldiers. Identifying the purposes of the tools was not easy as mostly only the handles remained, the iron having completely corroded away. Where tools had a characteristic form of handle, such as in probes and needles to help clean and sew wounds, or syringes of brass and pewter for urethral irrigations when treating gonorrhoea, or wooden spatulas to mix ointments in his brass mortar, their use can be identified. He had a chafing dish, a small charcoal brazier to heat ointments, and a pewter bleeding bowl to use with steel lances to make incisions to bleed patients, as it was believed that this balanced bodily humours and so helped heal fevers and infections. A boxwood needle enabled him to sew linen bandages, and eight bandages had, remarkably, survived because they were impregnated with healing oils and resins ready for use.[1]

The Surgeon's only piece of furniture was in the aft treatment room, and was a sloping wooden bench on which he dressed leg wounds. It had two long and two short legs, enabling the patient to sit on a chair beside the high end with his leg on the sloping bench. If the Surgeon was amputating, then the patient was held down by an assistant, leaving the Surgeon free to cut the flesh and bone. Curiously, chairs for the patient and Surgeon were absent.

His invasive surgery was carried out with knives and razors, so the cries from men being treated would have distressed the gunners on that main gun deck. He used a chisel or cauterising iron, and a bow saw to cut through limbs, whilst a leather strap with a buckle was used as a tourniquet to shut off the blood supply. For head injuries he had a trepanning tool to cut a hole in the skull by turning a metal tube with teeth at the edge. Injuries to hands and feet were common, and for this he had a wooden mallet with a cutting tool on a wooden chopping block to amputate fingers and toes. And when patients were recovering he had a small feeding flask, and a wooden spoon to measure amounts of food or medicine.

He also trimmed the beards of the more senior officers and gentlemen, as most men then, like Sir George Carew, grew fashionable beards, though, strangely, no scissors were found anywhere in the ship, perhaps because they would be of iron and had completely corroded away. For those who wanted a shave, the Surgeon had a brass bowl whose rim was shaped to fit under the chin, and a whetstone to sharpen his ten cut-throat razors. He also had a small brush and two combs of boxwood. Fern oil in a two-handled jug, and corked-glass phials possibly contained scented water or oils to freshen the skin after shaving.

His range of medicines enabled him to treat skin infections, such as scabies and ulcers, and to heal burns and wounds after surgery. For these he mixed a variety of materials including copper salts, sulphur and zinc, and used pine resin which is a natural antiseptic to help stop bleeding. His many ointment canisters of wood no doubt contained syrups, juices and camphor, none of which have survived, though analyses show that one canister contained oleoresin from pine and spruce trees that had been degraded by heat and blended with mercury, zinc, beeswax or other oils, to produce a soothing lotion. In a pewter flask he also had a blend of butter or tallow with a volatile oil or plant extract. Poppy and opium may have been used as pain killers, but they were not found.

The Surgeon was particularly busy in July for the fleet was infected with disease, as Lord Admiral Lisle described to the Duke of Suffolk on 1st August, 1545:

> There is a great disease fallen amongst the soldiers and mariners almost in every ship, in such sort that if the same should continue, which God forbid, we should have need to be newly refreshed with men. The disease is swelling in their heads and faces and in their legs, and divers of them with the bloody flux.

Suffolk told the King that he thought that the cause was 'the heat and the corruption of their victual by reason of the disorder in the provision'.[2] Dysentery and bloody flux were caused by rotting food that had been poorly salted and stored too long in that hot summer, as was demonstrated by the remains of weevils and flies in the fish and meat found in the *Mary Rose*.

Few of the Surgeon's non-medical personal possessions were in his sick-bay, presumably because they were in his living quarters in the sterncastle. His Surgeon's black, velvet cap or 'coif', reflecting his profession and social rank, was in his chest, as was his leather money pouch containing a few silver coins. But the one item that gives us a glimpse of him as an individual is a brass whistle, like a modern bird warbler, with which he probably taught a caged bird, most likely a canary or linnet, to sing. Perhaps this bird was in his personal cabin in the sterncastle.

A cabin of similar size to fit the deck's symmetry probably lay on the opposite, port, side of the deck in sector M7, though it was destroyed so we do not know whose it was. A personal chest that lay on the deck outside, and may have fallen from it, contained a leather flask for ale, a wooden bowl for serving food, a ceramic cooking pot, knives, a comb and several fishing floats and weights with two hand lines. We can imagine the owner, when not on duty, sitting quietly on the side of the ship holding his fishing line, hoping to catch his supper to pass to the cooks in the galley so he did not to have to eat the hardly edible salted fish from the ship's rotting supplies.

Further aft was the carpenters' cabin for three men, whose jobs were to maintain repairs, especially after a battle. They normally

Skeleton of the ship's dog, now called 'Hatch', found in the doorway of the carpenters' cabin on the main gun deck.

included a Master Carpenter and several carpenter's mates. Their cabin in the *Mary Rose*, was four metres long and 2.3 metres wide, and constructed with horizontally planked walls on a framework of timber beams. It had a sliding door eighty centimetres wide but only a one-and-a-half metres high facing inboard, which, when the *Mary Rose* sank, was held partly open by a small wooden wedge jammed between the door and its floor runner, leaving just enough room for a man to squeeze through.

The cabin was dark and illuminated by a lantern which had fallen to the deck from a hook or nail on a beam overhead. There were two wooden bunks, one on each side of the doorway, the aft bunk being a shelf wide enough for two men, presumably carpenter's mates, to sleep side-by-side. On it was a mattress of hay in a sack, and beneath the bunk was a chest with no lid, containing carpentry tools that included five caulking mallets. Next to it was a wicker basket with pieces of timber. The forward bunk was narrower, with room for only one man, perhaps the Master Carpenter. This too had a mattress of hay beneath a cover of red textile, and below the bunk was a store of more carpentry tools and pieces of timber. The cabin was so claustrophobic and airless that the carpenters had, perhaps unofficially, cut for themselves a small square ventilation port through the hull and neatly fitted it with a hinged lid.

Nobody was in the cabin except the carpenters' pet dog, a two-year old female mongrel that was probably tied up there and was drowned in the doorway. She probably kept down the rat population in that infested ship, the remains of black house rats being found on the upper and main gun decks and in the hold. No trace of cats, their main predator, was found on board.

Many carpentry tools were also found lying loose on their cabin floor, including planes with holes to hang them on the walls, and chisels that were thought to have been hanging on the wall just to the right of the doorway. Augurs were lying against the starboard side of the cabin where they had fallen during the sinking, though a whetstone was still perched on a shelf in the forward part of the cabin. Although the iron parts of the tools had corroded away leaving only the handles, Colin McKewan, a tools specialist, has managed to identify a considerable range throughout the ship, including augers, braces, chalk line reels, gimlets, axes or adzes, hammers, chisels, mallets, a joggle stick, a marking gauge, a measuring compass, planes, saws, a sawing horse, spokeshaves, tally sticks, rulers, whetstones, a grinding wheel and mount, and wooden tool holders.

A few personal items, also in the cabin, include fishing gear and a very fine folding backgammon board of oak, poplar and yew woods, with eight gaming counters of poplar wood and a leather shaker for dice. This game, popular in Europe at the time and then known as 'Pair of Tables', was probably stored in a bag as traces of red fabric were found with it.

Four personal chests containing more carpenter's tools lay outside the carpenters' cabin where they had fallen from the storage cabin on the port side, which itself had contained over eighteen personal chests. Some of these may have belonged to the carpenters, for one chest had an axe, a chisel, a saw, a whetstone and tool holders, with several personal grooming items including a comb, a manicure set, a mirror, a razor, a leather flask, a thimble ring, and probably a brush. This man obviously cared about his appearance. A second chest contained a brace, a plane and five spokeshaves, with decayed clothing represented by brass lace ends (aiglets), shoes, three silver coins, a dagger, a pouch, a seal, dice and a brush. The third chest had four tools whose iron parts had corroded away, plus a hammer, two planes and a whetstone, as well as a comb, a book, knife, basket, box, brush, a balance, a fishing float, probably handgun bolts and an inkpot. This man was educated and could read and write.

It is the owner of the fourth chest who is especially interesting, for although it contained an auger, a saw and two chisels suggesting that he was a carpenter, it also had a linstock and a priming wire for firing guns as if he was a gunner. But the presence of two Boatswain's calls indicate that he was a Boatswain who could turn his hand to carpentry and gunnery. Other things show that he was educated and fairly well-off, for they included clothing (represented by three aiglets), shoes, at least four silver coins, two knives, a dagger, two books, a pendant, several finger rings, and a dice. His chest was very fine with handles, its front being decorated with a crest.

The port side cabin opposite the carpenters' cabin, in which the personal chests were stored, had burst open as the sinking ship struck the seabed throwing the chests across the main gun deck, and at least five more fell through the damaged deck to the orlop deck immediately below, and four drifted along the main gun deck. This is shown by the concentration of chests in sectors M9 and M10, and in sectors O9 and O10 on the orlop immediately below, and in sectors U9 and U10 on the upper gun deck immediately above. Some chests had been smashed open, so the total number is not known, but the contents of sixteen chests shows that they belonged to people with practical skills in carpentry and gunnery, with some definitely being educated so that they could read and write. They were therefore men of at least modest status in the ship's company, and may have included gentlemen. For example, one man had navigating skills for his chest

A carrack by Johannes Stradanus showing gunport lids of the main gun deck being opened and closed by men on the upper gun deck, as is thought to have happened in the *Mary Rose*.

had two compasses and two dividers as well as swords. Another, found on the orlop deck contained a considerable amount of savings in gold and silver coins with his personal property, as will be described in the next chapter.

Also, opposite the carpenters' cabin there may have been the cabin of the Master Gunner, suggested by the concentration of gun equipment that fell to the starboard side, including nine linstocks to fire guns, three sets of semi-finished tampion reels and nine loose tampions with which to plug the ends of gun barrels, a shot gauge and a priming wire, nineteen lead shot, and an incendiary arrow that was to be thrown from one of the mast tops.

Between the cabins on this deck were some of the heaviest guns in the ship, each mounted on a wooden carriage. Three were uncomfortably wedged between the cabins and the rising timber knees that supported the deck, and were aimed out through rectangular gunports in the ship's side. Each gunport was about seventy-six centimetres wide and sixty centimetres high, with the gun tethered to iron ring bolts on the hull to minimise recoil when fired, and presumably by a further rope that was tied to a ring bolt in the deck, but so far the deck bolts have not been found.

Each gunport lid was hinged to the outside of the hull, and an iron lifting ring on its outboard face enabled men on the upper gun deck to pull the rope outboard to lift it open. A picture of a sixteenth-century carrack by Johannes Stradanus, an artist from Flanders who was alive in 1545, shows gunport lids being held open by ropes in precisely this way, with the ropes fastened to the upper rail of the ship. This explains the presence of a small square opening in the upper gun deck above each main gun for it enabled the gunners to shout to the men stationed above telling them when to pull or release the ropes holding the lids.

There was little space to change the angles of fire of the guns, including their elevation, by no more than three degrees. Consequently, the ship could only inflict damage on enemy vessels as it passed by, the varying types of gun used depending on the distance of the enemy. This means that the ship's Master was responsible for manoeuvring the *Mary Rose* to aim the guns in battle, and required great skill.

Gun equipment found on the deck included leather buckets for water to clean out barrels, gunpowder ladles to insert the charge, gauges to check shot diameters before loading guns, rammers to push cartridges and wadding down gun barrels, tompions to plug the ends of gun barrels and keep the gunpowder dry when the gun was not in use, gunpowder flasks to prime the touch holes and smouldering linstocks to fire guns. As their remains were scattered around the ship

The decks of the *Mary Rose* looking aft.

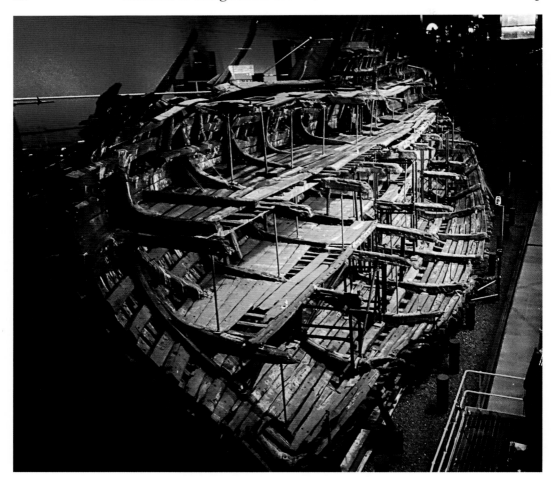

we do not know where they died, and the only barrel that probably contained gunpowder was found in an unlikely position at the forward end of the hold, close to the galley ovens.

A bronze gun on its wooden carriage, on the main gun deck.

There could be no space on this deck for forward firing guns to be situated in the bow, because the anchors were in the way, and therefore they are not shown there on the Anthony Roll. The guns were in pairs, on the starboard and port sides, with a mix of bronze and iron guns on this deck, all but one of them (in sector M8) being found fully loaded. The bronze guns fired cast iron shot to damage the hulls of enemy ships, but there were few examples of bar shot, two round iron balls joined by a short iron bar, to damage rigging. In contrast the wrought iron guns fired the smaller quantity of stone round shot, mostly of ragstone from the Maidstone district of Kent in south-east England, and although some had been carefully chipped to shape there was a quantity of roughly shaped shot.

A pair of two-ton bronze muzzle-loaded culverins on wooden carriages were situated in sector M3, one at each side of the vessel. The starboard gun, manned by the four gunners (FCS 74-77) already described, was still on its wooden carriage, together with a ladle and rammer to load gunpowder and shot. These muzzle-loaded guns had a range of roughly 420 metres, and had to be pulled inboard for reloading. The port side gun had broken loose from its rope fastening and had fallen to the starboard side in the sinking.

Nearby lay the skeleton of a man (FCS 78) who was in his mid-twenties, with a height 1.61 metres. and Ann Stirland described him as 'gracile, with delicate, poorly muscled bones'. So, he could have been a servant or gentleman, though it is difficult to understand what he was doing on this deck at the height of the battle. Perhaps he had drifted there.

Next aft, in sector M4, was an iron breech loading 'port piece' on a wooden carriage that could fire stone shot about 200 metres, and although its range was restricted, firing trials of a replica show that at 124 metres the stone shot was travelling at 284 metres per second so could have reached much further. The gun had its iron-breech cartridge chamber in position, but as the barrel was sealed with a wooden tompion it seems not to have been fully ready for use. Spare breech chambers lay on the deck next to the right wheel of the carriage, and nineteen of the nearby store of stone shot fitted this gun, though half were unfinished and would not have been as effective as the smoother finished ones. The remains of probably a gunner (FCS 91), a man 1.73 metres (5ft 8in) tall, with a very strong and robust skeleton, were also found here.

Another wrought iron port piece was in sector M5, with its spare chambers lying beside the right wheel of its wooden carriage. Close by were twenty-two stone shot for this gun, although half were roughly shaped and unfinished. The carriage for its port side counterpart gun had collapsed to starboard, showing that it originally supported a bronze cannon with a range of about 300 metres.

The body of an older man (FCS 89), perhaps an archer, lay on the deck beside the M5 gun. He was in his thirties and from the Mediterranean region, judging from the oxygen isotopes in his teeth, so he would be one of the hired mercenaries, probably from Spain. His spine, hips and knee joints were all damaged by physical wear and tear, and his left arm was more developed than his right as would be expected of an archer. He may have been on his way down from the upper gun deck to collect more arrows from the archery store on the orlop deck when disaster overtook him.

Another skeleton in sector M5 (FCS 84) was evidently of a Boatswain as he was apparently wearing his call or whistle. He was an older man in his thirties, about 1.63 metres tall and with strongly muscled fingers, but he had severe dental problems with caries and abscesses in both upper and lower jaws, so was in permanent pain. Perhaps he was checking on the readiness of the gun crews for the next attack on the enemy galley.

The bronze guns on the starboard and port sides of sector M6 were the shortest guns on the main gun deck because they had to be pulled inboard for reloading, and the space for this was restricted by the main mast and the ship's pump shaft. The starboard cannon, with a range of

300–350 metres, was probably made by the gunfounder Peter Baude.[3] Its port side counterpart, a bronze cannon royal, was made by Robert and John Owen in 1535.

The bodies of three men (FCS 68-70), possibly gunners, lay on the deck with these guns, and one of them had been crushed under a gun carriage as the ship heeled over. Even though they were in their twenties, their spines were so damaged by moving heavy loads that two had scoliosis. One of them (FCS 70) was wearing a leather jerkin.

It is doubtful if the staircase found in sector M6 was in its original position, for not only was it in the way of the M6 cannon when pulled inboard for reloading, but also a hatch in the upper gun deck there for access to the ladder would have made it difficult to get to the opening below the sterncastle.

In sector M8 was another wrought iron port piece gun on its wooden carriage, which had been slotted into an exceedingly narrow space between the cabins of the Surgeon and the carpenters. It had a range of about 200 metres and may have been fired at the French ship for it was the only gun in the ship that was found not fully loaded. Although the shot was in the barrel, its breech cartridge chamber lay on the deck together with its securing wedge, and in the sinking the gun had broken away from its carriage and fallen out through the open gunport.

Further aft in sector M10 was a muzzle loaded bronze demi-cannon, made by John and Robert Owen in London in 1542. It could fire iron shot at a range of about 300–400 metres, and was positioned awkwardly between the carpenters' cabin and a rising knee supporting the deck, making no sideways movement of the gun possible. Indeed, the space for it was so narrow that the right hand forward wheel of its wooden carriage had been cut smaller than the other three wheels, and part of the knee timber that helped support the deck had also been cut away to accommodate it. This was a particularly severe adaptation of the ship and it left the gun only able to fire somewhat towards the stern rather than exactly sideways. On the port side was a similar demi-cannon, which had fallen to the starboard side. It was made by the Italian gunfounder, Archangelo Arcano in London in 1542.

The final broadside gun, in sector M11, was another wrought iron port piece mounted on a carriage with spoked wheels. Although salvaged long ago, its carriage, rammers and gunpowder ladle remained making it clear what type of gun it was.

A pair of 'stern-chasing' guns pointing aft through the ship's flat transom stern on each side of the rudder, is shown on the Anthony Roll, and although these were not found, they may have been muzzle-loaded sakers with a range of about 300 metres, judging from a ladle and small rammers found there.

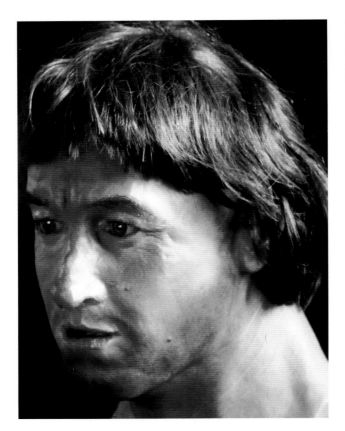

The reconstructed face of a man from the *Mary Rose*. He probably had a beard.

All of these guns and gunport lids reveal a great deal about how the *Mary Rose* operated as a warship, and reflect defects in the design of the ship, particularly in the overloading of guns so that the waterline was dangerously close to the open gunports. There was an inefficient system of opening and closing the gunport lids, which shows that the gunners were not in control of their safety. It also suggests that some of the guns may have been poorly tethered, so that they fell from the port side to starboard, which seems to support the contemporary comment by Edward Hall that the guns of the *Mary Rose* were 'unbreached'. It is possible, though, that the port side guns slid to starboard some time later after their tethering ropes rotted away. Nevertheless, when the unexpected combination of circumstances occurred on 19 July 1545 the men were unable to save themselves. The problem therefore lay not with the gunners or the crew, but with those who designed the ship. This will be explored further, but first we need to examine how the lowest parts of the ship, the orlop deck and the hold, were being used, for on these two areas depended much of the ship's stability that failed so tragically when the *Mary Rose* was heeled over by the strong gust of wind.

*Chapter Seventeen*

# FINAL MOMENTS: THE ORLOP DECK

At least twenty-four men died on the dark, cool orlop deck where so much of the ship's supplies and equipment were stored in fairly dry conditions below the waterline. Some of the men seem to have been collecting equipment ready for the next attack on the French galley, and others were preparing food for the next meal.

Their nightmare began as the ship suddenly lurched to starboard causing boxes of archery supplies and barrels of beef and beer to fall on them and extinguish their lighting. Injured and confused in the dark, they would have heard the roar overhead as water poured through the gunports onto the main gun deck, followed seconds later as the sea cascaded down through the central hatches. Within minutes the quickly rising water left them struggling to reach pockets of air trapped under the deck just above. Those who survived this initial onslaught had only seconds to live, and a few may even have experienced the jolt as the vessel struck the seabed with such force that the stern cut a trough into the mud. The brick ovens of the galley in the hold, and their two great brass cauldrons filled with scalding cooking water, fell apart and were thrown up through a ventilation opening in the orlop deck to add to the confusion. As the turbulence subsided, the clothed bodies of the men were left drifting slowly in the darkness. Their nightmare was over.

Much of the ship's content on this deck was found in a mess, with ropes tangled around smashed barrels, and food bones mixed with personal possessions and human remains. Some of the crew were still identifiable as skeletons wearing leather jerkins and shoes. Puzzled archaeologists tried to find some order in how things were originally stored, and attempted to identify those objects – such as coils of mooring cable, that had been in each compartment before the ship sank, separating them from those that had fallen or drifted in from elsewhere, including some personal chests, and even a large part of a gun carriage.

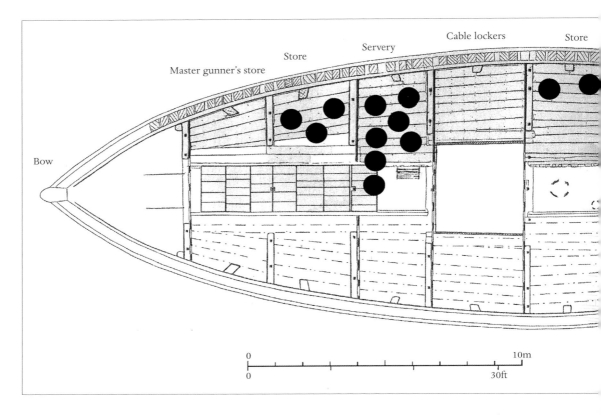

The storage areas may have been somewhat disorganised to start with, because food in barrels, sacks and baskets appear to have been stored near boxes of archery and gun equipment and spare rigging. Could this muddle show that the ship had been hurriedly re-supplied when the King arrived, so that many containers were simply shoved into the nearest storage places to await more careful storage later? Or did it reflect a loose system of control by the ship's command, and that this contributed to the disaster? Answers may lie in finding out who the men were and what they were doing.

Over half of the starboard side of the orlop deck, including its central hatches, has survived, the deck planks being of elm instead of the oak of the other decks. Fortunately, the Tudor shipwrights had inscribed the numbers II to VIII on the L-shaped rising knee timbers that held the deck beams. They showed that at some stage only one deck beam was missing from the bow, and that the entire deck was originally about thirty-five metres long and nine metres wide, narrowing towards each end. There were rows of stanchions on each of the main deck beams, but nowhere in the ship were there ventilation gratings used as safety features to stop men from falling below, as existed in later warships. This meant that the crew had to stumble around the orlop deck in dim candlelight, knowing that there was a

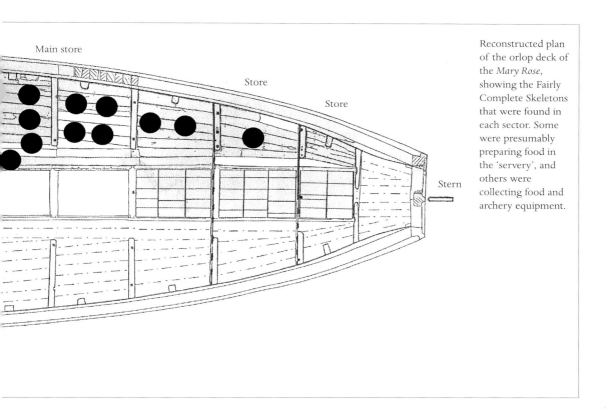

Main store

Store

Store

Stern

Reconstructed plan of the orlop deck of the *Mary Rose*, showing the Fairly Complete Skeletons that were found in each sector. Some were presumably preparing food in the 'servery', and others were collecting food and archery equipment.

serious risk of falling down an open hatchway. Curiously, only two lanterns not in storage were found in the entire ship, one in the carpenters' cabin on the main gun deck, and the other in a storage compartment on the orlop deck in sector O5. Otherwise, only three wooden candle-holders were found, one in the hold in sector H7 and the other on the orlop deck in sector O6, and the third in sector O4 of the orlop deck. These naked flames without the protection of a lantern are surprising because of the risk of fire, and it is expected that other lanterns must have been in use had presumably drifted away when the port side was eroded.

The crew's access to the hold from the orlop deck was down ladders through the hatches along the centreline. Each hatch, three metres long and half that wide, was closed by three wooden covers lying across the deck, with pairs of holes at opposite corners for lifting ropes. In the after part of the deck the covers had been engraved with the numbers from II near the stern to VIII further forward, enabling them to be replaced in the correct order. But others covers near the bow were not numbered, presumably because the ends of the ship were rebuilt and those covers had been replaced.

In the dark the men had to avoid barrels of beer and meat, and rows of narrowly spaced wooden stanchions across the orlop deck. How the crew moved between the ten compartments on this deck is far from clear as doorways in the partitions have not yet been found, so we have to wait until the wooden compartment walls are conserved and replaced in the ship before there are answers.

Although badly damaged, enough of the forward compartment, sector O1, has survived to show that this was part of the Master Gunner's store of gun equipment. Originally roughly triangular in shape, about four metres long and about five metres wide at its aft end, it contained spare gun carriage wheels and axles, cartridges and many wooden tampions to plug gun barrels. There was also an iron gun barrel and a cartridge chamber for a small gun. The much-damaged compartment in the hold immediately below also contained gunners' equipment, which had probably fallen from the orlop deck.

Immediately aft of this was the Boatswain's store, sectors O2 and O3, in which three men had died. The boatswain was responsible for maintaining sails, rigging, anchors and cables, and it seems that he or his mate was collecting equipment when the ship sank, which would explain why a 'call' or whistle on a silk ribbon was found with the skeletons. The skeletons of two of the men (FCS 72, 73) were aged eighteen to thirty and the third was a young lad (FCS 71) aged only thirteen to eighteen, and at least two of them were probably wearing leather jerkins. One of the men was 1.71 metres tall, but his back, hips and legs had been damaged by heavy manual labour, added to which he had old shin wounds that had healed. The other man also had a damaged back and left arm, in contrast to the teenager who showed no signs of damage as would be expected in a young person. This storage area measured six metres long and up to eight metres across, and was mainly filled with spare ship's rigging and pulley blocks. There was also a complete parrel assembly that enabled a timber yard to be raised and lowered, but it was waiting for repair. It had seven wooden ribs and thirty ball-like wooden roller wheels (trucks) mounted on rope, and may have been painted yellow, though it was scorched by friction and wear. Close by was a small spare mast 'top' only 1.45 metres wide and sixty centimetres high, with an opening of about thirty centimetres in the centre for the mast. Its sides were decorated with figure-of-eight patterns in pitch, and as it was too small for a man to climb onto it must have been purely decorative and would have come from the top of a mast. No tools were found, other than a metal pot containing pitch left over from a repair to the ship, so this was not where repairs were carried out.

A folded sail lay in the same compartment towards the bow, but it was so decomposed that it could not be lifted as a whole by the archaeologists, and had to be cut into blocks. Microscopic pollen grains show that its fibres were probably a mix of hemp and nettle, and around the edges of the sail was a rope, known as a 'bolt-rope' to stop the canvas from fraying, with loops, 'cringles', for attaching other ropes.

Apart from the Boatswain's equipment, there was a mix of items, some of which might have drifted here from elsewhere in the ship. This included twenty-eight decorative panels presumably from the fore-castle or sterncastle, perhaps to save them from damage during the battle, as well as a grindstone next to a wooden buoy or fender, and twenty wooden wedges. But two hand brushes, a shovel and a small cask on the end of which someone had roughly carved a grid of squares for the very old game of 'Nine Men's Morris', played by two people using counters, may have come from elsewhere.

Military equipment and spare clothing seems to have been kept here too, for as well as wooden tompions to seal the ends of gun barrels, there was also a stack of armour breastplates and leather straps from armour, and thirteen leather jerkins and fifteen leather shoes, five in pairs, that may have been stored in a sack.

A coiled anchor cable, perhaps for a reserve sheet anchor, lay at the after end of the compartment, so we can surmise that a similar one was stored on the eroded port side of the ship. This mooring equipment would explain the presence here of a large forked beam that may have been an anchor davit.

Surprisingly, parts of pig carcasses from at least thirty animals appear to have been stored in sacks in this compartment, some of the shoulder blades having holes in them as if they were sides of pork hung from the deck beams, though the holes might be too small for this. They were next to the servery. In this compartment were also traces of a previous food supply of cereal grain whose sweepings were found on the deck. Most of the grain was of rye, but as it was not fully mature it could not have been used. This is a reminder of the common complaint by Tudor naval officers that some food supplies that had been paid for by the Exchequer were simply not edible. This also links with the absence of bran as if instead of ship's biscuits the crew on this royal occasion was fed with fresh bread.

The six men (FCS 13-18) who died in the 'servery', sector O4, were presumably preparing food for distribution around the ship, a wooden candlestick being the only clue to how it was illuminated. About three metres long and nine metres across the deck, this was where some of the crew's tableware was kept, including wooden dishes, bowls, and oval baskets, as well as pewter plates and dishes each stamped 'GC' showing that they belonged to Vice-Admiral Sir George Carew. With them was found a pewter dish with the coat of arms of John Dudley,

Lord Lisle, the Lord Admiral, which had evidently been inadvertently brought by Carew's servants in the rush to get back to the ship after lunch with the King.

A ladder found propped against the starboard side of a central hatchway in the 'servery' gave access down to the two galley ovens in the hold below where food was cooked. It had been broken by falling logs and barrels when the ship sank. Another ladder led up two metres to the main gun deck above, and it seems strange that such a busy and vital place in the ship, where large quantities of food were stored, prepared and distributed, should simply have access ladders rather than a fixed staircase so that the cooks could carry the food safely. Working space in the servery was restricted by more than three hundred and seventy fuel logs, and forty-nine more that had spilled into the adjoining compartment, a cable locker.

Food in the servery included four barrels of beef lying close to a worn butcher's chopping block, and several ceramic and brass cooking pots. These showed that the diet of the men was as set out in the feeding list for Sundays. With them were two shovels and a wooden bucket for men to clean up any mess. One of the men (FCS 17) was an adult who may have been the Master Cook for his limbs had not suffered damage, unlike the rest who may have been 'deckmen' sailors.

The other four men (FCS 13-15, 18) were possibly waiting to distribute cooked food to their mates. One (FCS 16), was in his thirties and about 1.67 metres tall, and was evidently a gunner judging from the impression of a gunpowder flask for priming a gun on his jerkin. His body was found slumped against the compartment partition planks, but in life his spine, collar bones and pelvis had degenerated owing to hauling heavy loads. Moreover, his dental health was seriously painful as he had six abscesses in his upper jaw, an abscess in his lower jaw, and decayed teeth.

The other men had weakened backs and limbs, but no distinctive features. Of the two that were in their thirties, one (FCS 14) was 1.80 metres tall and possibly wore a leather jerkin, and had 'huge and extremely robust bones, with very well developed muscle attachments' though his clavicles (collar bones) reflect severe mechanical stress. The other man (FCS 18) was a bit shorter at 1.70 metres, and had a strained spine and pelvis, as did another man (FCS 13) who, although in his twenties, had damaged his upper left arm and both legs. Surprisingly, the final person (FCS 15), although a teenager, had injured his spine and both upper arms by heaving heavy loads. He was probably wearing a leather jerkin, and, with the others, may have owned some of the personal possessions around them, including knives, combs, coins, shoes and a rosary.

The cooks looked after a store of wooden tableware for the crew, including dishes, plates and bowls, some of which were probably kept inside a cask. In general, though, the crew used their own knives or daggers to cut their food which was served in wooden bowls, plates, tankards and spoons, some of which had owner's marks. They may well have been washed by their owners rather than be collected up by the cooks after meals.

The food in the ship tells us something about hygiene on board, for the fish were stored mostly in baskets in various parts of the ship, but this was going bad that hot summer and confirms contemporary records that rotting food was causing illness in the fleet. Flies had infested the fish leaving behind dead pupae, and a dung beetle, found in the compartment at sectors O2 and O3 where pork was stored, was presumably attracted by human faeces as a result of the compartment being used as a toilet. It is not surprising therefore that a flea found there was a reminder of the smell of unwashed sweaty human bodies must have permeated this crowded ship.

It is not clear where the crew ate their meals, for although contemporary records about the ship say that they were divided into messes of four men, no tables or benches were found presumably because space was so limited on the orlop and main gun decks so these can be discounted as feeding areas, as can the upper gun deck in the waist. Which means that the accommodation in the sterncastle, unfortunately almost completely eroded away, was probably used for feeding.

Documents referring to the crew of the *Mary Rose*, and to the other ships, make it clear that the men were served two meals, lunch and supper, each day. As lunch ashore in high status households was normally served at 11am, and supper at between five and six in the evening, this may have been applied only to the officers, leaving the crews to be fed on a rota system spread over several hours of the day.

The central opening (sector O5), three metres square in the orlop deck immediately over the galley ovens, allowed heat and steam to ventilate up into the ship, and added the smell of cooking as a pleasant relief to that of the rotting food, sweat, excrement and stale bilge water. Wooden partitions surrounded this opening, but as they have not yet been restored we do not know if any arrangements existed to enable cooked food to be hoisted up to the servery.

Aft of this was a formal 'locker' or storage place occupied by the cable seven centimetres thick, that presumably held the bower anchor in daily use. The coil filled the three metres square locker, though how it was lowered into here is not a clear. Various objects had drifted from the servery after the ship sank, including fuel logs, wooden dishes, baskets, a pewter plate and a medium sized cask. Also, one of the only two lanterns in the ship that could have been in use was also found here.

On the port side was presumably a similar compartment for the other bower anchor, but this has not survived.

Two skeletons (FCS79 and 80) were in the storage compartment in sector O6, a narrow area measuring only three metres fore-and-aft by nine metres across the ship, and they worked by the light of a candle held in a wooden holder, and seem to have been collecting food from the four casks of beef stacked on the starboard side. It must be remembered that the ship's main mast and main bilge pump shaft passed upwards through the centre of this compartment and restricted storage space.

The men were in their twenties, and one of them was 1.75 metres tall with his whole spine and pelvis seriously damaged by some trauma in his adolescence. The other was slightly taller, at 1.78 metres, and had a small healed wound in the top of his forehead, but he too had severe health problems in his spine and both upper arms, and suffered toothache, for five of his upper teeth and four of his lower teeth were decayed.

Many personal possessions had drifted or collapsed in from elsewhere, including a personal chest with traces of red and white paint, fifteen fuel logs from the servery and one of Sir George Carew's pewter plates, together with a few wooden dishes and tankards, and a large serving tankard that could carry beer to the crew. Particularly interesting were parts of two musical instruments, a musical tabor pipe and a drumstick, possibly from a broken personal chest.[1]

The main storage area for archery equipment and food was in the compartment in sectors O7, O8 and O9. Just over eight metres long and up to nine metres wide, it was separated by transverse rows of stanchions into three sectors. At least thirteen men died here, some of whom seem to have been archers collecting equipment, judging from four wristguards, and others may have been helping the cook. This would explain why some of the archery chests were open and partly empty, with arrows left strewn around as if the men had been overwhelmed while removing them. Of the ship's nine thousand six hundred arrows, reported on the Anthony Roll, we now know that they were stored in eight elm chests, each containing twelve hundred arrows, and that five chests were in this compartment with one more that had fallen into the hold. The remaining two were on the upper gun deck beneath the sterncastle where they were being used, so a total of 2,303 complete arrows was found in the ship together with parts of many more.

The *Mary Rose* is also listed as carrying two hundred and fifty long-

Reconstruction of the Fairly Complete Skeleton of a man from the lower part of the ship, with some of his clothing.

bows originally. Discoveries in the ship show that they were stored in five chests with fifty per chest, and that 172 longbows were found. The chests were each of elm, about 2.23 metres long, thirty-eight centimetres wide and about thirty-six centimetres high, with a rope handle at each end.

At least eleven barrels in this compartment appear to have held food and drink. One was a small cask containing two grape skins, suggesting that it originally contained wine, and another contained beef bones, presumably salted beef. Five of the casks contained traces of salted beef, and the two more barrels of beef found on the main gun deck immediately above, may have been thrown up from the orlop deck through the central hatches during the sinking. Cut marks on the bones showed that the beef had been chopped into blocks, presumably representing the two pounds weight, six for each man, of each piece in accordance with the food schedule of 1545.

These were parts of possibly 120–150 casks that were found throughout the ship, many of which would have contained beer for the crew, the alcohol being a preservative that replaced water that could not be drunk as it soon became stagnant. Most of the largest barrels were stored roughly amidships on the orlop deck and in the hold below the waterline where they added to the ballast loading for stability, but how they were laid out so as not to roll around in rough weather is not clear, particularly as relatively few wooden wedges to lock them in position were found with them. A few casks have been studied, the largest held 306–384 litres, the medium casks held 173–215 litres and small casks held 16–127 litres.

Otherwise on the deck in this compartment were many cod bones, representing fish that might have been stored in baskets. But the small selection of serving plates, bowls, dishes, a tankard and even a square wooden plate, a shape commonly used in the later navy that gave rise to the phrase 'a square meal', could have drifted from the servery.

At the rear of this compartment was a stack of seven or eight circular 'gun shields' of wood and metal, each about half a metre in diameter with a hole and fitting for a handgun through the middle. Above the gun hole was a small grill through which the gunner sighted on his target. Also, at the after end of the compartment was a large coil of mooring cable twelve centimetres thick that was softer than the other cables in the ship, as if it had not been impregnated with tar and was of such poor quality that it was not unusable.

A spare wooden main pump tube, eight metres long and thirty-two centimetres in diameter, had apparently fallen from fastenings on the underside of the main deck when the ship struck the seabed, and occupied the entire length of this compartment. How it was put there is puzzling, as it was necessary to remove some of the hatch covers on the main and orlop decks simply to get it in before fastening it in place. It had the same diameter as the housing slot in the pump well of the hold, and its length was enough to carry bilge water up to discharge into the ship's main drain or 'dale' just beneath the upper gun deck in the waist.

At least thirteen people were in this compartment, most of whom could have been deckmen judging from the poor state of their health. Three were (FCS 28, 29, 36) teenagers aged thirteen to eighteen who had already suffered hard lives. One had 'severe mid-back stress', with his arms and hips seriously damaged from excessive physical action. He was wearing a leather jerkin, and with him was a pocket sundial, a knife and buckle. Another had suffered from rickets when younger which had left him with bowed legs. He was wearing a leather jerkin and round-toed shoes. Finally, there was someone who was about 1.8 metres tall and had suffered wear and tear on his arms and legs, and was from northern Europe according to the oxygen isotope analysis of his teeth, so was probably English. He was found lying at the end of an arrows storage chest that had been partly emptied, as if he had died while removing them.

Six of the other men were in their twenties (FCS 26, 30-33, 87), and they too had damaged backs and limbs. One was about 1.75 metres tall, but as only the lower part of his body was found we can infer little else about him. Another had an old healed wound above his left ear, resulting from a blow from behind as if he had been injured in battle. The base of the spine of a third man, about 1.69 metres tall, was damaged by trauma years earlier, leaving an old healed compression fracture. He was in permanent pain, his right knee and the right side of his pelvis having been damaged, and he had an abscess on his upper jaw. Of two other men, one was 1.74 metres tall, and had spinal problems, and the other, wearing a leather jerkin, had strained his back and collar bones (clavicles).

There were also three men in their thirties (FCS 27, 35, 81), one of whom had a large and robust spine afflicted by severe arthritis, and he also suffered from two abscesses on his upper jaw as well as tooth decay. A forensic artist reconstruct his face from his skull, and it was round with a short stubby nose. Another man, who was 1.75 metres tall, had a strained back and hips, and decay in three of his lower back teeth. The third man, 1.72 metres tall, was particularly interesting as he

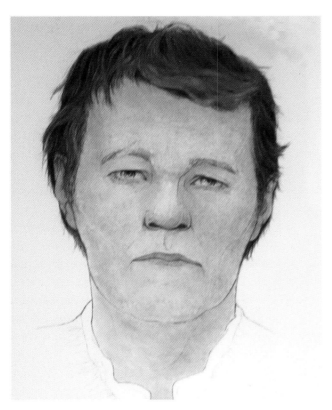

Reconstructed face of Fairly Complete Skeleton 27. *(Mary Rose Trust)*

was from southern Europe, judging from the oxygen isotope study of his teeth, so was probably Spanish. He was wearing a leather jerkin and had suffered physical hardship to his back, and had an old healed head wound at his right eyebrow.

Maybe the men in the compartment O8 were being led by the oldest man of the group who was over forty (FCS 38). We only know from his spine that had suffered from hard physical work, and that his teeth were in a good condition.

How the men were dressed remains unclear, though one man was wearing a calfskin jerkin laced in the front, with a chest size thirty-eight inches (96cm) and with a waist of thirty-five inches (90cm). He had a comb in the pocket on its left side. Otherwise, possessions found with the men included the usual knives, combs, a few coins, and a pouch containing a comb and a ring.

The orlop deck narrowed appreciably towards the stern, so that the compartment in sector O10 was only about three metres long by a little over six metres wide. A carpenter (FCS 88) seems to have been stationed here judging from the woodworking equipment scattered around. This included a chopping block, a whetstone for sharpening blades, a tool holder containing a ruler to hang on his belt, a hammer, chisel, plane, two mallets, four wooden wedges and a saw. He also had a stool, and a hand brush with which to sweep up wood shavings. His skeleton reflected very poor health, so that he was unable to serve as a sailor or soldier. He was in his thirties, and apart from his lower spine and hips having degenerated from a physically stressed life, he had suffered from Perthes disease in childhood, a softening of the tops of his leg bones which had left him with impaired mobility and a rolling gait as he walked, and was unable to straighten his back. A forensic artist has reconstructed his face from his skull, which had fairly long with well-proportioned features. In later times it was normal for carpenters to be stationed on the deck just below the waterline to repair damage to the hull made during battle, so it seems that this might be the case in the *Mary Rose*.[2]

Several personal chests in this compartment had presumably fallen from the chest store on the deck immediately above. One of them contained shoes, a wooden plate, a leather flask, and a comb. This chest had broken open as the ship sank, and it is possible that twenty-nine 'spiles' and 'shives' (wooden plugs and taps for bungs in barrels) immediately around may have fallen from it, though it is more likely that they were stored on the orlop deck for the crew to use when taking beer from the barrels stored in the hold. Another chest contained traces of clothing mainly represented by brass lace ends, braid and ribbon, and shoes as well as a sword, scabbard, beads, a rosary, a dice and possibly a key. A third chest contained more brass lace ends, a shoe and thigh boot, a dagger sheath, a comb, a knife, a besom brush, a piece of gunshot and a wristguard indicating that he was a soldier.

Yet another was an elm chest which contained about £3 in gold and silver coins, as well as the remains of clothing (indicated by two brass 'aiglets' or lace ends), a knife, a pin, a gun shield and possibly a tinder box. The gold coins included one half-angel of Edward IV (r. 1471–83) then worth four shillings, three angels of Henry VII and Henry VIII each worth eight shillings, and three half-sovereigns of Henry VIII each then worth ten shillings. There were also at least twenty-five silver coins, mostly groats, then worth four pence each, and half groats. With the total value of the cash in excess of one month's wage for the ship's Captain, this has been interpreted as Exchequer money held by the ship's Purser for the purchase of supplies for the ship, and the nearby skeleton (FCS 88) has been interpreted as the ship's Purser. This cannot be correct as, quite apart from the evidence that this was a personal chest, the Exchequer's funds would not be stored in that location or in a personal chest. Moreover, the skeleton of a man with poor health was in contrast to the Purser who was one of the most senior people on board whose accommodation quarters would be in the sterncastle where the ship's cash would have been stored in a very secure place. Also, the amount of cash is insufficient to cover the costs of maintaining the ship.

The final compartment, in sectors O11 and O12, lay at the extreme squared transom stern of the ship, and was only four metres long by five metres maximum width, narrowing to about two metres at the stern. This held the ship's store of lighting equipment and included candles of beef tallow, a small cask of tallow, and sixteen wooden lanterns, some of which had dropped into the hold immediately below when the ship sank. There was also a cask filled with a white substance that has not been identified, and illustrates that much more of the story of this ship has yet to be revealed.

Food also seems to have been stored here, including fish whose bones were found mostly in a cask. These were part of more than the 31,000 fish bones that were found in the ship, 90 per cent of which were of cod. Their heads had been removed showing that the fish had been gutted. Among those from the ship generally were just a few conger eels whose heads had not been removed, but whose bodies had been cut lengthways on either side of the backbone to give three flat fillets to aid speedy salt preservation. A few other fish that were served to the crew, whose bones were identified, were herring, haddock, hake, pollack, whiting and pouting, but as they were so few they show that sorting in general was only roughly done. In general the quantity of meat on each fish was fairly small, so, even assuming that this is a gross underestimate of the fish supply, the quantity of fish would not have lasted the crew for more than a week.

How the cooks and their staff in the servery had access to the food stored here is not clear, for it seems that they had to climb up onto the main gun deck, lift a hatch cover over this compartment and clamber down. This is but one of the issues that has yet to be answered, though the orlop deck already provides us with an amazing snapshot view of life on board the ship as men were caught by the disaster whilst in the middle of their daily duties. What we can say is that nothing irregular was apparently occurring on this deck that could have caused the disaster, so we must explore what was happening in the hold below where the ship's ballast and heavy goods helped to provide the ship's stability.

*Chapter Eighteen*

# FINAL MOMENTS:
# BODIES IN THE HOLD

Asurprising number of men were in the uncomfortable, dark, damp and smelly stores of the hold, whilst others were in the adjacent galley cooking food for the next meal. There were dangers in this U-shaped bottom of the ship where the limited headroom of 1.80 metres in the middle reduced towards the sides as the hull curved upward, and each of the compartments was separated by thin wooden partitions or bulkheads.

At least nine men were in the cooking galley, sectors H4 and H5, one of whom may have been a cook with the name possibly of Cooper. He had inscribed his name and trade 'Ny Coep coek' on a wooden bowl, and his name 'Ny Cop' on the lid of a wooden tankard and he is the only ordinary person in the ship whose name is known.[1] The cooking area was small, and although eight metres wide and extended six metres fore and aft along the ship, it was in reality smaller as two metres of its after end was occupied by two brick ovens, and a transverse row of wooden stanchions supported the orlop deck. This left the cooks a space of only 1.5 metres in front of the ovens in which to work, where two of the men were found (FCS 11, 12), the remainder being further forward as if waiting to carry the cooked food to the crew in the rest of the ship.

Cooking pots and implements with the remains of food were strewn around, the ovens had largely collapsed when the ship hit the seabed, throwing cemented red bricks and the two brass cauldrons in which the food was cooked upward through the large ventilation opening onto the orlop deck. Enough of the starboard brick oven remained mortared together to enable Christopher Dobbs to reconstruct each oven as originally being two metres fore and aft by 1.60 metres sideways and 1 metre high, with a hollow hearth where fuel logs were burned beneath a brass cauldron supported on two iron bars. The logs were fed through an arched opening in its forward face,

The hold of the *Mary Rose* (bottom right).

heating the starboard cauldron which held 600 litres of brew to its brim, though to stop spillage it probably held about 450 litres in normal circumstances, and the port oven which held about 360 litres to the brim, and about 250 litres when cooking. Moreover, the sides and back of the ovens were surrounded by wooden planking attached to upright posts.

The *Mary Rose* was stocked with at least 670 fuel logs, which is far more than she needed, as if she had been partly prepared for a long sea voyage. Each was about a metre long to fit into the hearths. The galley in the hold contained 155 logs ready for use and they were probably stacked up in the curved area between the ovens and the ship's sides. However, the main store of logs was in the servery on the orlop deck immediately above where 370 were found, and some others had drifted to other compartments.

The only piece of furniture in the galley was a roughly made stool with four legs that had chop marks in the top, as if it had been used to cut kindling to light the fire or to chop up food. Close by was the bellows to help with the lighting, and wooden shovels and ash boxes to help clear up any debris.

Christopher Dobbs was so fascinated by the cooking process that he supervised the building of a reconstruction oven, with a replica of the larger cauldron, to discover how it worked. He found that it did not need a chimney, and that the food cooked in the cauldrons might have

The reconstructed face of Fairly Complete Skeleton 12.
(*Mary Rose Trust*)

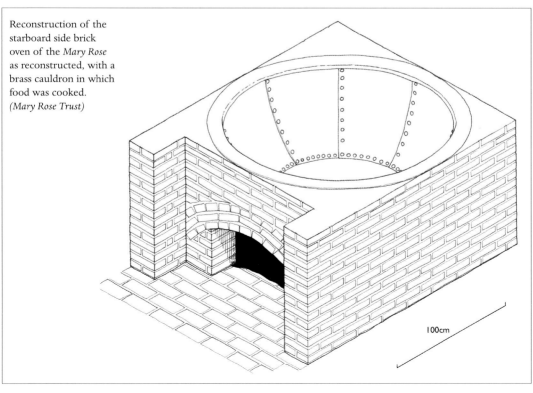

Reconstruction of the starboard side brick oven of the *Mary Rose* as reconstructed, with a brass cauldron in which food was cooked.
(*Mary Rose Trust*)

100cm

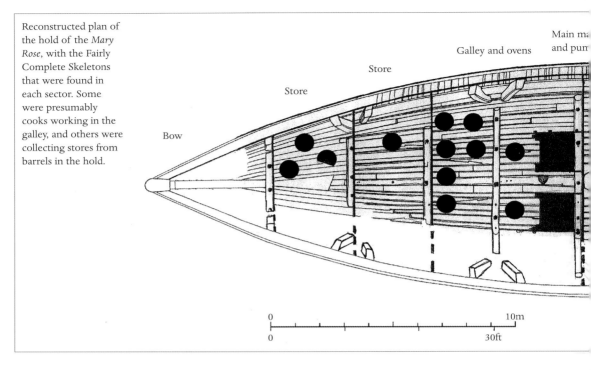

Reconstructed plan of the hold of the *Mary Rose*, with the Fairly Complete Skeletons that were found in each sector. Some were presumably cooks working in the galley, and others were collecting stores from barrels in the hold.

been kept in separate bags tied with wooden name tags, one of which he identified among the numerous wooden objects from the wreck, though it is uncertain if it was Tudor. It took three to five hours to heat the cauldron of 400 litres to 98 degrees Celsius. Thereafter, only two or three logs each hour were needed to keep the cauldron simmering, which accords with the fact that only five partly burnt logs were found in the ovens. Moreover, by pushing the ash to the back of the hearth, Dobbs was able to cook bread and pies on the hot brick floor at the front which explained why soot had coated the outer surfaces of some of the ship's cooking pots. He concluded that the oven 'was not a crude stove but was adaptable and sophisticated. It was capable of producing a wide range of cooked food for a large company of men of differing social status.'

In addition to the cooking pots there was a pewter colander to drain cooking water, a brass skimmer to remove unwanted froth and scum from the brew, a brass hanging kettle in which to boil water in front of the hearths, wooden ladles to serve food into bowls, buckets to distribute food to the crew, wooden troughs perhaps for kneading dough to make fresh bread, and wooden serving flagons for beer to be delivered to the crew. An iron spit for roasting meat was not found, but was also probably used.

A contemporary daily supplies list of food for the fleet enables us to work out the probable daily quota for each ordinary man per week:[2]

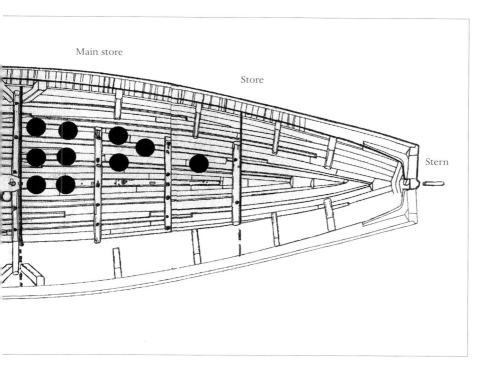

*Sunday:* 1 lb (0.45kg) fresh bread or 8 biscuits; 1 gallon (4.5 litres) beer; 2 pounds (0.90kg) of salted beef or 1lb of bacon; possibly peas.

*Monday:* 1 lb fresh bread or 8 biscuits; 1 gallon of beer; salted beef or bacon.

*Tuesday:* 1 lb fresh bread or 8 biscuits; 1 gallon beer; salted beef or bacon.

*Wednesday:* 1 lb fresh bread or 8 biscuits; 1 gallon beer; saltfish for 2 meals; cheese.

*Thursday:* 1 lb fresh bread or 8 biscuits; 1 gallon beer; salted beef or bacon; possibly peas.

*Friday:* 1 lb fresh bread or 8 biscuits; 1 gallon beer; saltfish for 1 meal; butter.

*Saturday:* 1 lb fresh bread or 8 biscuits; 1 gallon beer; saltfish for 2 meals; cheese.

The schedule to eat beef or bacon for supper that Sunday explains why beef and a few pig bones were found on the gravel floor of the galley, presumably having spilled from one of the cauldrons.

The cooks had to keep track of the food supplies, for although it was primarily stored on the orlop deck, some was stored elsewhere as if there was not enough time between the delivery of supplies and seeing the arrival of the French fleet. One of those other places, a standard location in ships generally, was in a barrel that was found hanging outboard on the starboard side of the sterncastle. This was known as the 'steep tub' in which salted meat was soaked in water to make it more palatable, and in the case of the *Mary Rose* it contained pork bones. A view of such a tub is shown in the picture of a carrack by the late fifteenth century artist 'WA'.[3]

Apart from the cooking requirements, the hold was primarily a storage area for heavy goods, particularly the barrels that presumably contained beer. Little water was needed in the ship as it quickly became sour, whereas the alcohol in the beer preserved it much longer. So, at the moment of sinking there were men in some of those storage compartments, and what they were doing is suggested by what was stored there.

The compartment just inside the bow, sector H1, was narrow and V-shaped in section, but so badly damaged that it was difficult to know what was stored there. Several barrels and parts of gun carriages had probably fallen from the Boatswain's store on the orlop deck above, and among them was a small barrel containing a black sediment, believed to be gunpowder.

Barrels from the *Mary Rose* probably held beer for the crew to drink.

At least three men (FCS 7, 8, 9) were in the next compartment, sector H2, another Boatswain's store forward of the galley. It was three metres long, about four metres wide at the forward end, about six

metres wide at the after end, and in it were parts of three small barrels of pitch or tar that would have been used to ensure that the seams of the decks remained watertight. With them was a small brass cauldron in which pitch or tar had been melted, and caused the perfect preservation of two iron nails. There were also some tools, including a mallet and chopping block, traces of coarse woven wool suggesting that four sacks were here, and some rigging fittings that included a ball and rib from a parrel, and pulley blocks.

Two of the men (FCS 8, 9) were in their twenties and thirties, and had damaged spines and arm and leg joints, with one having a fractured ball joint at the top of his left leg where severe violence had dislocated his hip in the past as if from a fall from the rigging. Otherwise, another man had two abscesses in his upper jaw, and yet another had seven abscesses. They were a sorry bunch of men. With them was a leather jerkin that had been patched, leather shoes, a dagger, lace ends from decayed textile clothing, two silver coins and a rosary of boxwood.

The third man (FCS 7), undoubtedly an archer, had one of the most complete skeletons in the ship. It is difficult to judge what he was doing in the hold, far from the fighting, as he was in his mid-twenties, about 1.76 metres tall (5ft 9in), and had the characteristic archery feature whereby the tips of both shoulder blades had not fused in a condition known as *os acromiale*. The repeated pulling on a longbow over the years had modified how his muscles and bones developed, especially on his upper arms, and an oxygen isotope study of his teeth shows that he probably grew up in northern Europe. It has been suggested that he might have worn the very fine archer's wristguard bearing the Royal Arms that was found in the Boatswain's store on the orlop deck immediately above. If so he may have been a high status royal archer, a Yeoman of the Guard. A similar wristguard was found on the main deck suggesting that he was not alone in the ship.

The storage compartment, sector H3, was forward of the cooking galley, and had only one man (FCS 10) in there. He was one of the smallest adult members of the ship, in his thirties and 1.61 metres tall (5ft 3in), and was notable for having painfully poor health, with spinal disk degeneration and trouble with his feet, and seven abscesses in his upper jaw, and caries in his teeth.

Aft of the galley were more storage areas. The first of these was the narrow part of sector H6 in which the main mast was stepped, and adjacent to it was the well for the main pump. Although the main mast was missing the socket for the rectangular step of the tenon at its base had survived in the timber keelson. This measured sixty-nine to seventy centimetres (27.5in) long x thirty-five centimetres wide, and thirteen centimetres deep, and the keelson itself was eighty-two centimetres (32.5in) wide at this point, so the foot of the mast was about seventy-six centimetres (almost 30in) in diameter.

The pump was also missing, but it slotted into a square 'well' eighty-four centimetres x 1.02 metres in the bottom of the ship next to the keelson. What the pump itself was like is shown by its replacement stored on the orlop deck, and was 8.22 metres long and 32.6 centimetres in diameter, with leather valves to lift the bilge water.

Over eight men (FCS 19-25, 37) were in the compartment in sectors H7, H8 and H9, with five wooden gallon flagons, as if they were due to fill them with beer from the barrels, though they seem not to have had time to insert the taps into the barrels. Here was the ship's main store of at least nineteen large barrels lying on top of the ship's gravel ballast, but they had broken open as the ash, willow or hazel hoops weakened, dispersing their content. They ranged in size from one that held 209 litres to a small one that contained 127 litres and had a government broad arrow incised on it, whilst another barrel was branded 'HR', so was the property of King Henry. It is possible that one might have contained gunpowder. Access for the men would be down a ladder, though that was not found, through a hatch from the orlop deck. This large dark and damp compartment was 8.5 metres long, nine metres wide at the forward end and seven metres wide at the after end, and in the dim lantern light the men would have seen three transverse rows of stanchions supporting the orlop deck. The damp smell of stale bilge water may well have pervaded the compartment.

They were a mix of young and middle aged men, two being teenagers, five were in their twenties, two in their thirties, and one is simply identified as 'adult'. All but one of them had damaged backs and limbs, suggesting that they were ordinary sailors who had suffered such serious and painful injuries in their short lives that, had they happened today the men would be off work for a long period. A teenage lad, for example, had suffered severe compression to his spine in a fall, and yet in this ship he had to continue working carrying loads that would only make him worse. A man in his twenties had a fractured spine and two of the men had spondylosis degeneration of the vertebrae joints, while another man had suffered a spiral fracture to his right leg. A man in his thirties had as an old wound on his shin that had healed.

One man (FCS 19) also in his thirties had the characteristic *os acromiale* feature of an archer where the end of his shoulder blade had not fused as an adult. What was especially interesting is that the oxygen analysis of his teeth show that he grew up in southern Europe, and so was probably a hired Spanish mercenary.

It is just possible that two men who were there were of higher-status judging from the presence of two pairs of thigh boots, traces of silk threads, a gold crown of 1529–32, a gold half sovereign, and three silver groats.

The final compartment at the stern, in sectors H10 and H11, was narrow and inconveniently V-shaped area in section, seven metres long, six metres wide at the forward end but only two metres wide at the stern. Nobody was there at the moment of sinking, and it is not clear what was being stored for, although there were at least three barrels, the one that contained candles had probably fallen from the lighting store on the orlop deck above, together with a basket of fish.

A man may have used the after end of this compartment as a toilet to account for a small concentration of cereal pollen in an area that was otherwise hardly used.[4] This is not surprising as later records mention that dark areas of sailing ships were sometimes used as unofficial toilets by their crews, to the extent that some vessels became notorious for their bad smell. This would have encouraged the colony of black rats on board the *Mary Rose* to spread disease by contaminating food.

It seems that there was nothing abnormal in the hold, though the gravel ballast as measured was insufficient to ensure the ship's stability. Much more study is required to understand the use of the hold, and part of this is to find the weight of everything.

## Chapter Nineteen

# WHO SANK THE *MARY ROSE?*

As the main gun deck gunners were not responsible for leaving their gunport open, we must look elsewhere to find who caused the loss of the ship. A great deal of credence has been given by historians to the account by John Hooker whose biography of Sir Peter Carew about thirty years later claims that Sir George Carew said just prior to the sinking that he had 'a sort of knaves he could not rule'. However, Hooker is a notoriously unreliable chronicler of the time, and was writing to extol the virtues of the Carew family. According to him Sir George Carew could not have been responsible for the loss of the ship, so in his view the next most likely culprit was the crew. This was unlikely, as there were severe punishments if they misbehaved, for the Rules of Orelon governed behaviour in ships at that time in northern Europe. Written on parchment, the rules were attached to the main mast of every ship, and were read out when necessary, so the crew of the *Mary Rose* knew that if anyone murdered someone on board he would be tied to his victim and thrown overboard; if someone argued with the Captain and drew a weapon, he would have his right hand cut off; a thief would be ducked two fathoms, about four metres, under water, then towed ashore at the stern of a boat and dismissed; and if a crew member fell asleep while on watch for a fourth time, he would be tied to the bowsprit with a biscuit, a 'can' of beer and a knife, and left to starve or cut himself adrift so that he fell into the sea and drowned. Consequently, it would be a foolish crew that ran the risk of such punishments.

Almost all of the ship's guns were found loaded as if they had been reloaded or simply not been fired. One gun even had its wooden tompion plug still in the end of its barrel, as if its gunners were not fully ready for battle. However, this does not explain why *all* of the gunports on the main gun deck seem to have been left open, though some could have been forced open by air bursting out of the sinking ship. Van der Delft, almost immediately after the sinking, said that a survivor had told him that the *Mary Rose* had fired her guns at the enemy vessel, so by the time that she sank almost all of her guns could have been reloaded. However, at least one starboard gun on the main gun deck seems as if it was in the process of being reloaded, as the shot was in the barrel, but the cartridge lay on the deck ready to be lifted into the breech. Historical records show that an experienced gun crew took roughly four-and-a-half minutes to reload similar big guns, so, it would seem that the engagement with the French galley could have happened only about five minutes before the gust of wind heeled the ship.

A comment, apparently made by Sir Walter Raleigh writing up to fifty years later, seems to reflect popular memory: 'In King Henry the eight' time … at Portsmouth the *Marie Rose* by a little sway of the ship in casting about, her ports being within sixteen inches of the waters, was overset and lost.'[1] Based on this we can calculate that the likely angle of heel at a waterline of 16 inches was only about 14 degrees.

Thanks to the discovery of the ship, we now know that the opening and closing of the gunport lids on the main gun deck depended upon men on the upper gun deck who manipulated the ropes.

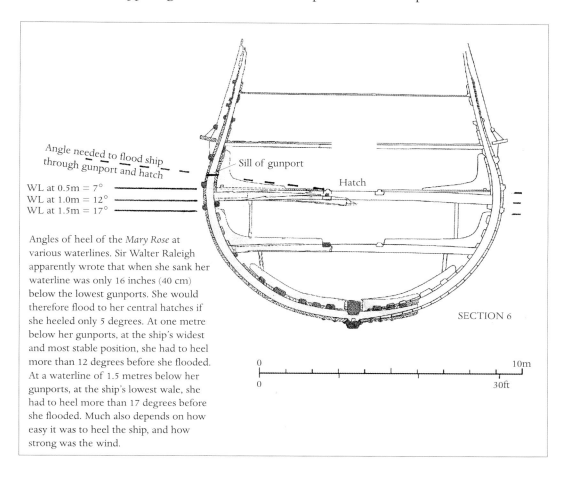

Angle needed to flood ship
through gunport and hatch

Sill of gunport

Hatch

WL at 0.5m = 7°
WL at 1.0m = 12°
WL at 1.5m = 17°

SECTION 6

0                                          10m

0                                          30ft

Angles of heel of the *Mary Rose* at various waterlines. Sir Walter Raleigh apparently wrote that when she sank her waterline was only 16 inches (40 cm) below the lowest gunports. She would therefore flood to her central hatches if she heeled only 5 degrees. At one metre below her gunports, at the ship's widest and most stable position, she had to heel more than 12 degrees before she flooded. At a waterline of 1.5 metres below her gunports, at the ship's lowest wale, she had to heel more than 17 degrees before she flooded. Much also depends on how easy it was to heel the ship, and how strong was the wind.

Communication was therefore essential between the gunners and the men above which was made through small hatches, fifty centimetres square, in the upper gun deck. So, in the heat of battle, could it be that the men operating the gunport lids simply did not hear the gunners below calling out for them to release the lids? Or could it be that the gust of wind that heeled the ship was so sudden and unexpected that there was no time to close the lids? Maybe, some of the men involved were hired foreign mercenaries who simply did not understand orders in English to close the lids. This last possibility fits a suggestion from a navigation specialist that the ship's Pilot could have been French, judging from where his equipment was manufactured.[2] If correct, then one can but wonder how he would feel as this English warship killed his countrymen. Could he have delayed telling the ship's officers of the approaching danger of running aground on Spitsand?

What seems clear is that the opening and closing system for the gunport lids of the *Mary Rose* did not allow the gunners to close the lids in an emergency. James Baker is said to have introduced gunports in English ships, and we know that he urged the King not to add more forward-firing guns to the *Mary Rose*.[3] Consequently, he might be to blame. At least the disaster made it clear that an alternative and more efficient method of closing the gunports was needed, the solution being seen in the Swedish warship *Vasa* that was built in 1628, for by then the responsibility for closing the gunports was transferred to the gunners.[4]

Edward Hall, the contemporary Tudor chronicler, pointed out that the guns of the *Mary Rose* were 'unbreached' which means that he had heard that they were not properly secured by ropes at the moment sinking. As the ship heeled this would have caused some of them to roll to starboard across the deck adding to the weight on that side and cause the vessel to heel even more. Alexzandra Hildred has examined the iron ringbolts in the ship's inboard side next to the gunports to reconstruct how the guns were held by ropes, and found that as the ropes had not survived, the securing arrangement is uncertain. Nevertheless, many of the port side guns had fallen to starboard, but whether this happened at the time of sinking or sometime later when the securing ropes had decayed, is unknown. It is assumed that there was a ring bolt in the deck behind each bronze muzzle loader to enable it to be pulled inboard for reloading as was done in later ships, but this bolt has not yet been found and shows that the reloading system needs further study. The iron breech loaded guns had a quite different system as they were loaded at the inboard end and did not need hauling inboard.

The *Mary Rose* was not alone in being rebuilt around 1536 and disaster did not overtake her slightly smaller sister ship *Peter Pomegranate* or the *Henry Grace a Dieu*, the 1,000 ton Lord Admiral's flagship that was rebuilt in 1540. The *Mary Rose* certainly had experience of battle as she was included in the battle plan against the French in June 1545, and was one of the largest warships in the navy. It seems inconceivable that he did not take part in the capture of the port of Boulogne in 1544, or in the naval attempts led by Lord Lisle to stop the French Armada assembling earlier in 1545.

There appears to have been a special problem in the *Mary Rose* on that day in 1545 which caused the disaster, and that her crew was not able to respond to the sudden and unexpected gust of wind that heeled her over as she was turning. This highlighted a weaknesses in her design and, showed that she was overloaded with guns so that her waterline was dangerously high.

The *Mary Rose* was a flawed ship whose rebuild around 1536 had been ordered and paid for by King Henry VIII as part of his plan to modernise his navy. He must have agreed the rebuild, although he had no practical experience of war at sea because his seafaring was limited to sailing between England and his possession of Calais in France. But this did not stop him telling his admirals how to conduct themselves in battle, or, as the Hatfield House letter shows, stop him influencing the design of his warships.

Henry's interest in warship design was even mentioned by the Ambassador, Eustace Chapuys, in a letter to the Emperor Charles V in 1541: 'the King has likewise sent to Italy for three shipwrights experienced in the art of constructing galleys, but I fancy that he will not make much use of their science as for some time back he has been building ships with oars according to a model of which he himself was the inventor'. Henry was also deeply interested in artillery and had employed foreign gunfounders. He also showed that he was particularly impressed by the French rowing galleys that carried a single heavy gun that could be fired forward at vulnerable sectors of the English ships. He therefore ordered similar 'row barges' to be built, but these were not ready until 1546, as Lord Lisle mentioned to Admiral d'Annebault.[5]

Henry was determined to improve his great warships, and not only overloaded *Mary Rose* with guns in 1545, but also he wanted yet more forward firing guns in her. She already had two 'slings' firing forward from the lower forecastle deck, two culverins firing from the forward face of the lower sterncastle deck, two sakers doing likewise from the middle sterncastle deck, and, it seems, two more similarly that were located on the upper sterncastle deck. But this was not enough, and the King's Master Shipwright, James Baker, and Benjamin Gonson, acting

Surveyor of the navy, had to hold him back by tactfully advising 'that there can be no more ordnance laid in the luff [forecastle] without the taking away of two knees and the spoiling of the clamps that beareth the bits [bitts], which will be a great weakening to the same part [the bow] of the ship'.[6]

It would be wrong to think of Henry as being ignorant about guns and ships, as he was surrounded by practical advisors, and his interest in the navy went right back to the start of his reign when in 1510 he ordered the construction of the *Mary Rose* and the *Peter Pomegranite*, and in March 1513 when he instructed his Lord Admiral, Sir Edward

King Henry VIII.
*(National Portrait Gallery)*

Howard, to race his fleet and to report back as 'you did command me to send your Grace word how every ship did sail'.

Henry believed that he knew best, and his personality became more forceful as he grew older, his omnipotent position enabled him to control anything in which he was interested without question. People feared him and were unlikely to report a faulty aspect in a major warship. Even Lord Admiral Lisle hesitated to make decisions during the Battle of the Solent without referring to the King. On 21 July 1545, after the French had landed on the Isle of Wight, he wrote to Henry from his flagship what must be one of the most obsequious letters in his life:

> I will not attempt, your majesty being so near, without your grace's consent to the same, albeit that I would for my own part little pass to shed the best blood in my body to remove them [the French] out of your sight. But have your grace no doubt in any hasty or unadvised or presumptuous enterprise that I shall make, having the charge of so weighty a matter under your majesty, without being first well instructed from your highness. For if I have any knowledge how to serve you in any kind of thing, I have received the same from yourself, and being so near the fountain [i.e. the King], and would die of thirst, it were little joy of my life.

In other words, he was saying that he would do nothing to remove the French from the Isle of Wight without having received the King's advice and approval.

Lisle had been promoted by the King as Lord Admiral of England on 27 January 1543, but he was uncomfortable in that post, as he expressed privately in a letter to a friend some years later: 'I do think I should have done his Majesty better service in some meaner office wherein to be directed and not to be a director.'

King Henry did interfere in naval matters. It was he who approved and paid for the order that the *Mary Rose* be modernised in 1536, and he must have approved the designs. It was he who paid for the new heavy guns, some of which carried his name and status 'supreme head of the Church in England'; it was he who no doubt agreed to convert her main deck into a gun deck, and approved the new gunports that were cut through the hull even though they proved to be dangerously close to the waterline. Henry VIII had driven the conversion of the *Mary Rose* beyond her safe capability, so it only needed an unfortunate set of circumstances, such as a delay in closing the gunport lids combined with a sudden gust of wind, for disaster to happen.

As Henry VIII sank the *Mary Rose* in 1545, it is no wonder that there is no record of any enquiry into what happened, as it would only implicate him. It was easier to blame the crew of the *Mary Rose*, for they could not reply. This would not be the last time that a crew was blamed for the design failures of others, as witness the loss of *MV Derbyshire* in 1980 during a violent storm in the Far East. It took an official enquiry ordered by John Prescott MP, then a government minister, some years later to find evidence of faulty hatch fittings in the wreck deep down on the seabed to exonerate the crew. Everyone feared Henry and his evil temper, and would think carefully before questioning his orders. Even when on his deathbed in January 1547, his doctors dare not tell him that he was dying for fear of being charged with treason.

*Chapter Twenty*

# LEGACY OF THE *MARY ROSE*

The loss of the *Mary Rose* was due to her being modified beyond her safe capabilities during one of the most exciting and important periods in human history when the Royal Navy was being founded, and sea routes to the rest of the world were being discovered. Added to which England was under threat from Catholic France, so King Henry was under enormous pressure. In 1519–22 the Portuguese explorer Ferdinand Magellan's ship *Victoria* was the first vessel to sail around the world, under the patronage of King Charles V of Spain, after which voyages laid the foundation of modern global trade. For this they needed appropriate ocean-going ships, and the *Mary Rose* helps to show how this was achieved.

The ship gives us is a unique window in on the time when small European states were beginning to coalesce into the larger nations that we know today. During the sixteenth century, Europe comprised rival kingdoms, like Spain, France, England and Scotland, and republics like Venice, Florence and Sienna, that were often involved in petty wars between each other. England, France and Scotland were at war with each other, and the *Mary Rose* took part in them all. But in the end we must wonder what was achieved at a large cost in human life.

In spite of these squabbles, the Catholic Church managed to bind loosely many of them together under the Pope, particularly in opposition to the Moslems of the Ottoman Empire, ruled by Suleiman the Magnificent, who threatened the eastern borders of Europe. And the Arabs of North Africa began to flex their muscles by embarking on a campaign of piracy and terror that was to last until the nineteenth century. In Christian Europe the situation was no better as the authority of the Pope was weakening, strengthening royal control and Protestantism so that eventually Henry VIII declared himself 'Supreme Head of the Church of England' in 1534. Henry seized and dissolved the monasteries, though it was not until 1538 that Pope Paul III published his excommunication from the Catholic Church. So, by 1540

England was isolated politically and religiously from the rest of Europe, and the wealth from selling the monastic lands in the 1530s gave Henry the money to finance his coastal defences and modernise his embryonic navy, including rebuilding the *Mary Rose*.

It was in the first half of the sixteenth century that the biggest changes occurred in the design, construction and armament of English warships, and this required the development of a more effective administration to maintain the Royal Navy. So, when the *Mary Rose* was built in 1510–12 she was one of the earliest of the very large ships in northern Europe to have edge-to-edge carvel planking nailed to great wooden ribs, replacing the medieval shipbuilding practice of overlapping clinker planking held together by iron rivets. This fundamental improvement allowed wooden ships to be built that were generally much larger and safer, and this even enabled square gunports to be cut through the planking without weakening the ship's structure. The success of this construction is reflected in the *Mary Rose*, and by its continued use in very large ships throughout the seventeenth, eighteenth and nineteenth centuries, as seen today in HMS *Victory*, until, in turn, wooden planks were replaced by iron and steel plates in the nineteenth century.

The original design of the *Mary Rose* as a floating fortress in 1512 was excellent as long as warships depended on light-weight archery and fairly small guns that were mainly mounted on high fore and stern castles. This emphasis on anti-personnel fighting enabled the *Mary Rose* to sail alongside an enemy vessel and drop her grappling hook to hold the two ships together so that her soldiers could board. Moreover, her archers and her anti-personnel guns could repel borders if an enemy ship attacked her. So, initially just a few heavy anti-ship guns that were mounted on the upper deck in the waist, as listed in her equipment inventory of 1514 when she had a total of sixty-five to sixty-eight anti-personnel guns and only eight to thirteen anti-ship guns. She was then at the pinnacle of naval technology, but that was not very different from warfare at sea in the fourteenth and fifteenth centuries. In 1340, for example, a naval battle took place off the Dutch town of Sluys between King Edward III of England (r. 1327–77) and King Philip VI of France (r. 1328–50) in a dispute over who was the legitimate King of France. In order to reinforce the French claim Philip had confiscated Edward's lands in Aquitaine, and, although the English won the sea battle by using archers and soldiers, in the long term, the English King lost his claim.

The discovery of the lower part of a merchant ship in Newport, south Wales, in 2002 has provided valuable information about how trading ships were then built in England in the middle of the fifteenth

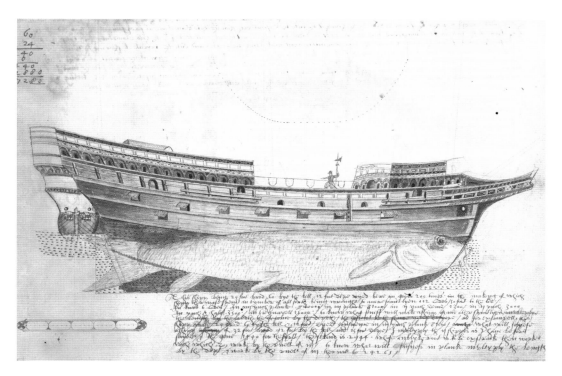

century. She may have been owned originally by a French or Portuguese merchant as she had a small silver coin minted in southeast France in 1447 placed for luck at the junction of her keel and stempost. She had clinker-built oak planks twenty centimetres wide and two to three centimetres thick fastened to ribs by wooden treenails, and was made watertight with a caulking of animal hair and tar. The majority of pottery sherds in the ship are of red coarse ware from the Alentejo region of Portugal, suggesting that she traded with that area, but she returned to Newport for repair sometime soon after 1459, and was abandoned in a creek inlet beside the tidal River Usk about twenty years later. She was smaller than the *Mary Rose* in that her keel was probably about thirty metres long, and she had a beam of at least eight metres. Her tall main mast fitted into a socket in the keelson and presumably carried a square sail, and she probably had a mizzen mast with a lateen sail, a foremast with a square sail, though fittings for these had not survived. However, there were loose fittings for wooden pumps, rigging blocks, deadeyes and rope. She was also lightly armed for there was a leather bracer for an archer found, and several stone shot with diameters ranging from two-and-a-half to four inches for anti-personnel guns to protect her from pirates. Personal possessions of the people on board included shoes, wooden combs, a bowl, a gaming piece and four other coins, all Portuguese, dating from the middle of the fifteenth century. There was also a merchant's counter, a jetton,

Galleons replaced carracks as the English warships in the latter half of the sixteenth century as they were more stable, and were designed to carry and fire ship-smashing guns. *(Pepys Library, Magdalene College, Cambridge)*

possibly part of a sandglass, and food bones of pig and cattle, with just a few bones of chicken, goose and duck.[1]

It is not known if she was a carrack, as on the Warwick Roll of about 1485, there are small guns poking over the gunwale of the upper deck in the waist. In war the Warwick ships had archers firing longbows and crossbows, and soldiers carrying spears who were prepared to board an enemy vessel. The larger ships are shown as having four masts, and on one there was a man in the main crow's-nest 'top' throwing rocks down onto an enemy crew.[2]

It is difficult to judge the size of these early ships, even though the royal records are excellent, as we do not know how tonnage was calculated. What we do know is what the ships did. For example, Henry V (r. 1413–22) wanted to ensure that he could control the English Channel, and so he built the *Trinite Royale* (c. 520 tons), the *Holigost* (c. 750 tons), the *Jesus* (1,000 tons) and the *Grace Dieu* (1,400 tons). Fortunately, the bottom of what is believed to be the *Grace Dieu* survives in the mud of the River Hamble near Southampton, and shows that the ship was huge judging from the thirty-eight-metre length of her keel compared with thirty-two metres for the keel of the *Mary Rose*. Records state that her main mast was about two metres in diameter with square sails, and that she had two other masts, one of which probably held a lateen fore-and-aft balancing sail near the stern, and a bowsprit at the forward end. She never fought against the French as peace was declared while she was being built, so she was mostly kept at a mooring in the River Hamble until in January 1439 she was struck by lightning and burnt.[3] Her construction was very different from the *Mary Rose*, mainly in that she had overlapping clinker planks held together by iron rivets in a complex of three layers and with a caulking of moss to make them watertight. The planks were fastened to narrowly spaced oak ribs by long wooden pegs or treenails.

Although there was no permanent English royal navy during most of the fifteenth century, warships were occasionally built for temporary purposes, such as by Edward IV (r. 1461–83) who had seven carracks, a caravel and a bark. Two of these were Spanish built, and another was Portuguese, and so probably followed the carvel edge-to-edge planking tradition of southern Europe in contrast to the clinker hulls of the English-built ships. It was only a matter of time before the superiority of carvel shipbuilding for the biggest ships was recognised and adopted in northern Europe, the *Mary Rose* being one of the first of that new style.

By the beginning of the sixteenth century the largest carracks had four masts, a foremast, main mast, mizzen mast and a bonaventure mast at the stern, as well as a bowsprit, and the main mast was then a massive structure of considerable diameter able to support large crow's-nest 'tops', from which soldiers could fire down on an enemy. This was why the archers and gunners in the waist of carracks were covered by a protective light timber roof, as in the *Mary Rose*.

Both the *Sovereign*, built by Henry VII in 1495 and rebuilt in 1509, and the *Mary Rose* built in 1510–12, reflect this stage of shipbuilding. Subsequent developments with bigger guns that fired ship-smashing shot made it obvious by 1536 that the *Mary Rose* needed updating so that she could carry heavier firepower. This emphasis on an extra weight of guns above the waterline could have caused instability, so it was necessary to reduce the thickness of the main mast in carracks. Henry VIII believed that his old carracks could be modernised, but he only succeeded in creating a situation whereby in the emergency faced by the *Mary Rose* her crew could not save themselves or their ship. A fundamental rethink of warship design was needed, based on how naval battles should be fought with heavy ship-smashing guns.

And so after 1550 a more appropriate ship, the galleon, became popular having begun its development earlier in the sixteenth century in Venice and in Portugal. Designed to carry heavy guns it had a long hull and low castles fore and aft. In the 1540s Henry VIII embraced the idea of having more manoeuvrable warships, and approved the building of two sailing 'galleasses', the *Anne Gallant* and the *Grand Mistress*, both of 450 tons, which are depicted on the Anthony Roll. They were transitional towards a galleon design though archers still manned the ships' waists behind shields, 'parvasses', and the upper-most decks were covered by anti-boarding netting, as in the old carracks.

Maintaining a large permanent navy required an efficient administration to deal with the finances, shipbuilding, and provide men and equipment to supply a fleet. In the early decades of his reign Henry had placed the care of his growing navy in the hands of Thomas Wolsey, the Lord Chancellor who was greedy for power, and then with Thomas Cromwell, Lord Privy Seal, who oversaw the rebuilding around 1536 of the *Mary Rose* and other warships. Under them was the Keeper or Clerk of the King's Ships, Robert Brigandine, who held that post under Henry VII, until the 1520s when he was succeeded by Thomas Spert and William Gonson. Their administration proved to be inadequate so in 1545 the King established a 'Council of Marine Causes', comprising seven senior officers in charge of ships, dockyards, guns, stores and rigging. They were all experienced in maritime logistical work and were well paid. This was so successful that it became permanent, so by the seventeenth century it was known as the Navy Board. Around 1650 it was separated into two parts, the Navy Board that administered the fleet and the dockyards, and the Admiralty that dealt with naval policy, command and discipline.

Throughout his reign Henry also appreciated the need for safety at sea, and he granted Pilots a royal charter in 1514 and established the Corporation of Trinity House of Deptford Strand initially to regulate Pilots on the Thames. Its first Master was Thomas Spert, who in the previous three years had been Master of the *Mary Rose*. In time Trinity House became the authority governing the safety of shipping generally in Britain, and still exists today.

Improvements in ship design and size in Europe had by the fifteenth century reached a point where the merchants and mariners of Portugal and Spain felt able to search for ocean routes to the wealth of spices, fine porcelain and silks in the Far East. Their main aim was to establish trading agreements with the Ming Emperor of Cathay, known to us as China, and so bypass the long Silk Road by land across the Middle East and northern India.

The Portuguese sailed south in the Atlantic hoping to discover a route eastward around Africa, and by 1441 had colonised the Cape Verde Islands and subsequently set up trading posts in Guinea, West Africa. In 1488 Bartholomew Diaz rounded the Cape of Good Hope, opening the way for Vasco da Gama to reach Malabar in 1498 and Goa in India in 1499, and lay the foundation of the Portuguese East India Empire. Pushing ever eastward the Portuguese reached Malacca by 1511, the Moluccas by 1512, China in 1516, and Japan in 1542–3.

The Spanish chose to sail west across the Atlantic to reach China, and when they reached the islands of the Caribbean and the mainland of central America they at first thought that they had reached Asia, hence even today these islands are still called the West Indies, and the natives of north America were called Indians. But they soon discovered that they were wrong, and that to reach Cathay they still had to sail across the world's greatest ocean, the Pacific.

It was Christopher Columbus, born in Genoa in 1451 but settled in Portugal, who won the support of the King of Spain to sail across the Atlantic, and in 1492 he reached Cuba and Haiti. There were already hints that this 'New World' existed, for the Vikings had found and briefly settled in Newfoundland around 1000 AD, and subsequent stories suggest that during medieval times Arab voyagers may have reached the West Indies. On his second voyage in 1493–6, Columbus discovered several West Indian islands including Guadalupe, Montserrat, Antigua, Porto Rico and Jamaica, and in 1498 he found Trinidad and sighted the mainland of South America for first time. On his last voyage in 1502–4 he explored the coast of Honduras and Nicaragua, and by the 1520s the Spaniards began settling there.

So when the *Mary Rose* entered naval service in 1512 the basic sea routes around the globe were beginning to be known, and experience in building very large ships meant that England could open up its own trade links with the Far East. However, the commanding positions of Portugal and Spain were such that their rivalry to reach Asia had to be arbitrated by Pope Alexander VI (r. 1492–1503). In 1493 he partitioned the world between them, initially drawing a north-south line down the middle of the Atlantic 100 leagues west of the Azores, west of which was a Spanish monopoly, and to the east was Portuguese. This line was later moved when a Portuguese fleet accidently found Brazil in 1500, while on its way to the Cape and India.

Both Henry VII and Henry VIII were aware of these discoveries and initially wanted England to join in by looking for a route to sail around North America. This got off to a good start when John Cabot, an Italian living in Bristol, was commissioned by Henry VII in 1496 'To discover hitherto unknown lands', which resulted in the discovery of Newfoundland and Nova Scotia.

Subsequently, with the approval of Henry VIII, Wolsey in 1520 devised a plan for a major expedition to find a passage around north America, and he offered Sebastian Cabot, son of John, then in Venice, a handsome reward if he would lead this, but Cabot refused. So, in 1521, he invited companies in London to finance a fleet, accompanied by a royal ship, and merchants were summoned to meet the King in the

Spanish silver pieces-of-eight, parts of which were found in the *Mary Rose*, were the world's first global currency. These are from an East India Company ship of the seventeenth century.

Drapers Company Hall in the City of London, where 'his grace would have no nay therein, but spake sharply to the Mayor to see it [the expedition] put into execution to the best of his power'. Some money was raised, but the cautious merchants refused.

Henry VIII lost interest, and instead declared war on France. Had he pursued this cause then the future of Britain could have been radically different. There were occasional unofficial English voyages of discovery, such as in 1527 when two ships sailed from Plymouth to North America. One was lost, the other reached Hudson Strait or Frobisher Bay before returning. And in 1536 a Master Hore set out from Gravesend with two ships for Newfoundland and Labrador as a private venture, but it was Henry's daughter, Elizabeth I, who would mainly encourage new voyages of discovery.

The situation in England was not all negative, however, for soon after the death of Henry VIII in 1547 some London merchants set up the Muscovy Company to trade with Russia and hoped to find an alternative route to Asia, this time eastwards around the icy north of Russia. It received a royal charter in 1555 and was England's first major chartered joint stock trading company. Moreover, Sebastian Cabot was one of those to encourage the formation of the Society of Merchant Venturers in Bristol, with a royal charter in 1552.

The result of all these European probing voyages was that the most successful route to the Far East was found to be around southern Africa. In 1600 some English merchants at long last took the major step that was to change British history and lay the foundation of its future wealth and Empire. They established the English East India Company and received a royal charter from Queen Elizabeth I. Two years later, merchants in Amsterdam created its greatest rival, the Dutch East India Company. They all needed well-designed ships able to carry large quantities of cargo, so further developments occurred in ship design, leaving the *Mary Rose* as a distant memory that marked the end of England's medieval seafaring adventures around Europe. These newer and more appropriate type of ship were the galleons.

Although Queen Elizabeth owned fewer warships than her father, Henry VIII, when in trouble she could call on at least two hundred and fifty merchant vessels of over 80 tons that she could arm. Moreover, developments in gunfounding technology enabled iron guns to be cast more cheaply than the bronze guns that were used in the *Mary Rose*. There were other improvements, such as by Hawkins who is credited with putting horsehair between a sheathing of thin planks over the wooden hull below the waterline to protect ships from the Teredo 'shipworm'. Efficient chain pumps superseded the elm tree pump of the type found in the *Mary Rose*, and in due course, galley ovens were moved up from the hold to the forecastle, where they were much safer. It was also found that the fourth mast, the bonaventure mizzen, was not needed. By the end of the sixteenth century Master Shipwrights, such as Matthew Baker, had begun to design ships on a more scientific basis.

Francis Drake left a unique impression on English seafaring history by sailing to the Caribbean in 1571 and seizing Spanish treasure. Between 1577 and 1580 he sailed around the world in his ship, *Golden Hind*, which was preserved in a special dock beside the River Thames at Deptford near London where her remains may be discovered in the future. English, Dutch and French 'privateers' and pirates began settling in the islands of the Caribbean to capture Spanish treasure carried in merchant ships across the Atlantic to Spain in the annual 'flota' convoy. This Spanish bullion fuelled global trade in which England, the Netherlands, Spain and Portugal took the lead during the seventeenth and eighteenth centuries. The Dutch succeeded in winning the highly valued Spice Islands of what is now Indonesia, and the British settled in India, each region eventually becoming part of the Dutch and British empires in the nineteenth century until they gained independence in the twentieth century. Both competed for control of the Cape, South Africa, as the half-way revictualling port, until that too gained independence from Britain in the twentieth century.

By mining precious metals in Central America, Spain created the world's first global currency, the Spanish silver 'dollar', respected for its quality in America, in Europe and in Asia. The Spanish also called the coins, essentially small ingots of silver, by their weight of 'eight reales', and they had sub-divisions of four, two, one-and-a-half reales. The English knew the largest of these coins as 'pieces-of-eight' because that number was stamped on them, and they have passed into legend with associations of piracy promoted by the story of *Treasure Island* and the film *Pirates of the Caribbean*. This is undoubtedly the most important coin in world history, as it was adopted by the USA as its currency, and the dollar is still an engine of world trade, though now mostly in an electronic form. Its origin lies in the age of the *Mary Rose*.

There are two small groups of objects discovered in the *Mary Rose* that are outstanding because they are signposts to the future direction of world history. The first are a few Spanish silver two-reale coins, each a quarter of a 'piece-of-eight' of a type that would soon finance world trade. Perhaps they were minted in Spanish central America. If so, they have a remarkable story, being mined by native slave labour, carried by mule train to the Caribbean, sailed across the Atlantic in a Spanish trading ship, and in Europe bought by merchants for trade. The second is a single cowrie shell, found in a seaman's chest, that had been

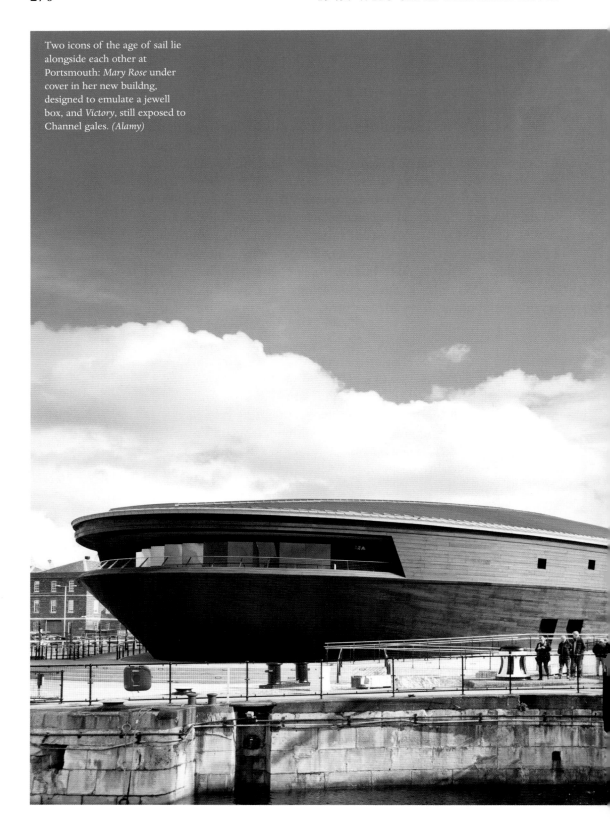

Two icons of the age of sail lie alongside each other at Portsmouth: *Mary Rose* under cover in her new buildng, designed to emulate a jewell box, and *Victory*, still exposed to Channel gales. *(Alamy)*

The remaining part of Polslo Priory, near Exeter, was the home of Sir George and Lady Mary Carew. After her husband died special arrangements were made to ensure that she received the income from here during her lifetime.

brought from the Red Sea or the Indian or Pacific oceans to reflect the discovery of the sea route to the Far East and the future ambition of Britain on a global stage.

It is fitting that the *Mary Rose* now lies in a dock alongside HMS *Victory*, in the same naval dockyard that gave birth to her five hundred years ago. The bows and arrows, bronze and wrought iron guns of the Tudor ship, contrast with great cast iron guns of Nelson's flagship 250 years later. Nearby is HMS *Warrior*, launched in 1860, which reflects the transition from wood to iron and from sail to steam in the nineteenth century. Modern British warships in service are also moored close to the *Mary Rose* and have missiles that can be fired with precision over hundreds of miles. After centuries of conflict, Britain, France, Spain, Portugal, and the Netherlands are now allies in Europe in a way that in Henry VIII's time would have been inconceivable.

The loss of Henry VIII's ship and crew has made possible the erection of the unique museum in which she is preserved and displayed. This is the legacy left to us by Alex McKee who found the ship and Margaret Rule who led the project, together with the enormous number of volunteers who carried out the excavation and recovery of the ship, and the Mary Rose Trust's trustees and staff. The handful of executive officers, who have raised huge sums of money to create the museum, and Prince Charles, as Patron of the Trust, have played a crucial part in the success of this very British project.

There is a curious post-script to the story of the *Mary Rose* for, while the public and royal court blamed the ship's crew for the loss, in private

King Henry evidently felt embarrassed by the death of Sir George Carew on 19 July 1545, for he engaged Lady Mary Carew as a lady in waiting to his daughters, the Princesses Mary and Elizabeth. Two years after the death of Henry in 1547 it was found necessary for Lady Mary to have financial protection, so, on 19 July 1549, on the anniversary of the death of her husband in the *Mary Rose*, the new King Edward awarded the priory and the manor of Polslo, her home just outside Exeter, to Sir John Dudley, the former Lord Admiral Lisle who had led the Battle of the Solent, and this subject to the 'life interest' of Lady Carew. This protection of Lady Mary by giving her the income from Polslo, was because she had married the colourful naval character Sir Arthur Champernowne in 1546 whose mother was a Carew.[4]

*Appendix A*

# SIZES OF THE MASTS AND YARDS

There had to be a relationship between the size of a large sailing ship's hull and the dimensions of her masts, yards and sails so that she remained stable. This was set out as a series of ratios that were eventually published in 1627, but could have been in use over eighty years earlier when the *Mary Rose* was rebuilt.[1] The basic ratio was that the length of the main mast was 2.4 times the ship's beam, which when applied to the *Mary Rose*, whose beam was 37.4 feet (11.4m), would make the lower part of her mast 89.76 feet (27.35m) long.

Moreover, as the diameter of the main mast of the *Mary Rose* would be one inch per three feet of its length, its diameter would be 29.92 inches (76cm).

Although the main mast of the *Mary Rose* is missing, the step or slot for its tenon at its base has survived in the keelson and is 27.5 inches (69cm) long, and keelson timber that supported the mast at that point is 32.5 inches (82cm) wide. This means that the main mast was between 27.5 inches and 32.5 inches (69–83cm) wide, which exactly fits the independent calculation of 29.92 inches (76cm) based on the 1627 rule. In view of this it seems likely that the traditional rule was applied to the *Mary Rose* during her rebuild in 1536. Assuming that this is true we can use the formula to calculate the dimensions of all masts and yards, with the exception of the bonaventure mizzen which had become obsolete before 1627, as follows:

## Lengths of the Masts of the *Mary Rose*
*Main mast:*

Length of the *main mast* is 2.4 times the ship's beam (37.4ft) = 89.76 feet.

The length of the *main topmast* is 60 per cent of the length of the main mast = 53.85 feet.

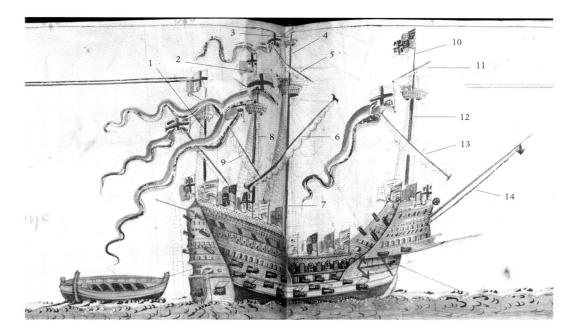

The length of the *main topgallant mast* was 42 per cent of the length of the main topmast = 22.61 feet.

## Foremast:

The *foremast* was 80 per cent of the length of the main mast = 71.80 feet.

The *fore topmast* was 60 per cent of the length of the foremast = 43.08 feet.

## Mizzen mast:

The *mizzen mast* was 50 per cent of the length of the main mast (assuming that it was stepped in the hold, which was not the case in the *Mary Rose*, so the figure has to be adjusted if stepped on a higher deck) = 44.88 feet.

The *mizzen topmast* was 50 per cent of the length of the main topmast = 26.92 feet.

## Bowsprit:

The *bowsprit* was 80 per cent of the length of the main mast = 71.80 feet.

## Diameters of masts:

The bottom of the *main mast* (before 1670) had a diameter of one inch per 3 feet in length = 29.92 inches diameter.

The *Mary Rose* on the Anthony Roll.

Key:
1. Bonaventure mast.
2. Mizzen topmast.
3. Main topgallant mast.
4. Main topmast.
5. Main topsail yard.
6. Main yard.
7. Main mast.
8. Mizzen mast.
9. Mizzen yard.
10. Fore topmast.
11. Fore topsail yard.
12. Foremast.
13. Foresail yard.
14. Bowsprit.

*(Pepys Library, Magdalene College, Cambridge)*

The *main topmast* had a diameter of $^{15}/_{16}$ inch per 3 feet of length = 16.82 inches.

The *main topgallant mast* had a diameter of $^{15}/_{16}$ inch per 3 feet in length = 7.06 inches.

The *foremast* (before 1670) had a diameter of one inch per 3 feet in length = 23.93 inches.

The *fore topmast* had the same diameter as the main topmast = 13.46 inches.

The *mizzen mast* had a diameter of one inch per 3 feet of length = 14.96 inches.

The *mizzen topmast* had a diameter of one inch per 3 feet of length = 8.97 inches.

## Lengths of Yards:

The *yard of the bowsprit* (before 1627) was $^{19}/_{21}$ the length of the main yard = 64.57 feet.

The *foresail yard* was 80 per cent of the length of the main yard = 67.8 feet.

The *fore topsail yard* was ½ the length of the fore yard = 33.9 feet.

The *main yard* was ⅚ the length of the keel (101.7ft) = 84.75 feet.

The *main topsail yard* was ½ the length of the main yard = 43.58 feet.

The *main topgallant yard* was ½ the length of the main topsail yard = 21.79 feet.

The *mizzen yard* was the same length as the mizzen mast = 44.88 feet.

## Diameters of the Yards:

The diameter of the *bowsprit sail yard* was ⅝ inch per 3 feet = 13.45 inches.

The diameter of the *fore yard* was ¾ inch per 3 feet in length = 16.95 inches.

The diameter of the *fore topsail yard* was ⅝ inch per 3 feet of length = 7.06 inches.

The diameter of the *main yard* was ¾ inch per 3 feet in length = 21.18 inches.

The diameter of the *main topsail yard* was ⅝ inch per 3 feet of length = 9.08 inches.

The diameter of the *main topgallant yard* was ⅝ inch per 3 feet of length = 4.53 inches.

The diameter of the *mizzen yard* was ½ inch per 3 feet of length = 7.48 inches.

*Appendix B*

# FAIRLY COMPLETE SKELETONS
# FROM THE *MARY ROSE*

This list is based on the study of the skeletons by Anne Stirland, and incorporates an analysis of the oxygen isotope in the teeth of a few men by Lynne Bell.[1] It includes associated objects, such as jerkins, listed by several other people.

It is assumed that where a Fairly Complete Skeleton (FCS) was found is where the person probably died, though it is possible that some bodies may have drifted from elsewhere after the sinking. However, it must be remembered that as some parts of the ship were partitioned into compartments it is unlikely that some bodies will have drifted far. Most were found in the same sector. The term 'Fairly Complete Skeletons' is not quite correct as they range from just a few bones of a single skeleton to almost a whole skeleton. The bones are generally well preserved, but there are a few that were heavily eroded in the sterncastle, so it is likely that they had fallen from higher up and had suffered damage while the upper part of the sterncastle was eroding away. Assuming that the massing of people (but not the total numbers) shown in the stations list of the *Henry Grace a Dieu* can be applied to other large ships like the *Mary Rose*, it seems that while at battle stations the soldiers were massed in the forecastle, in the waist, below the strerncastle, and in the fighting 'tops' on the masts, all ready to board the enemy vessel. This would account for the concentration of skeletons, thought to be soldiers, found on the upper gun deck beneath the sterncastle.

The health problems of the men only refer to those bones that were found, and not to the individual as a whole. Teeth found in skulls are often incomplete as some teeth had fallen out and could not be studied, and many skulls have lower jaws that are now missing. Consequently, our knowledge of the health of these men is somewhat limited. But, as a whole, the bones give us a unique partial view of the health of some of the men who served at the beginning of the permanent royal navy.

They show that the men were mostly in their twenties and had already generally suffered from strained backs and limbs due to the hard physical work involved. Moreover, as many of the skeletons were found below the upper gun deck, it is likely that they were mostly 'deckmen', and so are doubtful as representative of everyone in the ship, especially of the fitter 'topmen' who climbed the masts and yards to set the sails. This is also suggested by the presence of mostly slip-on shoes, though perhaps some men climbed the masts without shoes.

As many more human bones than those comprising the FCS were found, much more research is possible, especially using DNA to identify more FCS and confirm that all of the bones of FCS listed below really do belong to the same individual. Moreover, further oxygen isotope studies of teeth will add to what we know of where the men grew up, and better highlight what proportion of the men on board were foreign mercenaries. The small random selection of men already studied seems to show that many on board were foreign mercenaries who had been employed by King Henry VIII to supplement the English crew.

## Hold

### Sector H1, storage compartment:
This forward part of the ship was very badly damaged, and no FCS were found there.

### Sector H2, storage compartment:
**FCS 7:** Age 18-30. Height 1.76m (5ft 9in).
His shoulder blade has *os acromiale* where the bones are not properly fused, indicating that he was an archer. His finger and thumb bones were very well muscled. Unusual changes to his upper left arm and spine strongly suggest that he used a longbow. Health problems exist in his right clavical, his scapulae, his left humerus, his spine, left tibia and pelvis. His skull was found, and his face has been reconstructed. He was one of the most complete skeletons found in the ship. A leather jerkin was found on the skeleton, and it is possible that a highly decorated archer's wristguard found on the deck above may have been his.

**FCS 8:** Age 18-30. Height 1.68m (5ft 6in).
Most of this skeleton was found, and shows that he had health problems in his spine and in the pelvis joints to his legs. His upper jaw had two teeth with caries, and two abscesses.

**FCS 9:** Age and height unknown.
He had dislocated the top of his left upper leg bone for it was damaged from being forced out of his pelvis.

*Sector H3, storage compartment:*
**FCS 10:** Age 30-40. Height 1.61m (5ft 3in).
Health problems were noted on his spine, and at the ends of his ribs, pelvis, left shoulder, and in both feet. His skull was found with seven abscesses in the upper jaw, and caries on four teeth of the lower jaw.

*Sectors H4 & H5, cooking galley with two brick ovens:*
**FCS 1:** Age 18-30. Height 1.63m (5ft 4in).
A Potts fracture was in his left ankle, and severe Schmorl's nodes with arthritis in his spine. He may have been a cook.

**FCS 3**: Age 18-30. Height 1.77m (5ft 9in).
His sacrum reflected scoliosis to the left.

**FCS 4:** Age 18-30. Height 1.67m (5ft 5in).
His upper arms and lower legs show health problems.

**FCS 5:** Age 18-30. Height unknown.
His skull was pitted, and he had very poor dental health, with caries on seven teeth and five abscesses.

**FCS 6:** Age 18-30. Height 1.71m (5ft 7in).
There were health problems in the top of his left arm, his left elbow, the top of both legs, the top of his lower right leg, and in both ankles. A cut hose was found with him.

**FCS 11:** Age 30-40. Height 1.68m (5ft 6in).
Quite a lot of his skeleton remained, but his spine had double scoliosis and signs of stress due to age and work related causes. The top of his leg joints was damaged, and his sternum had an old healed partial fracture. His skull had three abscesses in the upper jaw, one tooth had caries, and in his lower jaw two teeth had caries.

**FCS 12:** Age 18-30. Height 1.68m (5ft 6in).
This man had heavy robust bones, and his skeleton was virtually complete. One of his lowest ribs had an old healed fracture, as if he had been struck from behind. His spine was very worn from stress, with all articulations enlarged on the right. There is possibly an old fracture on his left foot bone. His left and right knees had suffered torn ligaments, as if he had ripped both knee caps. His skull was found, with caries in four teeth of his top jaw, and in three teeth of his lower jaw. An oxygen isotope study of his teeth show that it is likely that he grew up in a hot climate, such as Spain. His face is recon-

structed by Richard Neave. He was found with his shoes, a knife and comb, and may have been a gunner.

**FCS 92:** Age 18-30. Height not known.
His lower jaw had one surviving tooth, and in it were caries. His jaw had five abscesses.

*Sector H6, storage compartment with foot of main mast and main pump:*
No bodies were found.

*Sectors H7, H8 &H 9, main storage compartment:*
**FCS 19:** Age 30-40. Height 1.67 (5ft 5in).
Both of his shoulder blades had *os acromiale* indicating that he was an archer. His spine was stressed, and the outer ends of his collar bones were damaged. An oxygen isotope examination of his teeth suggest that he was from southern Europe.

**FCS 20:** Age 18-30. Height unknown.
This incomplete skeleton showed that the man had health problems in both arms, and in the upper joint of the two bones of his lower right leg

**FCS 21:** Age 13-18. Height 1.68m (5ft 6in).
He had stressed his spine and knee joints, and his spine had a severe unhealed compression that suggests that it might have been caused by a fall.

**FCS 22:** Age 18-30. Height 1.65m (5ft 5in).
His spine had probable spondylolysis, and the tops of his legs were damaged.

**FCS 23:** Age 18-30. Height 1.70m (5ft 7in).
Stress is reflected by his spine and right arm. His lower jaw had one abscess.

**FCS 24:** Age 13-18. Height unknown.
He had health problems in his spine and in his right arm.

**FCS 25:** Age18+. Height unknown.
Both of his lower leg bones had a healed spiral fracture, suggesting that he might have fallen and was caught by the rigging.

**FCS 34:** Age 18-30. Height unknown.
Little of his skeleton was found, but he had health problems with his spine, pelvis and legs. His lower right leg bone had an old healed wound in mid shaft.

**FCS 37:** Age 18-30. Height 1.74m (5ft 8.5in).
Health problems exist in his pelvis, and his spine has a fracture (spondylolysis?). His skull is pitted on the top. He had good teeth on the upper and lower jaws.

**FCS 67:** Age 18-30. Height 1.66 (5ft 5in).
All of his long bones had well-developed joints.

*Sectors H10 & H11, storage:*
No bodies were found.

## Orlop Deck
*Sector O1, storage compartment:*
As the ship's structure was very damaged at the bow, it is not surprising that no bodies were found in this sector.

*Sectors O2 & O3, storage compartment:*
**FCS 71:** Age 13-18. Height not known.
Few of his bones were found. His MtDNA haplotype may be M, and he may have been wearing an unusually well-finished leather jerkin for a small person, with a pocket on the inside, and round-toed shoes.

**FCS 72:** Age 18-30. Height not known.
Some stress is reflected by his spine and left arm.

**FCS 73:** Age 18-30. Height 1.71m (5ft 5.7in).
His pelvis shows stress, and the shins of both lower leg bones have what look like old wounds.

*Sector O4, servery:*
**FCS 2:** Age 13-18. Height 1.70m (5ft 7in).
His skeleton shows that had health problems in the upper right arm.

**FCS 13:** Age 18-30. Height unknown.
Possible damage existed in his spine, upper left arm, joints at the top of both legs, and in his right knee joint.

**FCS 14:** Age 30-40. Height 1.8m (5ft 11in).
He had huge and extremely robust bones, but his collar bones reflect severe stress. His poor health is reflected by damage to his spine, his right arm bones, the joint at the top of his right leg, and to both lower leg bones. With him was a leather jerkin, and possibly a rosary.

**FCS 15:** Age 13-18. Height unknown.
Much of his skeleton survives, and there is little trace of health problems, except that his spine and upper arm bones show signs of stress. With him was a leather jerkin.

**FCS 16:** Age 30-40. Height 1.67m (5ft 5in).
He was found lying over collapsed partition planks, with his spine and ribcage still in his leather calfskin jerkin. The jerkin had stitches for the cross of St. George, and there was the impression of a gunpowder flask on the leather skirt flap of the jerkin at waist level, where it presumably hung from a belt or chord. A comb and pocket sundial were found with him and suggest that he was a man of some status. He had a thimble ring which was found with his finger bones. His spine, sacrum and sternum had degenerated possibly due to lifting heavy weights. His skull showed that some of his teeth had been lost in his lifetime. He had six abscesses and two teeth with caries on his upper jaw, and one abscess and two teeth with caries on his lower jaw. He seems to have been a soldier or gunner.

**FCS 17:** Age 18+. Height unknown.
He had little sign of health problems.

**FCS 18:** Age 30-40. Height 1.70m (5ft 7in).
He had a stressed spine and problems with his pelvis.

*Sectors O5, cable lockers at the sides of the ship, and a central ventilation gap:*
No bodies were found.

*Sector O6, storage compartment:*
**FCS 79:** Age 18-30. Height 1.75m (5ft 9in).
His whole spine was stressed, and there was damage to his pelvis suggesting that he had had an accident in adolescence which had led to the poor fusion of his pelvis.

**FCS 80:** Age 18-30. Height 1.78m (5ft 10in).
His spine and both of his upper arms were stressed. In his skull were

nine surviving upper teeth, five of which had caries, and in his lower jaw were seven teeth, four of which had caries. He has a small healed depression on his forehead that may be an old wound.

*Sectors O7, O8 & O9, main storage compartment:*
**FCS 26:** Age 30-40. Height 1.75m (5ft 9in).
His skeleton revealed that he had health problems in both legs.

**FCS 27:** Age 30-40. Height unknown.
His spine was large and robust. His skull had two abscesses and four caries in the upper jaw, and caries in three teeth in the lower jaw. He may have been wearing a leather jerkin.

**FCS28:** Age 13-18. Height unknown.
His spine had spondylolysis and damage reflecting severe mid-back stress. His arms, elbows and pelvis also had health problems. He was wearing a leather jerkin.

**FCS 29:** Age 13-18. Height unknown.
His spine shows slight health problems, and his lower leg tibiae were bowed as if he had suffered childhood rickets. He was found with a leather jerkin, and a single round-toed shoe.

**FCS 30:** Age 18-30. Height unknown.
He had health problems in his upper right arm and spine. His skull had an old healed wound above the left ear, as if he had been hit from behind.

**FCS 31:** Age 18-30. Height 1.69m (5ft 6in).
Most of the lower part of his skeleton remained. His spine had an old healed compression fracture at its base, and there was a health problem in his right leg knee joint. His skull had one abscess and one tooth with caries. His lower jaw did not survive.

**FCS 32:** Age 18-30. Height 1.74m (5ft 8in).
Little of this skeleton survives, but it shows health problems in his spine. No skull was found, but his lower jaw had seven teeth that were healthy. He was found with a single round-toed ankle boot and a single square-toed shoe.

**FCS 33:** Age 18-30. Height unknown.
His spine and collar bones reflect health problems. He was found with a leather jerkin.

**FCS 35:** Age 30-40. Height 1.75m (5ft 9in).
He had health problems in his spine and pelvis. There was pitting on top of the skull, and although he mostly had good upper and lower teeth, he did have caries in three of his lower teeth at the back.

**FCS 36:** Age 13-18. Height 1.80m (5ft 11in).
He had health problems with upper arms and lower legs, and he was found with round toed shoes.

**FCS 38:** Age 40+. Height unknown.
His spine was stressed. His lower jaw was found and its fourteen teeth were healthy.

**FCS 81:** Age 30-40. Height 1.72m (5ft 7in).
His spine was stressed. Of his ten remaining upper teeth four had caries, and there was one abscess in his upper jaw, but his five surviving lower teeth were healthy. An oxygen isotope study suggests that he grew up in southern Europe, so he may have been a Spanish mercenary. He was found with a leather jerkin.

**FCS 87:** Age 18-30. Height 1.70m (5ft 7in).
His spine was stressed, but otherwise his skeleton seems healthy.

### Sector O10, storage compartment:
**FCS 88:** Age 30-40. Height not known.
He may have been a carpenter prepared to repair the ship if she was damaged by enemy gunfire near the waterline, since in the same area were found some carpentry tools. It has been suggested that he was the ship's Purser, a senior member of the ship's complement, but that is not possible as he was in such poor health that his mobility was impaired and he had suffered from hard labour. Moreover, the gold and silver coins found in a chest, have traditionally been associated with him simply because they were found nearby. But this was a personal chest, so the coins could not be Exchequer money to maintain the ship. In fact, the chest could have drifted from the chest store on the main gun deck immediately above.

His poor health is reflected by changes to the top of his leg bones which suggest that he had Perthes disease in childhood. This is where the top of the thigh bone softens, and although it had healed it could have left him with a limp. In later life his spine and hips had become stressed due to the hard labour that he had suffered. His face has been reconstructed.

*Sectors O11 & O12, storage compartment:*
No bodies were found.

## Main Gun Deck
*Sector M1:*
This forward part of the ship was largely destroyed, so no bodies were found.

*Sector M2-M3, including the forward cabin:*
**FCS 82:** Age 18-30. Height 1.68m (5ft 6in).
This man was probably an archer who had fallen from the upper gun deck down the companion way stairs that were attached to the aft face of the Forward Cabin. There was evidence of muscle stress on his pubis, and near him was found an ivory wristguard used by archers that might have been his. Much of his skeleton remains, and two of eleven surviving teeth in his skull had caries. Seven of his lower teeth were healthy. He had a large bone tumor on his left wrist, and sclerosis in his back. He was found lying on the main gun deck, and appeared to be wearing an elaborate jerkin of cattle and goat skin tied with an elaborate leather belt. The jerkin was found laced up on the left side with silk thread. His chest size was 112cm (44in), and his waist was 108cm (42.5in). With him were a comb and shoes.

**FCS 83:** Age 18-30. Height 1.82m (5ft 11in).
His pubis was stressed, possibly because he too was an archer. His spine had suffered some compression thereby causing both Schenermann's disease and Schmorl's nodes. His muscle attachments were very well developed, but his spine was noticeably stressed mid-section. With him was a large leather jerkin that he may have been wearing, and on his right side was a bundle or quiver of arrows tied with a strap. He lay aft of the stairs with his arms out, and with his lower left leg drawn up as if he was kneeling. He was wearing shoes, in one of which was found his foot bones. His skull survives, and his eight surviving upper teeth are healthy. He was apparently wearing a side-fastened leather jerkin stitched with silk thread.

*Sector M3:*
**FCS 74:** Age 18-30. Height 1.69m (5ft 6in).
There is little doubt that this man was a gunner as his spine shows an extraordinary amount of stress, as if he had suffered extreme loading. He was trapped against the main gun deck on the starboard side, and was wearing a jerkin, a belt and shoes.

**FCS 75:** Age 18-30. Height 1.70m (5ft 7in).

He was probably part of a gun crew with FCS 76 and 77, and had a severely stressed spine. He had damaged his right elbow which restricted its use. This had given him osteoarthritis probably in his adolescence. His right arm bone was very thick and strong, with muscle attachments that were very well developed. He wore a finger ring bearing the letter 'K'. With him were a silver coin, a comb, a decorated knife sheath, a pewter spoon, and a wooden bowl.

**FCS 76:** Age 18-30. Height not known.

His spine was stressed, and he is thought to be part of a gun crew with FCS 75 and 77.

**FCS 77:** Age 18-30. Height 1.68m (5ft 6in).

He had a very stressed spine due to extreme pulling, pushing and lifting forces so that his vertebrae had the appearance of a much older man. All ligament insertions were very well developed. He is thought to be part of the gun crew with FCS 75 and 76.

**FCS 78:** Age 18-30. Height 1.61m (5ft 3in).

He had gracile bones that were delicate and poorly muscled, so he may have been a gentleman or servant.

*Sector M4:*

**FCS 84:** Age 30-40. Height 1.63m (5ft 4in).

He may have been a Boatswain as he was found on the main gun deck with a Boatswain's call or whistle. With him was a also pair of squared-toed shoes. Much of his skeleton was found, his hands having very developed finger attachments. In his skull were nine upper teeth only one of which had has caries, though there was an abscess in his upper jaw. Of five teeth that survived in his lower jaw only one had caries, but there was one abscess.

**FCS 91:** Age 18-30. Height 1.73m (5ft 8in).

He had a very strong and robust skeleton, and was possibly a gunner.

*Sector M5:*

No bodies were found.

*Sector M6:*

**FCS 68:** Age 18-30. Height 1.74m (5ft 8in).

The joints of his left arm, right shoulder and lower legs showed stress.

**FCS 69:** Age 18-30. Height not known.

His spine was stressed and had traces of scoliosis. His skull and lower jaw survive, with some upper and lower teeth, all of which were healthy.

**FCS 70:** Age 18-30. Height 1.78m (5ft 10in).

He may have been an archer, for he seems to have been wearing a leather jerkin, and may have been wearing an archer's wristguard decorated with the Royal Arms. He apparently carried a comb in a pouch. A longbow lay beside him, with a scabbard and a sword hanger with an attached pomander. He had scoliosis of the spine, and possibly Scheuermann's disease. His skull survives with sixteen teeth, ten of which had caries. His lower jaw also survives with three teeth, one of which had caries.

*Sector M7:*

**FCS 86:** Age 18-30. Height 1.61m (5ft 3in).

This man had a stressed spine. His skull and lower jaw were found and although eight upper teeth were healthy, of thirteen teeth that survive in his lower jaw six had caries. A rosary and an arrow spacer lay near this man.

*Sector M8:*

**FCS 85:** Age 18-30. Height 1.65m (5ft 5in).

No health problems were found on this man's skeleton.

*Sector M9:*

No bodies were found.

*Sector M10:*

**FCS 89:** Age 30-40. Height 1.76m (5ft 9in).

He had a stressed spine, and his left arm was more developed than his right arm. His hips and knee joints were stressed, and his skeleton was like that of an older man. He may have been a gunner.

*Sector M11:*

No bodies were found.

*Sector M12:*

No bodies were found.

## Upper Gun Deck

*Sector U1:*
The forward part of the ship was completely eroded away, so no bodies were found.

*Sector U2:*
Although no bodies were found, it is likely that FCS 82 and FCS 83, probably archers, had been on the upper gun deck just before the ship sank. In the sinking they may have fallen through a hatch (now eroded) and down the surviving stairs on the aft side of the Forward Cabin, so that they were found in sector M2 of the main gun deck.

*Sector U3:*
There were no bodies. This sector marked the forward end of the ship's waist.

*Sector U4:*
No bodies were found in the ship's waist.

*Sector U5:*
No bodies were found in the ship's waist.

*Sector U6:*
No bodies were found at the after end of the ship's waist.

*Sector U7:*
This sector marked the forward end of the sterncastle that covered the upper gun deck. The men listed in sectors U7 to U10 appear to have been mainly armed soldiers waiting to board an enemy vessel.

**FCS 65:** Age 18-30. Height 1.72 (5ft 7in).
There was severe strain on the spine of this man, who may have had Scheuermann's disease. His MtDNA haplotype, derived from his mother, was possibly H.

**FCS 66:** Age 18-30. Height 1.77m (5ft 9in).
His pelvis was damaged, and his right upper leg bone was found twisted, bowed and flattened, and had a dropped head, as if to suggest that it was fractured or dislocated in his youth. His left lower leg bone was thickened as if he had been wounded years earlier.

*Sector U8:*
**FCS 60:** Age 13-18. Height not known.

He had few bones.

**FCS 61:** Age 18-30. Height 1,68m (5ft 6in).
The bottom of his upper left leg bone was healed from damage.

**FCS 62:** Age 18-30. Height 1.72m (5ft 7in).
He had few bones.

**FCS 63:** Age 18-30. Height 1.70m (5ft 7in).
His spine and sacrum had marked scoliosis, and the left side of his pelvis suggests that he had a torn attachment, possibly resulting from heavy lifting.

**FCS 90:** Age 18+. Height 1.69m (5ft 6in).
Both of his lower legs were bowed.

*Sector U9:*
**FCS 39:** Age 18-30. Height 1.70m (5ft 7in).
The top of his right leg was damaged, possibly after his death, by severe violence which had forced it out of the pelvis socket. The upper teeth in his skull were healthy, though two at the back had caries.

**FCS 40:** Age 18-30. Height 1.76m (5ft 9in).
His spine showed stress, and there were health problems in his pelvis. His upper jaw had four abscesses and there were caries in two teeth. In his lower jaw were five abscesses, and there were caries in two teeth.

**FCS 41:** Age 18-30. Height 1.74m (5ft 8in).
His spine and pelvis show signs of stress. His upper leg bones were bowed, suggesting that he had healed rickets in his childhood.

**FCS 43:** Age 18-30. Height 1.79m (5ft 10in).
Stress had affected his left arm, pelvis and legs.

**FCS 44:** Age 30-40. Height 1.80m (5ft 11in).
He had osteoarthritis and a stressed spine, pelvis and arms. His right elbow had been severely damaged, but there was new bone growth showing that this had occurred some weeks before the ship sank.

**FCS 47:** Age 18-30. Height 1.74m (5ft 8.5in).
Both of his lower legs were bowed, and the base of the spine was damaged, suggesting that he had rickets in his childhood, though it is possible that he had an adult form of rickets.

**FCS 48:** Age 18-30. Height 1.70m (5ft 7in).
His lower legs were stressed. With him was a leather jerkin with an applied scalloped decoration to the skirt, a wooden spoon, a leather pouch, a kidney dagger, chain mail, and a boarding pike.

**FCS 49:** Age 18-30. Height 1.74m (5ft 8.5in).
His right arm was more robust than his left.

**FCS 50:** Age 18-30. Height 1.72m (5ft 7in).
He had a stressed pelvis, and his arms were robust and well-muscled.

**FCS 51:** Age 18-30. Height 1.78m (5ft 10in).
Both of his legs were bowed, and his spine had Scheuermann's disease. His pelvis was stressed.

**FCS 52:** Age 18-30. Height 1.72m (5ft 7in).
Few of his bones were found.

**FCS 54:** Age 18-30. Height 1.70m (5ft 7in).
Few of his bones were found.

**FCS 55:** Age 13-18. Height not known.
A reasonable amount of his skeleton survived, and he showed no sign of stress or damage.

**FCS 56:** Age 13-18. Height not known.
Few of his bones were found.

**FCS 57:** Age 18-30. Height not known.
Few of his bones were found.

**FCS 58:** Age 18-30. Height not known.
Few of his bones were found.

**FCS 59:** Age 18-30. Height not known.
Few of his bones were found.

*Sector U10:*
**FCS 64:** Age 18-30. Height not known.
Severe ossification existed in the lower part of his spine. His skull had eight surviving teeth, six of which had caries.

*Sector U11:*
No bodies were found.

*Sector U12:*
No bodies were found.

## Sterncastle Decks

The very eroded state of FCS 42, 45, 46 and 53 shows that they had been exposed to tidal erosion higher up in the sterncastle, in the region where the ship was originally steered and commanded by officers. They had evidently fallen onto the upper gun deck when the sterncastle broke up.

*Sector U9:*
**FCS 42:** Age 18-30. Height 1.70m (5ft 7in).
His spine was stressed.

**FCS 45:** Age 18-30. Height 1.67m (5ft 5in).
His right arm and left leg were stressed.

**FCS 46:** Age 30-40. Height 1.66m (5ft 5in).
His upper arms were stressed.

**FCS 53:** Age 18-30. Height 1.68m (5ft 6in).
His pelvis and parts of legs and arms survive, and they are gracile, suggesting that he was a gentleman.

*Sterncastle:*
Four pear-shaped decorative dress hangings or buttons covered in red silk were found in sector U9 with part of a disintegrated silk garment, several threads of which were attached to the spine of a skeleton. Dress, or Sumptuary Laws of Henry VIII decreed that only a knight or son of a lord were entitled to dress themselves in red silk, so these items suggest that they are the remains of a person of noble rank, such as Vice-Admiral Sir George Carew or Roger Granville. His remains may be identified in future by comparing his DNA with that of modern members of the families.

## Forecastle Decks

The forecastle had completely eroded away as an intact structure, so no human skeletons were found.

# ENDNOTES

## INTRODUCTION

1. The main publications relating to the *Mary Rose* are: Marsden 2003; Gardiner 2005; Marsden 2009; Hildred 2011; Jones 2015; Knighton and Loades 2000; Knighton and Loades 2002; Knighton, Fontana and Loades 2002; McElvogue 2015.
2. Potter 2011; Knighton and Loades 2002; McElvogue 2015.

## CHAPTER 1

1. Found in sector U4.
2. Marsden 2009, p. 164.
3. Ibid., p. 392.
4. Marsden 2003, pp. 181-2.
5. Horsey 1841, p. 43.
6. Bellay 1569.
7. Hooker 1595 in Marsden 2003, pp. 181-2.
8. Gardiner 2005, pp. 447-8, 493.

## CHAPTER 2

1. *CSP*, in Marsden 2003, p. 150, no. 2. The 1546 picture of both ships on the Anthony Roll show that the *Mary Rose* and her sister ship *Peter Pomegranate* were both carracks.
2. Ibid., p. 150, no. 3.
3. Ibid., p. 150, nos. 8, 9.
4. Ibid., pp. 167-70, no. 106.
5. Friel 1995, pp. 142, 155.
6. Oman 1963, pls. xv-xvii.
7. Laughton and Lewis 1960, p. 254.
8. Salisbury 1961; Oppenheim 1896b, p. 47.
9. *CSP*, in Marsden 2003, pp. 150-1, nos. 10-23.
10. Knighton and Loades 2000, pp. 139-42.
11. Oppenheim 1896b.
12. *CSP*, in Marsden 2003, p. 151, no. 20.
13. Oppenheim 1896a, p. 62.
14. Knighton and Loades 2000, p. 42.
15. Marsden 2003, p. 9.
16. Hildred 2011, pp. 882-92.
17. *CSP*, Henry VIII, p. 287; Rule 1983, pp. 13-15.
18. *CSP*, in Marsden 2003, p. 156, no. 27.
19. Ibid., p. 156, no. 55.
20. Nelson 2001, p. 43.

## CHAPTER 3

1. Spont 1897.
2. *CSP*, in Marsden, pp. 151-2, nos. 24, 32.
3. Ibid., p. 153, nos. 37, 38.

4. Ibid., p. 152, nos. 28, 31.
5. A detailed description of the battle is in Knighton and Loades 2002, pp. 10-68.
6. *CSP*, in Marsden 2003, pp. 152-3, nos. 35, 36, 39.
7. Ibid., p. 152, no. 35; Moorhouse 2005, p. 73.
8. Ibid., p. 153, no. 36.
9. Ibid., p. 154, no. 40.
10. Ibid., pp. 156-8, no. 58.
11. Ibid., pp. 156-8, no. 58.
12. Ibid., pp. 156-8, no. 60.
13. Ibid., p. 158, nos. 60, 61.
14. Ibid., pp. 158-9, no. 61.
15. Ibid., p. 160, nos. 63, 64.
16. Ibid., p. 162, no. 72.
17. Ibid., p. 162, no. 73.
18. Ibid., p. 163, no. 78.
19. Ibid., p. 164, no. 83.
20. Ibid., p. 165, no. 91.
21. Sadler 2006.
22. *CSP*, in Marsden 2003, p. 166, no. 94.
23. Ibid., pp. 166-7, no. 105. It has been incorrectly suggested elsewhere that a picture by Anthony Anthony of Brighton refers to this attack.

## CHAPTER 4

1. *CSP*, in Marsden 2003, pp. 167-70, no. 106.
2. Ibid., p. 170, no. 107.
3. Ibid., p. 170, no. 109.
4. Ibid., p. 171, no. 113.
5. Ibid., p. 114.
6. Ibid., p. 172, no. 120.
7. Salisbury 1961.
8. *CSP*, Henry VIII, 1714, p. 762; *CSP*, in Marsden 2003, p. 174, no. 130.
9. *CSP*, in Marsden 2003, p. 175, nos. 135, 136.

## CHAPTER 5

1. Nelson 2001, pp. 43-4.
2. *CSP*, in Marsden 2003, p. 176, no. 138.
3. Dobbs and Bridge 2009.
4. *CSP*, in Marsden 2003, p. 176, no. 139.
5. *CSP*, Henry VIII, *Acts of the Privy Council*, 21 August 1545; Oppenheim 1896a, p. 73.
6. Oppenheim 1896a, pp. 73-4.
7. *Fragments of Ancient Shipwrightry* 1582.
8. *CSP*, Henry VIII, *Acts of the Privy Council*, 22 April 1548; Oppenheim 1896a, p. 73.
9. Dobbs and Bridge 2009.

10. Knighton and Loades 2000, pp. 42-3. McElvogue has suggested that the gunports might be original features from when the ship was built, though evidence indicates that they were probably added later. See McElvogue 2015, p. 18.

11. Marsden 2009, p. 363. The rising knees beside the main deck gunports have been tree-ring dated as follows: at M3 it is after 1526 (no sapwood), at M4 after 1530 (13 sapwood rings remain) and at M8 the knee dates from after 1528 (23 sapwood rings remain).

12. Knighton and Loades 2002, pp. 101-05.

## CHAPTER 6

1. *CSP*, 10 April 1544, Privy Council to Hertford.
2. *CSP*, 28 April 1544, fleet instructions; Hall 1548.
3. Corbett 1905.
4. *CSP*, 6 June 1513; Knighton and Loades 2002, text 29.
5. *CSP*, 22 May 1544; Potter 2011, p. 349.
6. Potter 2011, pp. 1-7, where plague is discussed.
7. *CSP*, 7 May 1545, St. Mauris to Cobos.
8. Potter 2011, p. 353.
9. Potter 2011, pp. 353-4.
10. Hall 1548, p. 863.
11. Potter 2011, p.350.
12. *CSP*, 7 May 1545, St. Mauris to Cobos.
13. Potter 2011, p. 354.
14. Ibid., p. 356.
15. Ibid., p. 360.
16. Marsden 2003, p. 177, no. 144.
17. Hall 1548, p. 863.
18. *CSP*, 27 July 1545, St. Mauris to Cobos.
19. Ibid., 27 July 1545, St. Mauris to Cobos.
20. Potter 2011, p. 375.
21. Ibid., p. 376.
22. Bellay 1569, vol. IV.
23. *CSP*, 24 July 1545, Delft to Emperor.
24. Bellay 1569.

## CHAPTER 7

1. *CSP*, 24 July 1545, Delft to Emperor.
2. *CSP*, 21 August 1545, Scepperus and Delft to Queen Dowager.
3. Gardiner 2005, p. 266.
4. *CSP*, 19 July 1545, news to be sent to the Emperor.
5. Gardiner 2005, pp. 250-63.
6. *CSP*, 24 July 1545, Delft to Emperor.
7. Ibid.
8. Ibid.
9. MRT 2010, p. 7.
10. Cowdray engraving.
11. MRT 2010, p. 5.
12. Gardiner 2005, pp. 593-4.
13. Corbett 1905.

14. Knighton and Loades 2000.
15. Ibid.
16. Ibid.
17. Pulvertaft 2016, pp. 331-5.
18. *CSP*, in Marsden 2003, p. 177 no. 144; *CSP*, Addenda I-II, 1697, p. 569.
19. Knighton and Loades 2000, p. 65.
20. Ibid, pp. 34-7.
21. Bellay 1659.
22. *CSP*, 24 July 1545, Delft to Emperor.
23. Ibid.
24. Ibid.
25. Embarkation painting.
26. Knighton and Loades 2000, pp. 72-3.
27. MOD 1965, p. 105.
28. Goodman 2015, pp. 121-2.
29. Gardiner 2005, pp. 441, 489-96.
30. *CSP*, 24 July 1545, Delft to Emperor.
31. *CSP*, in Marsden 2003, pp. 181-2, no. 168.
32. Corbett 1905; Knighton and Loades 2000, p. 159.
33. *CSP*, 24 July 1545, Delft to Emperor.
34. *CSP*, 23 July 1545, Russell to Privy Council.
35. *CSP*, 24 July 1545, Delft to Emperor.
36. Ibid.
37. Ibid.
38. Gardiner 2005, pp. 492-3.
39. *CSP*, 23 July 1545, Russell to Privy Council.
40. *CSP*, 24 July 1545, Delft to Emperor.
41. Ibid.
42. Bellay 1569.
43. Ibid.
44. Knighton and Loades 2000, p. 159.
45. Potter 2011, p. 376 An early illustration of a *Contarina* is in Abulafin 2003. However, as a succession of Venetian galleys had this name there is no certainty that this particular vessel was in the Battle of the Solent in July 1545.

## CHAPTER 8

1. Corbett 1905; Knighton and Loades 2000, p. 159; *CSP*, in Marsden 2003, p. 177, no. 145.
2. Marsden 2009, p.392.
3. Ibid., pp. 198-204.
4. Ibid., pp. 203, 206.
5. Smith 1627, p. 34.
6. *DNB*, 'Sir George Carew'.
7. Granville 1895. However, some details are given about Roger Granville that are disputed, particularly as to whether or not he was knighted.
8. *DNB*, 'Sir George Carew'.
9. Gardiner 2005, p. 97, fig. 2,76, objects nos. 81A4518-81A5421.
10. Gardiner 2005, p. 19.
11. Object 81A0689.

12. Gardiner 2005, p. 113.
13. Ibid., pp. 439, 449, 492-3.
14. Object 81A2573, sector M8.
15. Gardiner 2005, p. 666.
16. *CSP*, in Marsden 2003, p. 178, no. 149; *CSP*, 24 July 1545, Delft to Emperor.
17. Smith 1627, p. 34.
18. Ibid., p. 35.
19. Gardiner 2005, p. 22.
20. An excellent account of this is given in Goodwin 2012, pp. 132-61.
21. FCS 8 (sector H2), 9 (H2), 19 (H7), 20 (H7), 22 (H7), 23 (H8), 25 (H8), 26 (O7), 27 (O7), 30 (O7), 31 (O7), 32 (O7), 33 (O8), 34 (O8), 37 (H7), 67 (H9), 72 (O3), 79 (O6), 80 (O6), 81 (O9), 87 (O7).
22. Gardiner 2005, p. 92.
23. Ibid.
24. Ibid., pp. 22-55. FCS 33 (sector O8) was found with leather jerkin 82A5034.
25. Pietsch 2005, p. 13. The average age and height of boys then was – age 12 (4ft. 3ins.), 13 (4ft. 4ins.), 14 (4ft. 6ins.), 15 (4ft. 7 ins.), 16 (4ft. 9 ins.), 17 (4 ft. 10 ins.), 18 (4 ft. 11 ins.), 19 (5 ft.).
26. Gardiner 2005, pp. 47-8; Object 81A2592.
27. Smith 1627, p. 36.
28. Gardiner 2005, pp. 46-8.
29. Ibid., pp. 422-96.
30. Ibid., p. 593.
31. Ibid., p. 255, 262.
32. Smith 1627, p. 35.
33. Oppenheim 1896b, p. 258.
34. Gardiner 2005, pp. 284-5.
35. Ibid., pp. 281-284.
36. Knighton, Fontana and Loades 2017.
37. Smith 1627.
38. Ibid., pp. 37-40; Knighton and Loades 2000, pp. 113-58; Goodwin 2012, pp. 130-53.
39. Smith 1627, p. 38.
40. Ibid.
41. Knighton and Loades 2000, pp. 139-42.
42. Harland 1984, p. 237.
43. Smith 1627, pp. 12, 35.
44. Marsden 2009, p. 377.
45. Ibid., p. 379.
46. Marsden 2003, p, 162, no. 73.
47. Marsden 2009, p. 278, fig, 15.7, object 15A0104.
48. Ibid., pp. 261-2.
49. Oman 1963, pl. XV-XVII.
50. Embarkation painting.
51. Knighton and Loades 2000, pp. 139-42.
52. Smith 1627, pp. 34-5.
53. Goodwin 2012, p. 118.

CHAPTER 9

1. Admiralty tidal predictions for 19 July 1545 on the Julian calendar (29 July on the modern Georgian calendar).
2. Oppenheim 1986a, p. 80.
3. Ibid.
4. *CSP*, 24 July 1545, Delft to Emperor.
5. Smith 1627, pp. 58-60.
6. *CSP*, 19 July 1545, Paget to Russell.
7. Hall 1548, p. 863.
8. *CSP*, 24 July 1545, Delft to Emperor.
9. Potter 2011, p. 377; Bellay 1569.
10. Hildred 2011, p. 156, 903 states that gun M8 was found partly loaded.
11. See also Potter 2011, p. 376; *CSP*, 24 July 1545, Delft to Emperor.
12. *CSP*, 24 July 1545, Delft to Emperor.
13. Ibid.
14. Corbett 1905.
15. Bellay 1569.
16. *CSP*, 16 August 1545, intelligence from France.
17. Knighton and Loades 2000, pp. 64-79.
18. Bellay 1569.
19. *CSP*, 24 July 1545, Delft to Emperor.
20. Bellay 1569.
21. Oglander 2017.
22. Ibid.
23. *CSP*, 24 July 1545, Delft to Emperor.
24. *CSP*, 21 July 1545, Privy Council to Lord Admiral.
25. *CSP*, 21 July 1545, Privy Council to Anthony Anthony.
26. Hall 1548, p. 863.
27. Wriothesley 1895, p. 158.
28. Bellay 1569.
29. *CSP*, 21 July 1545, Privy Council.
30. *CSP*, 21 July 1545, Lisle to Henry VIII.
31. *CSP*, 24 July 1545, Delft to Queen Dowager.
32. Bellay 1569.
33. Ibid.
34. *CSP*, 24 July 1545, Delft to Emperor.
35. *CSP*, 23 July 1545, Privy Council.
36. *CSP*, 24 July 1545, Delft to Emperor; *CSP*, 25 July 1545, Russell to Privy Council.
37. Bellay 1569.
38. *CSP*, 26 July 1545, Vaughan to Lord Cobham.
39. Carr Laughton 1916.
40. *CSP*, 24 July 1545, Paget to Buckler and Mount.
41. *CSP* (incorrectly dated) 22 July 1545, Gawge to Justices; *CSP*, 26 July 1545, Sir John Gage and Sir Edmund Peckham to Lord Cobham. Sir John Gage's house was Firle Place, inland from Seaford.
42. *CSP*, 25 July 1545, Privy Council.
43. *CSP*, 26-27 July 1545, Privy Council.
44. *CSP*, 27 July 1545, Russell in Dartmouth to Paget in Portsmouth.

45. *CSP*, 27 July 1545, Mayor and Burgesses of Saltash to Russell.
46. *CSP*, 28 July 1545, St. Maurice to Cobos.
47. *CSP*, 31 July 1545, Lord Poynings to Henry VIII.

### CHAPTER 10

1. *CSP*, 7 August 1545, Lisle to Paget.
2. Ibid., Russell in Exeter to Paget.
3. *CSP*, 17 August 1545, Russell in Exeter to Privy Council.
4. *CSP*, 7 August 1545, St. Mauris to Cobos.
5. Potter 2011, p. 385, fn. 156 for sources of the French account of the battle.
6. *CSP*, 11 August 1545, Lord Poynings in Boulogne to the Lord Deputy of Calais.
7. *CSP*, 7 August 1545, Lisle to Paget.
8. *CSP*, 11 August 1545, Privy Council.
9. *CSP*, 12 August 1545, Lisle to Henry VIII.
10. *CSP*, 15 August 1545, Lisle to Henry VIII; Potter 2011, p. 383.
11. *CSP*, 18 August 1545, Lisle to Henry VIII; Potter 2011, pp. 384-5; *CSP*, 25 August 1545, Paget to Norfolk, quoted in Potter 2011, pp. 383-4; *CSP*, 16 August 1545, Lisle to Bellingham.
12. Potter 2011, p. 385; *CSP*, October(?) 1545, St. Mauris to King of the Romans; *CSP*, 17 August 1545, Delft in Guildford to Emperor.
13. *CSP*, 17 August 1545, Lisle to Gage.
14. *CSP*, 18 August 1545, Lisle to Henry VIII.
15. Potter 2011, pp. 387-8 for a discussion on the effect on the French people.
16. *CSP*, 21 August 1545, Lisle to Paget.
17. *CSP*, 21 August 1545, Lisle to Henry VIII.
18. *CSP*, 20 August 1545, Lisle to Lord St. John (Sir William Paulet).
19. *CSP*, 11 September 1545, Lisle, Seymour and Lord St. John to Henry VIII.
20. *CSP*, October? 1545, St. Mauris to the King of the Romans. The date of the attack is discussed in Potter 2011, p. 387, fn. 165.
21. *CSP*, 11 September 1545, Lisle, Seymour and Lord St. John to Henry VIII. The infected ships were listed in a book of the fleet, with those that were infected indicated by a *: the *New Hulk* of Lubeck, *Jesus* of Lubeck, *Christopher* of Dansck, *Pawncye*\*, *Ann Galauntet*, *Murrey*, *Mary Hamburg*\*, *Lesse Galey*\*, *Sweepstake*, *Pellycane*\*, *Strikill* of Dansk, *Mynyon*, *Salamander*\*, *Unycorn*\*, *Swalowe*\*, *Jenett*, *Fawcone Lisle*\*, *Christopher Benett*, *Evangelist Jud*\*, *Lyone*, *Dragon*, *Mary Fortune*, *Phenyx*\*, *Hynd*, *Marlion*, *Less Pynnes*, *Ronagers Pynnes*, *Greyhound*, *Fawcon*, *Roo*, *Sakre*, *George* of Totnes\*, *Hare*, *Unycorne* of Poole.
22. *CSP*, October? 1545, St Maurice to the King of the Romans.

23. *CSP*, French Embassy no. 1384; *CSP*, 31 August 1545, Privy Council to Wotten.
24. *CSP*, 15 May 1546, Lisle to Sir William Petre.
25. Ibid.

### CHAPTER 11

1. References to the salvage of the *Mary Rose* in 1545–1546 are given in Marsden 2003, pp. 20, 179-82, and in Knighton and Loades 2003, pp. 121-33.
2. See Horsey 1841.
3. *CSP*, in Marsden 2003, p. 182.
4. Ibid., pp. 21-9.

### CHAPTER 12

1. The rediscovery of the *Mary Rose* and what followed is described in Marsden 2003, pp. 30-9. Also in McKee 1968, and in Rule 1983.
2. Marsden 2003; Gardiner 2005; Marsden 2009; Hildred 2011; Jones 2005.
3. Knighton and Loades 2002; Stirland 2005; McElvogue 2015.
4. Potter 2011.

### CHAPTER 13

1. Knighton and Loades 2000, pp. 42-3.
2. Embarkation painting; Nelson 2001, p. 40.
3. Marsden 2003, p. 28.
4. Smith 1627.
5. Marsden 2003, p. 162.
6. Marsden 2009, pp. 377-8.
7. Ibid., p. 149.
8. 370 logs were found on the orlop deck servery in sector O4, with 49 in the adjacent compartment O5. 90 were in the galley in sector H5 with the ovens, and 65 were adjacent in sector H4. Otherwise they were scattered nearby as follows: in sector H2-5 logs, H3-4 logs, H6-8 logs, H7-16 logs, H8-8 logs, H9-1 log; O2-2 logs, O3-3 logs, O6-15 logs, O7-2 logs, O8-6 logs, O9-3 logs, O10-3 logs; M3-5 logs, M4-10 logs, M5-5 logs.
9. Oppenheim 1896a, p. 80.
10. Dobbs in Marsden 2009, pp. 119-23.

### CHAPTER 14

1. Hildred 2011, pp. 223, 227-36.
2. Knighton and Hildred 2011, pp. 942-5; Marsden 2009, pp. 277-8.
3. Gardiner 2005, p. 19.
4. Ibid., pp. 381-2.
5. Marsden 2009, p. 252.
6. Pulvertaft 2016.
7. Hildred 2011, pp. 522-9.

**CHAPTER 15**
1. Marsden 2003, p. 178, no. 149.
2. Smith 1627, p. 12.
3. Gardiner 2005, p. 599.
4. Ibid., pp. 85-6.
5. Stirland 2002.
6. Carr Laughton and Lewis 1960, p. 270; Marsden 2009, p. 379.
7. Marsden 2009, pp. 197-209.

**CHAPTER 16**
1. Gardiner 2005, pp. 171-224.
2. *CSP*, 1 August 1545, Suffolk to Henry VIII.
3. Hildred 2011, p. 52, but see also p. 903 which says that it was not loaded.

**CHAPTER 17**
1. Gardiner 2005, p. 227.
2. Goodwin 2012, p. 118.

**CHAPTER 18**
1. Gardiner 2005, pp. 446-8, 493. The bowl was from sector U8 on the upper gun deck, and the tankard was from sector M9 on the main gun deck.
2. Ibid., pp. 422-96.

3. Marsden 2009, fig. 20.1, p. 369.
4. Gardiner 2005, p. 626.

**CHAPTER 19**
1. Marsden 2009, p. 392.
2. Ibid., p. 347.
3. Ibid., pp. 377-8.
4. Hocker 2011.
5. *CSP*, 15 May 1546, Lisle to Petre.
6. Marsden 2009, pp. 377-8.

**CHAPTER 20**
1. Jones and Stone 2018.
2. Friel 1995, p. 155.
3. Ibid., pp. 10-11.
4. *DNB*, 'Sir George Carew' and 'Sir Arthur Champernowne'; Orme 2014.

**APPENDIX A**
1. Smith 1627 and 1691.

**APPENDIX B**
1. Bell, Lee-Thorp and Elkerton 2009a; Bell, Lee-Thorp and Elkerton 2009b.

# BIBLIOGRAPHY

Abulafin 2003: Abulafin, D (ed). *The Mediterranean in History*. Thames and Hudson.

Bell, Lee-Thorp and Elkerton 2009: Bell, L., J. Lee-Thorp and A. Elkerton. 'The Sinking of the Mary Rose Warship: A Medieval Mystery Solved?'. *Journal of Archaeological Science*, 36, pp. 166-73.

Bell, Lee-Thorp and Elkerton 2009: Bell L., J. Lee-Thorp and A. Elkerton. '"Sailing Against the Wind". Reply to Mullard and Schroder, "True British Sailors": A Comment on the Origin of the Men of the Mary Rose'. *Journal of Archaeological Science*, 37, pp. 683-6.

Bellay 1569: Bellay, M. 1495–1559: *Les memoires de Mess. Martin du Bellay*, vol. IV. Paris 1569. A selective translation is in *Memoirs of Martin du Bellay*, extracted by Percy Stone, reprinted from Isle of Wight County Press, 2 November 1907.

Bennell 2000: Bennell, J. 'The Oared Vessels', in Knighton & Loades 2000, pp. 34-7.

Besly 2005: Besly, E. 'Coins and Jettons', in Gardiner 2005, pp. 250-63.

Carr Laughton 1916: Carr Laughton, L. 'The Burning of Brighton by the French'. *Trans. Royal Historical Society*, pp. 167-73.

Carr Laughton and Lewis 1960: Carr Laughton, L. and Lewis, M. 'Early Tudor Ship-guns'. *Mariners' Mirror*, 46, pp. 242-85.

Corbett 1905: Corbett, J. *Fighting Instructions 1530–1816*. Navy Records Society, XXIX.

Cowdray engraving. See Ayloffe, J. 'An Account of Some English Historical Paintings at Cowdray, in Sussex'. *Archaeologia*, 3, pp. 239-72.

CSP: *Calendar of Letters and Papers, Foreign and Domestic of the Reign of Henry VIII, preserved in the Public Record Office, the British Museum and Elsewhere*. HMSO. Also, *Calendar of State Papers and Manuscripts Relating to English Affairs Existing in the Archives of Venice*. Volume II, 1509–1519. Edited by R. Brown, London, 1867.

DNB: *Dictionary of National Biography*.

Dobbs and Bridge 2009: Dobbs, C. and Bridge, M. 'Construction and Refits: Tree-ring Dating the *Mary Rose*', in Marsden 2009, pp. 361-7.

Embarkation c1540: *Embarkation of Henry VIII at Dover*. Painting at Hampton Court.

Friel 1993: Friel, I. 'Henry V's *Grace Dieu*, and the Wreck in the River Hamble near Bursledon, Hampshire'. *International Journal of Nautical Archaeology*, 22, pp. 3-19.

Friel 1995: Friel, I. *The Good Ship, Shipbuilding and Technology in England 1200–1520*. British Museum Press.

Gardiner 2005: Gardiner, J. with Allen, M. (eds). *Before the Mast: Life and Death Aboard the Mary Rose*. Mary Rose Trust, volume 4.

Goodman 2015: Goodman, R. *How to be a Tudor: A Dawn to Dusk Guide to Everyday Life*. Penguin.

Goodwin 1992: Goodwin, J. *Bonchurch from A-Z*. The Bonchurch Trading Company.

Goodwin 2012: Goodwin, P. *HMS Victory, 1765–1812 (First Rate Ship of the Line). Owners' Workshop Manual*. Haynes Publishing.

Granville 1895: Granville, R. *The History of the Granville Family Traced Back to Rollo, First Duke of Normandy*. William Pollard and Co.

Hall 1548: Hall, E. *Chronicle: Containing the History of England*.

Hamilton Papers, *Letters and Papers Illustrating the Political Relations of England and Scotland in the XVI Century*. Edited by Joseph Baine. Volume IX. General Register Office, Scotland.

Harland 1985: Harland, J. *Seamanship in the Age of Sail*. Conway Maritime.

Harris 2014: Harris, O. 'The Generations of Adam: The Monument of Sir Gawen Carew in Exeter Cathedral'. *Church Monuments*, XXIX, pp. 40-71.

Hildred 2011: Hildred, A (ed). *Weapons of Warre: The Armaments of the Mary Rose*. Mary Rose Trust, volume 3.

Hocker 2011: Hocker, F. *Vasa: A Swedish Warship*. Medstroms Bokforlag.

Hooker 1595: Hooker, J. *The Lyffe of Sir Peter Carew, late of Mohonse Otrey, in the Countie of Devon, Knyghte, whoe dyed at Rosse, in Irelande, the 27th of November, 1575, and was buryed at the Cettie of Water Forde, the 15 of December, 1575; collected by John Vowell, al's Hoker, of the Cetie of Excester, Gent. partly upon the credible reporte of others, and partly wch he sawe and knewe hyme selfe*. Published by Phillips (1839), pp. 96–151.

Horsey 1841: Horsey, S. *A Narrative of the Loss of the Royal George at Spithead, August 1783*. Horsey.

Jones 2015: Jones, M. *For Future Generations: Conservation of a Tudor Maritime Collection*. Mary Rose Trust.

Jones and Stone 2018: Jones, E. and Stone, R. *The World of the Newport Medieval Ship*. University of Wales Press.

Kelland and Holt 2014. Kelland, N. and Holt, P. *Surveying, Excavating and Raising the Mary Rose*. Sonardyne.

Knighton 2000: Knighton, C. 'The Manuscript and its Compiler', in Knighton, Fontana and Loades 2000, pp. 3-11.

Knighton and Hildred 2011: Knighton, C. and Hildred, A, in Hildred 2011, pp. 942-5.

Knighton and Loades 2000: Knighton, C. and Loades, D. (eds). *The Anthony Roll of Henry VIII's Navy*. Navy Records Society and British Library.

Knighton and Loades 2002: Knighton, C. and Loades, D. *Letters from the Mary Rose*. Sutton.

Knighton, Fontana and Loades 2017: Knighton. C., Fontana, D., and Loades, D. (eds). 'More Documents for the Last Campaign of the Mary Rose'. *The Naval Miscellany*, 8, pp. 49-84.

Lees 1984: Lees, J. *The Masting and Rigging of English Ships of War 1625–1860*. Conway.

Loades 1992: Loades, D. *The Tudor Navy: An Administrative, Political and Military History*. Scolar Press.

Loades and Fontana 2017: Loades, D. and Fontana, D. 'More Documents for the Last Campaign of the Mary Rose'. *Naval Miscellany*, 8, pp. 49-84.

McElvogue 2015: *Tudor Warship Mary Rose. Anatomy of the Ship Series*. Conway.

McKee 1968: McKee, A. *King Henry VIII's Mary Rose*. Souvenir.

McKee 1973: McKee, A. *King Henry VIII's Mary Rose: It's Fate and Future: The Story of One of the Most Exciting Projects in Maritime Archaeology*. Souvenir.

McKee 1982: McKee, A. *How We Found the Mary Rose*. Souvenir.

Marsden 2003: Marsden, P. *Sealed by Time: The Loss and Recovery of the Mary Rose*. Mary Rose Trust, volume 1.

Marsden 2009: Marsden, P. (ed). *Mary Rose: Your Noblest Shippe*. Mary Rose Trust, volume 2.

MRT 2010: *Mapping Portsmouth's Tudor Past*. Mary Rose Trust.

MOD 1965: *Your Navy: Past and Present*. Ministry of Defence.

Moorhouse 2005: Moorhouse, G. *Great Harry's Navy*. Phoenix.

Nelson 2001: Nelson, A. *The Tudor Navy: The Ships, Men and Organisation, 1485–1603*. Conway.

Oglander 2017: Oglander, J. ( 1585–1655). *Narrative of the Invasion of the Isle of Wight, July 1545*. Isle of Wight County Press, 30 November 1907; re-published with corrections in Knighton, Fontana and Loades 2017, pp. 81-4.

Oman 1963: Oman, M. *Medieval Silver Nefs*. Victoria and Albert Museum.

Oppenheim 1896 a: Oppenheim, M. *A History of the Administration of the Royal Navy and of Merchant Shipping in Relation to the Navy from 1509 to 1660 with an Introduction Treating of the Preceding Period*. Bodley Head. Republished 1988 by Gower Publishing.

Oppenheim 1896 b: Oppenheim, M. (ed). *Naval Accounts of Henry VII, 1485–8, 1495–7. Navy Records Society*, VIII.

Orme 2014: Orme, N. *The Churches of Medieval Exeter*. Impress Books.

Pietsch 2004: Pietsch, R. 'Ships Boys and Youth Culture in Eighteenth-century Britain: The Navy Recruits of the London Marine Society'. *The Northern Mariner*, XIV, no. 4, pp. 11-24. Canadian Nautical Research Society.

Potter 2011: Potter, D. *Henry VIII and Francis I: The Final Conflict, 1540–1547*. Brill.

Pulvertaft 2016: Pulvertaft, D. 'The Figurehead/Badge of the Mary Rose 1510–1545'. *Mariners Mirror*, 102.3, pp. 331-5.

Rodger 2004: Rodger, N. *The Safeguard the Sea*. Harper Collins.

Rule 1983: Rule, M. *The Mary Rose: The Excavation and Raising of Henry VIII's Flagship*. 2nd ed. Windward/Conway.

Sadler 2006: Sadler, J. *Flodden 1513: Scotland's Greatest Defeat*. Osprey.

Salisbury 1961: Salisbury, W. 'The Woolwich Ship'. *Mariners' Mirror*, 47.2, pp. 81-90.

Smith 1627: Smith, J. *The Seaman's Grammar*.

Spont 1897: Spont, A. *Letters and Papers Relating to the War with France 1512–1513*. Navy Records Society.

Stirland 2005: Stirland, A. *The Men of the Mary Rose: Raising the Dead*. Sutton Publishing.

Stone 1907: Stone, P. *Two Accounts of the French Descent on the Isle of Wight under Claude d'Annebault, July 1545, Extracted from the Memoirs of Martin du Bellay, 1513–1546*. Isle of Wight County Press.

Weinstein et al 2005: Weinstein, R., Gardiner, J. and Wood, J. 'Official Issue or Personal Possessions', in Gardiner 2005, p. 489-96.

Wilson 2000: Wilson, T. 'The Flags', in Knighton and Loades 2000, pp. 28-30.

Wriothesley 1895: Wriothesley, C. *A Chronicle of England*. W. Hamilton (ed). Volume 1. Camden Society.

# INDEX